Brazilian Ronaldinho celebrates scoring for Barcelona against Athletic Bilbao, during their Spanish Liga match, played at the Camp Nou stadium in Barcelona, Spain.

LONDON, NEW YORK, MUNICH,
MELBOURNE, AND DELHI

**Senior Designer** Guy Harvey
**Senior Editor** Catherine Saunders
**Editor** Julia March
**US Editor** Margaret Parrish
**Editorial Assistants** Jo Casey and Darren Nelson
**Designers** Jon Hall and Dan Bunyan
**Publishing Manager** Simon Beecroft
**Category Publisher** Alex Allan/Siobhan Williamson
**Production** Amy Bennett
**Production Editor** Siu Chan

Body illustration pp.28-29 by Medi-Mation
Statistics pp.128–147 by Aidan Radnedge

First published in the United States in 2008
by DK Publishing
375 Hudson Street, New York, New York 10014

08 09 10 11 12 10 9 8 7 6 5 4 3 2 1
FD159 – 12/07

A catalog record for this book is available from the Library of Congress.

ISBN: 978-0-7566-3434-6

Reproduced by Media Development and Printing Ltd., UK
Printed and bound in China by Hung Hing.

The publisher would like to thank Steve Ellis for high res work, Will Jones and Martin Copeland for
picture research, Ann Barrett for the index, Louise Hughes for legal advice, and Dr. Robert Marshall
for medical guidance.

Discover more at
www.dk.com

*Ecstatic Greek fans celebrate winning the
UEFA European Championship in 2004.
Greece beat the host Portugal 1–0.*

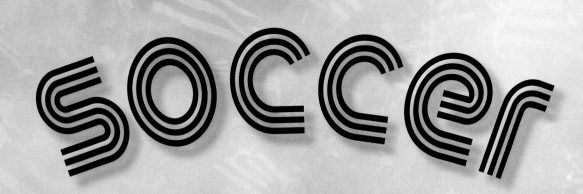

# soccer

# THE ULTIMATE GUIDE

**Written by** Martin Cloake, Glenn Dakin,
Adam Powley, Aidan Radnedge,
and Catherine Saunders

# CONTENTS

Italy celebrates its 5–3 penalty shootout victory over France in the 2006 World Cup Final.

A group of children play soccer barefoot, overlooking Rio de Janeiro, Brazil.

# THE BEAUTIFUL GAME

"FOOTBALL IS ONE OF THE WORLD'S BEST MEANS OF COMMUNICATION. IT IS IMPARTIAL, APOLITICAL, AND UNIVERSAL. FOOTBALL UNITES PEOPLE AROUND THE WORLD EVERY DAY. YOUNG OR OLD, PLAYERS OR FANS, RICH OR POOR, THE GAME MAKES EVERYONE EQUAL, STIRS THE IMAGINATION, MAKES PEOPLE HAPPY AND MAKES THEM SAD."

FRANZ BECKENBAUER, WORLD CUP
WINNING PLAYER AND COACH

Football, soccer, fussball, futebol, futbol, voetball—whatever we call it, it's the same beautiful game. For many of us it is, quite simply, the greatest game on Earth. Its popularity has spread across the globe to every tiny island and remote wilderness. It is a game for everyone. The love of the game brings people together—whether it is to play it, watch it, or just debate endlessly the referees' decisions! Rich and poor, boys and girls, young and old, everyone can play the game. Best of all, you don't need any fancy equipment. All you need is a ball...

## ABOUT THE BOOK

This guide to the beautiful game has it all—from the history of the game to the anatomy of a player, the greatest teams to the most famous players, the most prestigious competitions to the die-hard fans. However, soccer is an ever-changing game: every effort has been made to verify all facts and statistics—they are correct at the time of going to press, but may be subject to change at any future time.

# ORIGINS OF SOCCER

## FIFA

World soccer is governed by FIFA (Fédération Internationale de Football Association). Founded in 1904, FIFA oversees the organization and development of the game around the world and also oversees the World Cup, including the allocation of its hosts. FIFA's headquarters are in Zürich, Switzerland, and its current president is Joseph "Sepp" Blatter. Today, FIFA has more than 200 member countries.

No one can say precisely when, how, or even why the game of football, or soccer, developed. Games resembling soccer can be traced back as far as the ancient Chinese, Greek, and Roman civilizations. However, the rules of these games differed widely—from the number of players, to the handling of the ball, and the size of the goal. A standard set of rules was needed, and eventually the English took on the job. In 1863, the English Football Association was formed and it published the "Laws of the Game." This meant that every team could play by the same rules, creating the foundation for the way soccer is played today, all over the world.

## CUJU

The first game believed to have involved players kicking a ball was an ancient Chinese game called cuju. Popular in the 2nd century BCE, the object of cuju was to kick a leather ball through a hole in a piece of silk held up by two 30 ft (10m) poles.

## DID YOU KNOW?

*More countries are members of FIFA than of the United Nations (an organization that aims to promote international cooperation).*

## KEMARI

The Japanese sport of kemari developed from the Chinese game cuju. It was first played in about 600 CE, but has been revived in modern times. The object of kemari is to keep the ball in the air. The game is unique because all the players must work together, so there are no winners or losers.

## MEDIEVAL SOCCER

In the Middle Ages soccer games were popular throughout Europe. However, they were often little more than mass brawls between neighboring towns or villages. By the 16th century, soccer was also being played in English "public" schools (schools that charged tuition). Although this helped the game to develop, each school had its own set of rules, which made it very difficult for them to play each other.

By 1881 some teams had begun to wear coordinated uniforms.

## DEVELOPING GAME

By the end of the 19th century, soccer was growing rapidly in popularity. Once again, it was the British who helped to spread the game around the world, first to continental Europe and then to South America, North America, Africa, Asia, and Australasia.

At first players were just talented amateurs, but in 1885 they became professionals and, therefore, could be paid. Organized leagues and cup competitions were formed, and games attracted huge crowds. In 1901, more than 110,000 fans watched Tottenham Hotspur and Sheffield United in the English FA Cup Final.

# THE MODERN ERA

*"THE ONLY THING THAT HAS NEVER CHANGED IN THE HISTORY OF THE GAME IS THE SHAPE OF THE BALL."*

DENIS LAW, FORMER SCOTLAND STRIKER

Throughout the 20th century the game of soccer has continued to develop across the globe and in the last thirty years it has become big business, thanks to worldwide TV coverage and lucrative sponsorship deals. Today, the top players are highly trained superstars, earning massive salaries for their talents, both on and off the field.

It was a very different story for footballers in 1900. Above, West Bromwich Albion players enjoy a training session—a brisk walk in their suits! In 1901 the English FA set the maximum wage for a soccer player at a lowly £4 a week.

**1880s**

In the 1880s teams began to wear coordinated uniforms for the first time. They were usually long shorts with knee-length socks and knitted jerseys.

**1900s**

After 1901 players were allowed to show their knees so shorts became shorter. Striped shirts with collars also became fashionable.

**1930s**

During the 1930s, shorts became even shorter and also baggier. There was more variation in uniform style.

**1950s**

In the 1950s, soccer fashions began to take off. Lightweight fabrics were introduced and uniform design became more colorful and daring.

**1960s**

By the 1960s cleats and uniforms were more lightweight. In the 1960s plain uniforms were fashionable, since they showed up better under the floodlights.

**1970s**

During the 1970s, teams asserted their individuality with distinctive uniforms. They also began to realize the marketing potential of gear sponsorship and replica shirts.

## THE BALL

The first soccer balls were inflated pigs' bladders or skins stuffed with straw or sawdust. In the 19th and early 20th centuries, balls were made of animal bladders wrapped in leather. They often lost their shape during a game and became heavy in wet conditions. Modern balls are lighter and are usually made of leather or plastic with a special waterproof coating. Match balls must be 27–28 in (68–70 cm) in circumference and weigh 14–16 oz (410–450 g).

## CLEATS

Early players nailed studs into their heavy leather work boots and the soccer cleats were heavy, ankle-high leather boots. Lighter, shorter cleats, made of a mixture of leather and synthetic materials, were first introduced in the 1960s. Today's cleats use the latest technology, They are light, and sleek, with plastic studs.

### 1980s
During the 1980s uniform fabrics became even more lightweight, but for many the decade was defined by the players' hairstlyes. Curly perms and the "mullet" (below) were the height of fashion.

### 1990s
The 1990s saw a trend for bright colors and crazy patterns. Thankfully, this fad had passed by the end of the decade.

### 1970s
In the 1970s, players began wearing numbers on their shorts. Although with shorts this tiny, it is a wonder they found space...

## DREAM TEAM

It's not just the game that has developed over the years, but the players and uniforms have changed too—from the long shorts and perfectly groomed moustaches of the 19th century to the long hair and tight shorts of the 1970s and the high-tech, ever-changing gear of the 21st century. Check out this all-time fantasy eleven of professional players through the ages.

### 2000s
In the 21st century replica gear and sponsorship deals are even bigger business. Most teams have at least three uniforms that they change every season.

### 2000s
Even in the 21st century, players still make some serious fashion mistakes. Cameroon's one-piece uniform in 2004 earned it a fine and a points deduction from FIFA.

# WOMEN'S SOCCER

## "THE FUTURE OF SOCCER IS FEMININE."

FIFA CHIEF EXECUTIVE SEPP BLATTER

Today, there are more than 26 million female soccer players in the world and it is women who have led soccer's long-awaited advances in the US and China. Although the first women's professional league collapsed in the US in 2003, it appears to have been only a temporary setback. Semiprofessional domestic leagues have sprung up all over the world, and international tournaments such as the Women's World Cup have become compelling fixtures in the soccer calendar.

No one, man or woman, has scored more international goals than Mia Hamm, with 158.

### DICK, KERR'S LADIES

The first ever women's international was played in 1920 between France and a team of factory workers from Lancashire, England, who had defeated male players at the Dick, Kerr and Co.'s base in Preston. Dick, Kerr's Ladies became a touring sensation and they used their games to raise money for injured World War I soldiers. The team played on until 1965 as Preston Ladies, despite many obstacles such as the English FA banning women from using official fields between 1921 and 1971.

### MIA HAMM

US star player Mia Hamm is more famous than most of her male counterparts. She spearheaded US victories in the 1991 and 1999 Women's World Cup finals and is her country's top scorer. Now retired, Hamm and her strike partner Michelle Akers were the only women included in Pelé's 2004 list of the 125 greatest living soccer players.

China striker Sun Wen has had to settle for several second-place finishes behind US soccer players—in the 1999 World Cup, and a series of end-of-year prize-givings. However her goal-scoring and passing abilities finally received top billing when FIFA named her the Woman Player of the Century in 2002, although she still had to share the title with American Michelle Akers.

### KARREN BRADY

has proved the sceptics wrong by making a success of England's Birmingham City since taking over as managing director in 1992, at the age of 23. She has paved the way for other women to work in soccer as referees and game commentators.

WOMEN'S DREAM TEAM? 1. Bente Nordby (Norway) 2. Kerstin Stegemann (Germany) 3. Sandra Minnert (Germany) 4. Hege Riise (Norway) 5. Carla Werden Overbeck (US) 6. Steffi Jones (Germany) 7. Kristine Lilly (US) 8. Michelle Akers (US) 9. Mia Hamm (US) 10. Sun Wen (China) 11. Julie Foudy (US)

## BIRGIT PRINZ

Germany forward Birgit Prinz has won an unprecedented hat trick of FIFA Women's Player of the Year prizes in 2003, 2004, and 2005. Her seven goals helped Germany win the Women's World Cup for the first time in 2003 and she was instrumental in its 2007 victory. In 2005 Prinz and Inka Grings fired Germany to their fourth consecutive UEFA Championship trophy. Italian club Perugia tried in vain to sign her for their men's team in 2003.

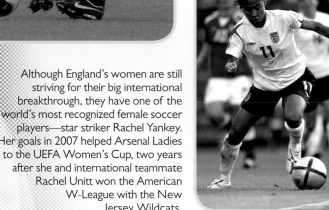

Like Birgit Prinz, Sweden's Hanna Ljungberg was wanted by Serie A's Perugia, but turned them down. Ljungberg is a skillful and hard-working forward, but despite talents such as her and Swedish top scorer Pia Sundhage, Sweden's women have had to settle for finishing runners-up in the 2003 World Cup and at two European Championships.

Although England's women are still striving for their big international breakthrough, they have one of the world's most recognized female soccer players—star striker Rachel Yankey. Her goals in 2007 helped Arsenal Ladies to the UEFA Women's Cup, two years after she and international teammate Rachel Unitt won the American W-League with the New Jersey Wildcats.

*Women were banned from playing soccer in Brazil until 1975.*

### ONE TO WATCH

China forward Ma Xiaoxu made history when she was voted Asia's Young Soccer Player of the Year in 2006—ahead of the continent's men. Although she has been nicknamed "Sun Wen Junior" she names veteran US midfielder Kristine Lilly as her heroine. Ma Xiaoxu's late equalizer and opening spot-kick in the shootout helped China to win the 2006 AFC Women's Asian Cup final against Australia.

### DID YOU KNOW?

*Brazilian Milene Domingues, the ex-wife of Ronaldo, is a soccer wife with a difference. In 1997, she set a women's world ball-juggling record when she kept a soccer ball in the air for more than nine hours and six minutes with a total of 55,187 touches! After Ronaldo joined Real Madrid in 2002, she too moved to the Spanish capital—but signed for city rivals Atlético instead in a record $400,000 transfer.*

### MARTA

Brazilian midfielder Marta Vieira da Silva had her cleats imprinted in cement outside Rio's Maracanã Stadium after Brazil beat the US in the 2007 Pan American Games. FIFA Women's Player of the Year in 2006, Marta plays her club soccer for Sweden's Umeå IK since there is no women's league in Brazil.

# PLAYING BY THE RULES

**"MY JOB IS NOT TO CHANGE THE GAME BUT MAKE IT WORK TO EVERYONE'S SATISFACTION."**
REFEREE PIERLUIGI COLLINA

*Italian Pierluigi Collina was widely considered to be the best referee in the world until he retired from the game in 2005.*

Soccer is a simple game. It is based on 17 laws first agreed to in 1863, which have been revised and updated to fit in with the modern game. The rules are the same whether you are playing in your local park or in the World Cup Finals. A game lasts for 90 minutes and is contested by two teams, each with 11 players. One player on each team must be a goalkeeper and the winner is the team that scores the most goals. Check out the glossary on p. 148–149 for extra information.

## GAME OFFICALS

A referee ensures that the rules of the game are followed. He or she is supported by two assistants, one on each touchline. Assistant referees carry a flag to signal infringements such as offside or a foul. Being a game official is a tough job and requires skills such as physical fitness (game officials must keep up with play at all times), good eyesight, and the ability to make split-second decisions while under pressure.

## CARDS

Free kicks are awarded for minor fouls and infringements, but for persistent or serious breaches of the rules, referees will show a yellow card. Two yellow cards in a game result in a red card and the player must leave the field for the rest of the game. A serious foul will result in an immediate red card.

## FOULS

When one of the laws of soccer is broken, it is generally known as a "foul." The most common types of foul are tackles in which the player (deliberately or accidentally) trips or makes contact with the opposition player rather than the ball. Other common fouls are handball, obstruction, and dangerous play.

LA Galaxy's Kyle Martino (right) fouls DC United's Fred and earns a red card. If a foul occurs inside the penalty area, a penalty kick will be awarded.

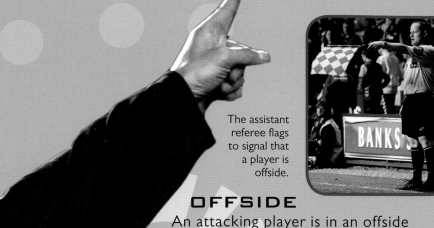

The assistant referee flags to signal that a player is offside.

## OFFSIDE

An attacking player is in an offside position if he is closer to the goal line than the ball and the second-to-last opponent. (The last opponent is usually the goalkeeper.) However, offside is judged from the moment the ball is played, not when it is received and it is only an offense if the player gains an advantage, is interfering with play, or affecting his opponent.

## KEY

1 Goal line
2 Goal
3 Six-yard box
4 Penalty spot
5 Eighteen-yard box
6 Center spot
7 Center circle
8 Halfway line
9 Corner arc
10 Touchline

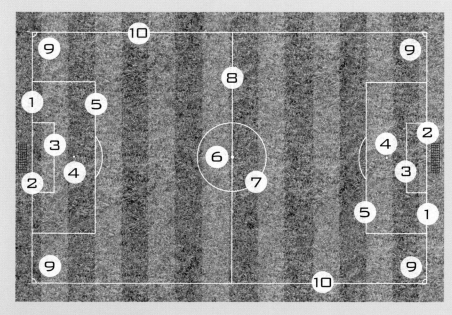

## THE FIELD

Above is an illustration of a typical soccer field, with the key areas marked. According to the Laws of the Game, not all fields have to be the same size. They must be rectangular, and between 100 and 130 yards (90 and 120 meters) long and between 50 and 100 yards (45 and 90 meters) wide. One part of the field must always be the same size—the goal. It must be 8 feet by 8 yards (2.44 meters high and 7.32 meters) wide.

## THE LAWS OF SOCCER
Here are some key rules of the game.

### THE REFEREE
The referee's decision is always final. He or she can only reverse a decision (usually on the advice of the assistant referee) immediately after the incident, if play has not been restarted.

### THE PERIOD OF PLAY
A 90-minute match is divided into two equal halves of 45 minutes, with a halftime interval of not more than 15 minutes. Extra time is added on to each half to make up for stoppages such as substitutions and injuries.

### IN AND OUT OF PLAY
A ball is only out of play if the whole of the ball has crossed the touchline or goal line, whether it is on the ground or in the air. It is in play if it rebounds off a goalpost, crossbar, corner flag, or even the referee, as long as it lands on the field of play.

### SCORING
A goal is scored when the whole of the ball crosses the goal line, between the goalposts and underneath the crossbar, as long as none of the Laws of the Game have been infringed. The winning team is the one that scores the most goals. If the score is equal at the end of the game, it is known as a "draw."

### PENALTIES
Infringements on the attacking team in the penalty area usually result in a penalty kick—a one-on-one shot with the goalkeeper. The ball is placed on the penalty spot and the penalty taker steps forward. The goalkeeper faces the kicker but must remain on the goal line. All other players must stand outside the penalty area, behind the penalty spot. As soon as the penalty is taken the ball is in play but the penalty taker cannot strike the ball again until it has touched another player.

### SUBSTITUTIONS
Before a game begins, each team can name a number of substitute players (the number varies between competitions). Of these named substitutes a fixed number (usually three) can be brought on during the course of the game, if the referee consents.

# THE CLUB

> "EVERYONE PLAYS THEIR PART. IF WE WIN ANYTHING, THEN IT WILL BE TOGETHER, NOT AS INDIVIDUALS."
>
> FORMER PORTO AND CHELSEA MANAGER JOSE MOURINHO

Although the players are the ones who grab the glory, the headlines, and the big fat salaries, a soccer club is about more than just the team. The club is a business and many people work behind the scenes to ensure that it is profitable off the field as well as successful on the field. From the people who sell the game day tickets to the people who negotiate big-money sponsorship deals, everyone plays a part in the club's success. Take a look at this pyramid—it shows how the average club is structured and who does what.

## BIG MONEY

In the 21st century, soccer is big business. Russian billionaire Roman Abramovich (right) bought England's Chelsea FC in 2003. With billions of dedicated fans around the globe, lucrative sponsorship deals, and potentially enormous revenues from TV, it is hardly surprising that many big companies and wealthy business people are eager to invest in soccer clubs.

## STRUCTURE

Not all clubs are run in exactly the same way. Some are privately owned, while others have shareholders and a Board of Directors. Some have a Director of Football and head coach instead of a manager. However, this illustration should give you some idea of just how many different people are involved in the smooth running of a soccer club.

### THE TEAM
The team is picked from a squad of players. Squad size varies from about 20–30 (there are no set rules) and this system provides cover for injured players.

### YOUTH TEAM
Most clubs want to find and keep young soccer talent so many have academies, development programs, and under-18 teams.

### RESERVES
Every player in the squad needs to be game ready. Reserve team games give players who are not in the first 11 a chance to play and also help injured players to regain their sharpness.

### ASSISTANT MANAGER
The assistant manager works closely with the manager and the team. If a manager is fired, the assistant may take temporary charge of the team.

### MANAGER
A manager or head coach is in charge of the first team. He controls training, picks the team, and sets the tactics. At some clubs, he also scouts for new players and handles transfer negotiations.

### OTHER COACHES
The reserve and youth teams also have dedicated coaches. They will liaise with the manager and discuss which players may be ready to move into the first team.

### GEAR MANAGER
Most teams have two or three different uniforms and it is the gear manager's job to ensure that every member of the squad has complete gear for every game.

### PRESS OFFICER
The press officer has the vital job of liaising with the media—TV, newspapers and magazines—to ensure that facts about the club are reported correctly.

### GROUND STAFF
A team of expert ground staff ensures that the field is in peak condition at all times, from the depths of winter to the height of summer.

### HEALTH AND FITNESS
Many different people look after the health and fitness of the players, from team doctors and physiotherapists to fitness and skills coaches.

## BUSINESS STAFF
Some people handle the commercial side of the business. These include accountants, hospitality and events coordinators, development managers, and administration staff.

## MARKETING AND PUBLICITY
The club's image is very important. The marketing and publicity department handle everything from merchandising to promotional events and campaigns.

## STADIUM STAFF
From catering staff and program sellers to guards who keep the crowds safe and well behaved, it takes hundreds of staff to run the stadium.

## TICKET OFFICE
For most clubs, demand for tickets greatly exceeds the number available, so it is the job of the ticket office to coordinate all ticket sales.

## COMMUNITY LIAISON
A club is part of its local community. The liaison team organizes community events to develop local links and help the club to feel part of the area it represents.

## FINANCIAL DIRECTOR
Executive Directors are often given responsibility for key areas of the club. A vital role is the Financial Director, who must oversee all financial aspects of the club.

## VICE CHAIRMAN
The Vice Chairman is the Chairman's second-in-command and will take charge of Board meetings if the Chairman is unable to attend.

## CHAIRMAN
The Chairman is the head of the Board of Directors. Some Chairmen are involved in the day-to-day running of the club, while others leave it to a Chief Executive or Managing Director.

## CHIEF EXECUTIVE
A Chief Executive or Managing Director deals with the day-to-day running of the whole soccer club. He or she is answerable to the Chairman and the Board.

## EXECUTIVE DIRECTOR
An Executive Director is employed by the club. He or she is involved in the day-to-day running of the club. A club may have any number of Executive and Non-Executive Directors.

## NONEXECUTIVE DIRECTOR
Most soccer clubs are controlled by a Board of Directors. A Nonexecutive Director attends Board meetings and acts as an adviser but is not employed full-time by the club.

## FANS
The loyal fans who support their teams through good times and bad are the heart and soul of any club.

FANS

FANS

FANS

FANS

FANS

FANS

FANS

FANS

FANS

FANS

FANS

FANS

# THE TEAM

"THERE ARE TWO CERTAINTIES IN LIFE. PEOPLE DIE, AND FOOTBALL MANAGERS GET THE SACK."

EOIN HAND, REPUBLIC OF IRELAND
MANAGER 1980–1985

The day-to-day running of a soccer team is hard work! Keeping a talented squad of individuals fit, healthy, happy, playing well and working together is a tough job. Players might get injured or they might go off their game for a few matches; they might have a better offer from another club, or they might not fit in with the style or direction in which the manager wishes to take the club. In the modern game expectations are high, but the rewards are even higher.

## THE MANAGER

The manager (or sometimes the Head Coach) is the boss of the team. He takes charge of training, picks the team, and decides the tactics. It is a high-pressure role and too many bad results can cost a manager his job. Dutch manager Guus Hiddink (above) has an impressive resume that includes PSV Eindhoven, Fenerbahçe, Valencia, Netherlands, Real Madrid, Real Betis, Republic of Korea, Australia, and Russia. Manchester United's Sir Alex Ferguson is a rarity in soccer management—he has been in his job for more than 20 years.

*FC Barcelona lines up before a preseason match against Internazionale in August 2007.*

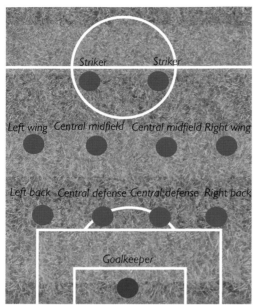

Striker    Striker

Left wing  Central midfield  Central midfield  Right wing

Left back  Central defense  Central defense  Right back

Goalkeeper

**4-4-2** This illustration shows a traditional 4–4–2 formation: four defenders, four midfielders, and two strikers. There is a flexibility within this formation as midfielders can play deep to provide defensive cover or even sit just behind the strikers in an attacking 4–4–2 formation.

## TACTICS

Tactics and formations vary depending on the abilities of the players in the squad, the nature of the opposition, and the manager's style of play. They can even be changed during the course of a game to protect a lead or provide more attacking options. There are many different styles of play but here are three of the most common formations.

**4-5-1** This formation involves four defenders, a five-man midfield, and a lone striker and is primarily used when a team wants to keep possession of the ball and prevent the other team from scoring. It is particularly useful in home games when away goals count and the home team needs to stop the visitors from scoring.

**4-3-3** This attacking formation involves four defenders, three midfielders, and three strikers. The emphasis is on attack with this style of play so it is only really used against weak opposition or when chasing a goal during a match.

## THE CAPTAIN

The manager chooses one player to be the leader on the field. Known as the captain or "skipper," this player is usually one of the oldest or longest-serving members of the team, such as Germany's Oliver Kahn (above). He has no official authority but wearing the captain's armband for club or country is a great honor. Captains must also participate in the prematch coin toss that decides who plays at which end.

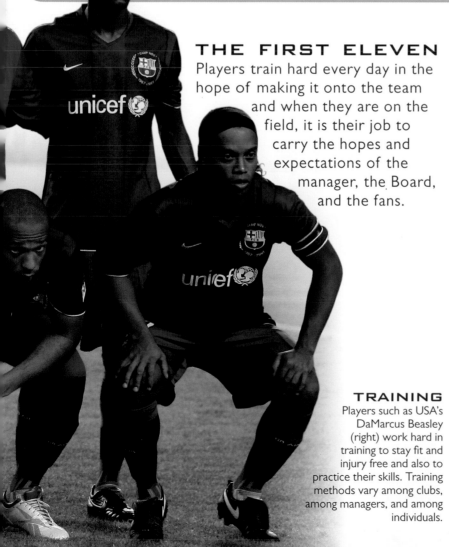

## THE FIRST ELEVEN

Players train hard every day in the hope of making it onto the team and when they are on the field, it is their job to carry the hopes and expectations of the manager, the Board, and the fans.

### TRAINING

Players such as USA's DaMarcus Beasley (right) work hard in training to stay fit and injury free and also to practice their skills. Training methods vary among clubs, among managers, and among individuals.

19

## PUNCHING

The only kind of punch that is allowed in a soccer match is a punch by the goalkeeper to the ball, in the area. In high-pressure situations, the goalkeeper may not be able to catch the ball cleanly, so he must punch it away. It is important to get height and distance on a punch so that the goal threat is cleared. A poor punch can rebound off a player and end up in the back of the net!

*Italy's Gianluigi Buffon punches clear of Germany's Miroslav Klose in the 2006 World Cup semifinals.*

# GOALKEEPERS

## "IF YOU'RE A GOALKEEPER, IT DOESN'T MATTER WHAT YOU SAVE THE BALL WITH— IF YOU KEEP IT OUT, IT'S NOT A GOAL."

FORMER REPUBLIC OF IRELAND AND LIVERPOOL DEFENDER MARK LAWRENSON

Goalkeepers are in a way the odd-ones-out of the soccer team. For a start, they wear a different uniform (to distinguish them from the rest of the team) and are the only players permitted to handle the ball in open play. Moreover, they are often all that stands in the way of a certain goal—a great save and the goalkeeper is the hero; a clumsy fumble and he is the villain!

## DIVING SAVE

Goalkeepers need quick reactions, agility, and the courage to put themselves in dangerous situations. If the ball comes at them from a low angle, the goalkeeper must make a diving save, as France keeper Grégory Coupet demonstrates (right).

## REACTIONS

Goalkeepers must always be alert and ready to react to goal threats. Sometimes they have to improvise, as Polish keeper Jerzy Dudek does with a point-blank stop against France in a friendly match in 2004.

## CATCHING

When catching the ball, it is important to take it firmly and cleanly. Here, US goalkeeper Kasey Keller (above) clutches the ball safely to his body in a friendly game against Germany in 2006.

## DID YOU KNOW?

*There have been many spectacular saves, but probably none more inventive than former Colombian goal-keeper René Higuita's famous "scorpion kick." It occurred during a friendly match between Colombia and England at Wembley in 2003. Instead of catching an England cross, Higuita performed this acrobatic kick (right).*

## UNDERARM THROW
Netherlands goalkeeper Edwin van der Sar (above) demonstrates the underarm throw, which is perfect for moving the ball a short distance.

## OVERARM THROW
Brazil goalkeeper Dida (above) uses an overarm throw to launch a quick counterattack. This technique requires accuracy, strength, and power.

## INDIVIDUAL STYLE
Goalkeepers are famous for their individuality and eccentricities, but probably none more so than former Mexico goalkeeper Jorge Campos. (left). Despite his short stature (5 ft 6 in/1.68 m) Campos was extremely agile and earned 130 caps for his country. He was famous for his his eye-catching uniforms, which he designed himself, and his occasional fondness for playing as a striker, all of which helped to make him a cult figure with fans around the world.

## DISTRIBUTING THE BALL
In addition to being the last line of defense, a goalkeeper can be the launch pad for an attack. He must be able to distribute the ball effectively and accurately whether it is with his hands or his feet. Above, England goalkeeper Paul Robinson aims a massive goal kick up the field toward the strikers. Robinson once scored directly from a long-range kick!

## PENALTIES
For most goalkeepers, penalties are the ultimate test. This one-on-one situation favors the attacker and gives the goalkeeper very little chance of glory. Even if he correctly guesses which way the attacker will shoot, a well struck penalty is virtually impossible to save. However, some goalkeepers have a reputation for saving penalties, such as Portugal keeper Ricardo (right).

Ricardo saves a penalty from England's Frank Lampard during Portugal's penalty shootout victory in the 2006 World Cup quarterfinals.

## TACKLING

A tackle is the most direct way of winning the ball back from the opposition and breaking down an attack. Tackles must be from the side or the front, never from behind, and timing is vital to win the ball cleanly and safely.

*Chelsea's Ricardo Carvalho makes a sliding tackle on his international teammate, Manchester United's Cristiano Ronaldo.*

# DEFENSE

## "STRIKERS WIN YOU GAMES, BUT DEFENDERS WIN YOU CHAMPIONSHIPS."

FORMER ENGLAND MIDFIELDER AND NOW CLUB MANAGER, JOHN GREGORY

Although strikers and midfielders often steal all the glory, the defense is the backbone of the team. Defenders must be strong, aware, skillful, and cool under pressure. However, it is important for every player to know how to defend as during a match any player could find themselves needing to make a goal-saving tackle or goal-line clearance.

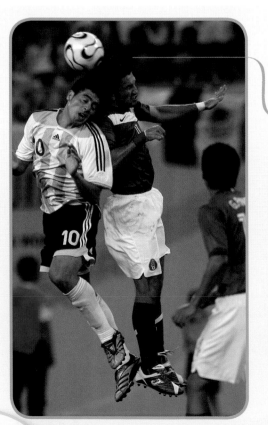

*Argentina won the match 2–1 thanks to goals from Hernán Crespo and Maxi Rodríguez.*

## HEADING

Defenders need to have a strong physical presence, particularly in the air. Here Mexico's José Fonseca (right) rises above Argentina's Juan Riquelme (left) to head the ball during the 2006 World Cup Finals. An effective defensive header should travel as far and as high as possible.

## TEAM DEFENDING

An important part of good defending is organization. Whether it is trapping the attacker offside, marking for a corner or just covering for each other, defenders must work together. Here Ronaldinho of Brazil prepares to take a free kick from just outside the area, but first he must get past England's defensive wall.

## WINNING THE BALL

Sometimes a defender doesn't even have to make a tackle to win the ball—by reading the game or marking tightly he can intercept a pass or steal the ball right off an attacker's toes! Pace and skill can also help the defender to stay one step ahead of the attacking player.

### DID YOU KNOW?

*Defensive football was not popular during the 19th century and teams favored all-out attack instead. In 1872 the first ever international game took place. It was between Scotland and England. England fielded seven or eight forwards and played either a 1–1–8 or 1–2–7 formation while Scotland had six forwards in a 2–2–6 formation. Rather surprisingly the match ended in a 0–0 draw!*

*Italy's Fabio Cannavaro (right) beats France's Franck Ribéry (left) to the ball in the 2006 World Cup final.*

*Fabio Cannavaro lifted the World Cup in 2006 as Italian captain. He was also named World and European Footballer of the Year in 2006.*

## STRENGTH

Strength and determination are key parts of a defender's game. Winning headers, making tackles, and passing under pressure all require strength as well as skill and good technique. Above, France defender Lilian Thuram (right) uses his strength and body size to shield the ball from Spain striker Fernando Torres (left) in a 2006 World Cup Finals match.

# MIDFIELD

*"THE MIDFIELD IS THE MOST CRUCIAL AREA OF THE GAME, THE ONE WHERE MATCHES ARE WON OR LOST."*

MANCHESTER CITY MANAGER SVEN-GÖRAN ERIKSSON

The midfield is the engine of the team. Midfielders provide a vital link between defense and attack, tracking back and making tackles to win the ball and then driving forward with vision and awareness. Some midfielders embody all these attributes, while others have more specialized roles. A "holding" midfielder plays a defensive game, while an attacking midfielder may play just behind the strikers. It is the job of a winger to make runs on the outside of the field, beating defenders and supplying accurate crosses.

### PACE AND POWER
Attacking midfielders like Spain's Cesc Fàbregas (above, left) need pace to outrun defenders, strength to hold off challenges, and the skills to supply accurate passes.

### TACKLING
The midfield is a key area of the field and winning the ball in this area can quickly turn defense into attack. This means that tackling is often a vital part of a midfielder's role. Here, France midfielder Patrick Vieira (right) stretches beyond Portugal's Luis Figo (left) to take the ball from him.

*Argentina defensive midfielder Javier Mascherano is admired for his passing and tackling skills.*

### PASSING
Passing and distribution are also important skills for a midfielder. Whether it is having the vision to play a cross-field pass and set up an attack or calmly passing the ball out of defense, a midfielder needs to blend creativity with coolness under pressure.

### DID YOU KNOW?
*Many midfielders claim that they work the hardest out of everyone in the team and they certainly cover the greatest distance. In fact a top level midfielder covers more than 6 miles (10 km) per game.*

## WING PLAY

Wingers play on the far sides of the field, making attacking runs, beating defenders, and supplying accurate crosses to the strikers. They need speed, strength, and versatility, plus excellent dribbling and passing skills. Manchester United and Portugal's Cristiano Ronaldo (right) is one of the world's finest wingers.

*A prolific goalscorer, Ronaldo is a skilled header of the ball and often takes free kicks.*

*Ronaldo is versatile and can play on the right or left wing.*

*Ronaldo is also famous for his stepovers and tricks that bamboozle defenders.*

## GOALSCORING

Midfielders, especially attacking ones, must also be able to score goals. After a penetrating forward run or fast-paced attack a midfielder can often find himself in a goal-scoring position. Above, France midfielder Franck Ribéry confidently rounds the stranded Spain goalkeeper Iker Casillas to score.

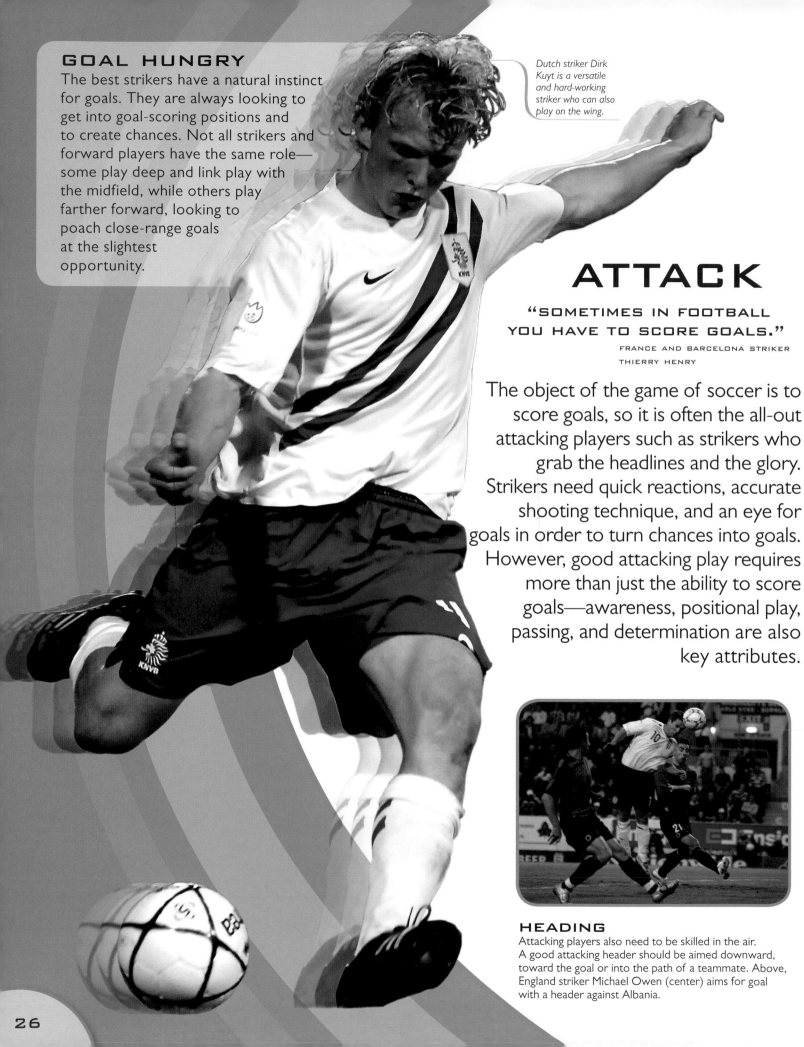

## GOAL HUNGRY

The best strikers have a natural instinct for goals. They are always looking to get into goal-scoring positions and to create chances. Not all strikers and forward players have the same role—some play deep and link play with the midfield, while others play farther forward, looking to poach close-range goals at the slightest opportunity.

*Dutch striker Dirk Kuyt is a versatile and hard-working striker who can also play on the wing.*

# ATTACK

## "SOMETIMES IN FOOTBALL YOU HAVE TO SCORE GOALS."

FRANCE AND BARCELONA STRIKER
THIERRY HENRY

The object of the game of soccer is to score goals, so it is often the all-out attacking players such as strikers who grab the headlines and the glory. Strikers need quick reactions, accurate shooting technique, and an eye for goals in order to turn chances into goals. However, good attacking play requires more than just the ability to score goals—awareness, positional play, passing, and determination are also key attributes.

## HEADING

Attacking players also need to be skilled in the air. A good attacking header should be aimed downward, toward the goal or into the path of a teammate. Above, England striker Michael Owen (center) aims for goal with a header against Albania.

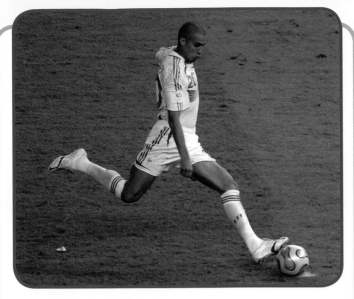

## PENALTIES

A penalty is a high-pressure situation so nerves can play a huge part. Most players choose their spot before they strike the ball and hope that the goalkeeper dives the wrong way. Above, France striker David Trézéguet takes a penalty in the 2006 World Cup final but unfortunately hits the crossbar.

## SWERVE

Being able to strike the ball in different directions takes great skill. Above, England striker Wayne Rooney turns his body and strikes across the ball to produce a fierce swerve shot. This kind of shot is very difficult for goalkeepers to save.

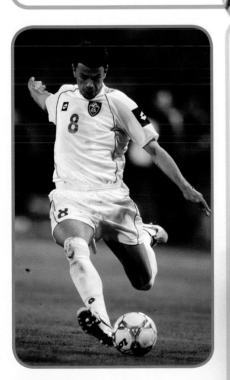

## SPECTACULAR GOALS

Scoring a goal is great, but scoring a spectacular goal is even better! Powerful shots from a distance, strikes conjured from the most impossible angles, or impressive solo skill all make fantastic goals. Below, Roma and Italy's Franceso Totti attempts an acrobatic overhead shot with his back to goal.

## DID YOU KNOW?

*Pelé never played at England's Wembley Stadium. So when filming an ad there long after he had retired, he couldn't resist the opportunity of scoring a "goal" on the famous Wembley turf.*

*An overhead kick requires great balance, good technique—and a lot of confidence!*

## PASSING

Whether it is an attacking pass or a shot on goal, timing and accuracy are vital. A pass must be accurately delivered to reach the intended teammate and perfectly timed to reach the target while he is in an onside position. Above, Serbia striker Mateja Kežman launches a long-range attacking pass.

# BODY MATTERS

## "FOR A PROFESSIONAL SPORTSMAN, BEING INJURED IS LIKE LIVING IN A STRANGER'S BODY."

FORMER FRANCE MIDFIELDER ROBERT PIRÈS

A player's body is the tool of his trade so he must look after it. This means working hard in training, eating the right foods, and living a healthy lifestyle. Professional players won't get far without natural talent, but agility, speed, strength, and power are also must-haves for modern players. Take a look inside the body of a superfit player and see how it works, then check out some common soccer injuries. WARNING: SENSITIVE READERS MAY WANT TO SKIP THIS PAGE!

## DID YOU KNOW?

In 1998, Republic of Ireland striker Robbie Keane ruptured his knee cartilage after stretching to pick up his TV remote control.

Arsenal's Steve Morrow broke his collarbone falling off teammate Tony Adams' shoulders while celebrating the 1993 League Cup final win.

When DR Congo striker Lomana LuaLua scored a goal for Portsmouth in 2006, he celebrated with his trademark somersault but sprained his ankle on landing.

## WARM-UP

Players train regularly during the soccer season. They must not only practice their soccer skills, but also work on their strength and stamina. At the beginning of every training session and before a match, players prepare their muscles and increase their heart rate with special warm-up and stretching exercises.

Warm-ups prepare the body for more strenuous activity and can help to prevent injury. When the game or training session is over, players "warm down" to allow their bodies to recover gradually.

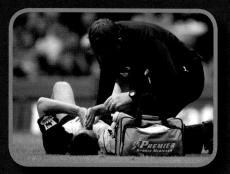

**THE PHYSIO** (short for physiotherapist) treats injuries during a game. He or she is only allowed on the field if the referee gives permission. The physio also helps players recover from long-term injuries using treatments such as massage and specially developed exercise programs.

## FAKING IT

Players might suffer hard or dangerous tackles during a game, but sometimes the reaction can be worse than the foul! What FIFA diplomatically calls "simulation" is the kind of play-acting that belongs on a cinema/movie screen, not a soccer field. Theatrical dives while clutching a supposedly injured body part are designed to fool the referee into penalizing the opposition. Unfortunately, it sometimes works...

## FOOT

From sprained ankles to broken toes, damaged tendons, or severe bruising, the foot and ankle area of the body can take a lot of punishment during a soccer game. A particularly common injury is the broken metatarsal (right). The five metatarsals are the long bones that attach the toe bones (phalanxes) to the bones near the ankle (collectively known as the tarsals). The metatarsals are usually broken by impact, e.g., a mistimed tackle or a bad landing.

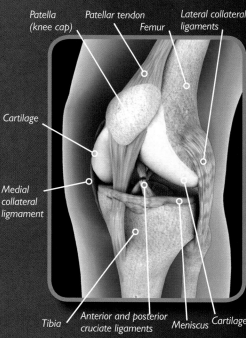

Patella (knee cap) · Patellar tendon · Femur · Lateral collateral ligaments · Cartilage · Medial collateral ligmament · Tibia · Anterior and posterior cruciate ligaments · Meniscus · Cartilage

## KNEE

Sharp turns when all the weight is borne by the knee can damage the meniscus (known as cartilage damage), while turns, awkward landings, and over extending can damage the cruciate and medial ligaments.

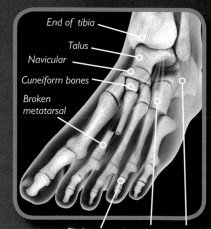

End of tibia · Talus · Navicular · Cuneiform bones · Broken metatarsal · Phalanx · Cuboid · Calcaneus

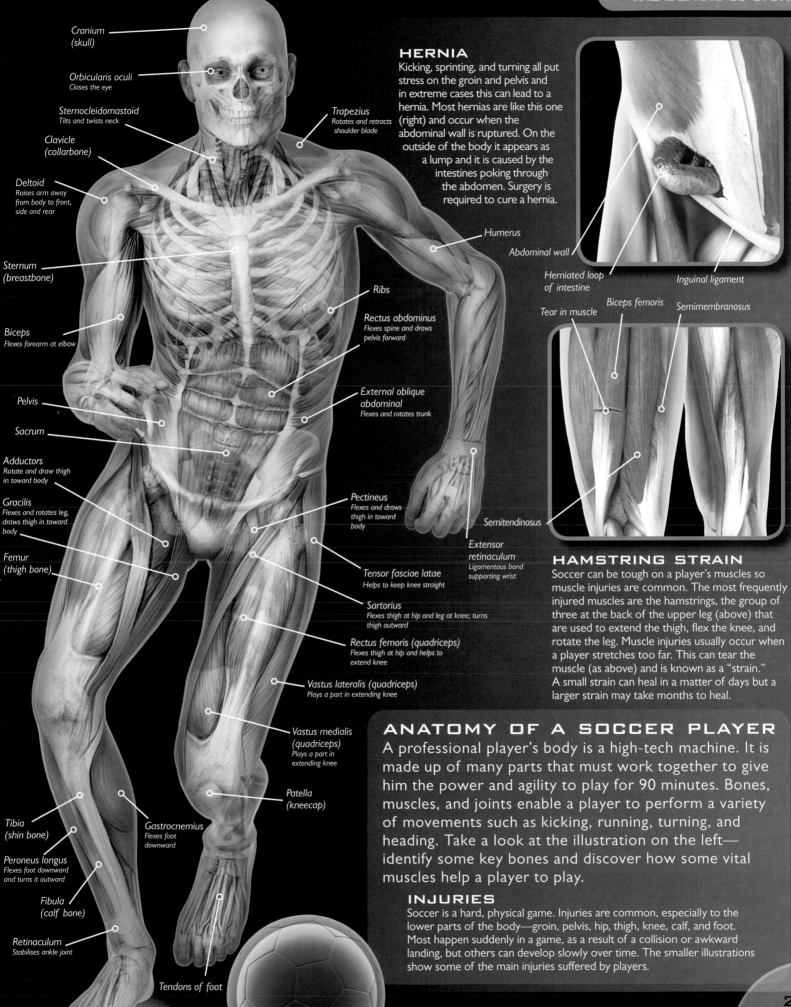

Cranium
(skull)

Orbicularis oculi
Closes the eye

Sternocleidomastoid
Tilts and twists neck

Clavicle
(collarbone)

Deltoid
Raises arm away
from body to front,
side and rear

Sternum
(breastbone)

Biceps
Flexes forearm at elbow

Pelvis

Sacrum

Adductors
Rotate and draw thigh
in toward body

Gracilis
Flexes and rotates leg,
draws thigh in toward
body

Femur
(thigh bone)

Tibia
(shin bone)

Peroneus longus
Flexes foot downward
and turns it outward

Fibula
(calf bone)

Retinaculum
Stabilises ankle joint

Trapezius
Rotates and retracts
shoulder blade

Humerus

Ribs

Rectus abdominus
Flexes spine and draws
pelvis forward

External oblique
abdominal
Flexes and rotates trunk

Pectineus
Flexes and draws
thigh in toward
body

Semitendinosus

Extensor
retinaculum
Ligamentous band
supporting wrist

Tensor fasciae latae
Helps to keep knee straight

Sartorius
Flexes thigh at hip and leg at knee; turns
thigh outward

Rectus femoris (quadriceps)
Flexes thigh at hip and helps to
extend knee

Vastus lateralis (quadriceps)
Plays a part in extending knee

Vastus medialis
(quadriceps)
Plays a part in
extending knee

Patella
(kneecap)

Gastrocnemius
Flexes foot
downward

Tendons of foot

## HERNIA

Kicking, sprinting, and turning all put stress on the groin and pelvis and in extreme cases this can lead to a hernia. Most hernias are like this one (right) and occur when the abdominal wall is ruptured. On the outside of the body it appears as a lump and it is caused by the intestines poking through the abdomen. Surgery is required to cure a hernia.

Abdominal wall

Herniated loop
of intestine

Inguinal ligament

Tear in muscle

Biceps femoris

Semimembranosus

## HAMSTRING STRAIN

Soccer can be tough on a player's muscles so muscle injuries are common. The most frequently injured muscles are the hamstrings, the group of three at the back of the upper leg (above) that are used to extend the thigh, flex the knee, and rotate the leg. Muscle injuries usually occur when a player stretches too far. This can tear the muscle (as above) and is known as a "strain." A small strain can heal in a matter of days but a larger strain may take months to heal.

## ANATOMY OF A SOCCER PLAYER

A professional player's body is a high-tech machine. It is made up of many parts that must work together to give him the power and agility to play for 90 minutes. Bones, muscles, and joints enable a player to perform a variety of movements such as kicking, running, turning, and heading. Take a look at the illustration on the left— identify some key bones and discover how some vital muscles help a player to play.

### INJURIES

Soccer is a hard, physical game. Injuries are common, especially to the lower parts of the body—groin, pelvis, hip, thigh, knee, calf, and foot. Most happen suddenly in a game, as a result of a collision or awkward landing, but others can develop slowly over time. The smaller illustrations show some of the main injuries suffered by players.

# EUROPE

Formed in 1954, the Union of European Football Associations (UEFA) now has 53 members. It is the most powerful of the world soccer confederations and has 13 World Cup Finals places. Former Soviet countries Georgia, Armenia, Kazakhstan, and Azerbaijan are members of UEFA and so is Israel, although they are not technically part of Europe.

**"AT A TIME WHEN EUROPE IS SEEKING TO DEFINE ITSELF, NOTHING CONTRIBUTES MORE TO THIS QUEST THAN ITS LOVE FOR OUR SPORT."** FIFA PRESIDENT MICHEL PLATINI

Over the years, intensely competitive leagues such as Serie A in Italy, the Premier League in England, La Liga in Spain, and the Bundesliga in Germany have produced many top-class players. This has made Europe a powerhouse of international soccer with many strong national teams, even from comparatively small nations such as Portugal and the Czech Republic. Today, the money and prestige of European league soccer attracts the world's greatest stars to the continent.

NORTHERN IRELAND

REPUBLIC OF IRELAND

## FANATICS

European fans are increasingly using soccer as a way of celebrating—and sometimes spoofing—their national stereotypes. While patriotic Norwegians, Swedes, and Danes dress as Vikings, many English fans favor the medieval knight look, while proud Scottish fans like to dig out their family tartan!

PORTUGAL

SPAIN

## THE ORANJE

Any city that has hosted a major soccer tournament will remember any visiting Dutch fans. Famous for the crazy orange outfits, these loyal fans often make sure that their team has the brightest and loudest support, both on and off the field.

# ENGLAND

*"GOD BLESS WHOEVER INVENTED FOOTBALL. IT WAS THE ENGLISH, I THINK. AND WHAT A FANTASTIC IDEA IT WAS."* ITALIAN STRIKER, PAOLO ROSSI

The FA was formed in 1863. The official badge features three lions, which are from the royal coat of arms and the Red Rose of Lancaster, the official emblem of England.

Credited as the founders of modern soccer, England is the oldest international team in the world, alongside Scotland. These two countries played the first ever international match in 1872. England did not play outside the British Isles until 1908 and did not enter the World Cup until 1950. Despite perennially high hopes, the team has only won one major tournament—the 1966 World Cup, in England.

## MOMENT OF GLORY

England's finest hour came on 30 July, 1966, at Wembley Stadium. As 98,000 fans roared it on, the team took a famous victory in the World Cup final against West Germany. England won a thrilling game 4–2 after overtime. Some people say that Hurst's second goal (England's third) did not cross the line, but USSR linesman Tofik Bakhramov ruled that it did.

Striker Geoff Hurst scored three goals, and remains the only player to have scored a hat-trick in a World Cup final. England's other goal was scored by Martin Peters.

*England captain Bobby Moore proudly holds up the Jules Rimet trophy.*

Former England striker Gary Lineker is the only English player to top the scoring charts at a World Cup Finals. His six goals at Mexico '86 included a hat-trick against Poland.

Michael Owen was 18 when he scored a wonder goal against Argentina in the 1998 World Cup Finals. He ran from the center circle, through the Argentinian defense, and shot into the top corner. England still lost the second round match 4–3 on penalties.

ENGLAND DREAM TEAM? 1. Gordon Banks 2. Alf Ramsey 3. Ray Wilson 4. Glenn Hoddle 5. Bobby Moore 6. Billy Wright 7. Stanley Matthews 8. Bobby Charlton 9. Gary Lineker 10. Jimmy Greaves 11. Tom Finney

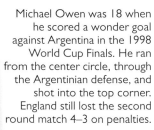

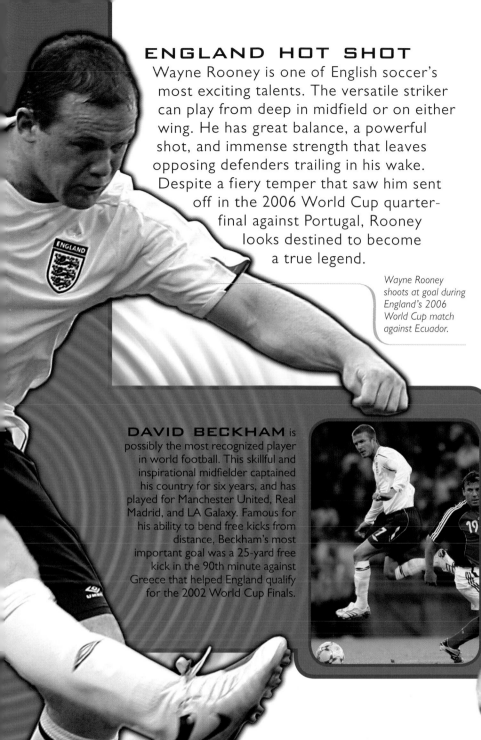

# ENGLAND HOT SHOT

Wayne Rooney is one of English soccer's most exciting talents. The versatile striker can play from deep in midfield or on either wing. He has great balance, a powerful shot, and immense strength that leaves opposing defenders trailing in his wake. Despite a fiery temper that saw him sent off in the 2006 World Cup quarter-final against Portugal, Rooney looks destined to become a true legend.

*Wayne Rooney shoots at goal during England's 2006 World Cup match against Ecuador.*

**DAVID BECKHAM** is possibly the most recognized player in world football. This skillful and inspirational midfielder captained his country for six years, and has played for Manchester United, Real Madrid, and LA Galaxy. Famous for his ability to bend free kicks from distance, Beckham's most important goal was a 25-yard free kick in the 90th minute against Greece that helped England qualify for the 2002 World Cup Finals.

## FACT FILE: ENGLAND

### NICKNAME
The Three Lions

### TOP GOAL SCORERS
1. Bobby Charlton 49 (1958–1970)
2. Gary Lineker 48 (1984–1992)
3. Jimmy Greaves 44 (1959–1967)
4. Michael Owen 40 (1998–present)
5. Tom Finney 30 (1946–1958)
= Nat Lofthouse 30 (1950–1958)
= Alan Shearer 30 (1992–2000)

### MOST APPEARANCES
1. Peter Shilton 125 (1970–1990)
2. Bobby Moore 108 (1962–1973)
3. Bobby Charlton 106 (1958–1970)
4. Billy Wright 105 (1946–1959)
5. David Beckham 99 (1996–present)

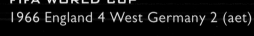

### TROPHIES/HONORS
#### FIFA WORLD CUP
1966 England 4 West Germany 2 (aet)

## KEY MEN

John Terry (left) and Steven Gerrard are two of the current England team's key players. Terry is a brave, powerful central defender whose commanding performances on the pitch have led to him being made captain of his club, Chelsea, as well as his country. Gerrard is a gifted and hard-working midfielder with an eye for creating and scoring goals. His never-say-die attitude makes him a firm favorite with both Liverpool and England fans.

Originally built in 1923, Wembley Stadium is the home of English soccer. In 2007 a new structure was opened and with 90,000 seats it is the second largest stadium in Europe.

## DID YOU KNOW?

*Stanley Matthews achieved a series of "firsts"—he was the first Football Writers' Association Footballer of the Year (in 1948), the first European Footballer of the Year (in 1956), and the first footballer to be knighted (in 1965).*

*Billy Wright played in 70 consecutive England internationals between October 1951 and May 1959, a national record.*

# FRANCE

Famed for skill, flair, and entertainment, French soccer has always placed more emphasis on attack rather than the physical and tactical style favored by other European nations. Yet for all the undoubted talent of its soccer players, France did not lift an international trophy until the 1984 European Championship. However, since then the national side has won the World Cup and the European Championship for a second time, providing a strong challenge to Brazil's domination of the modern game.

The Fédération Française de Football was founded in 1919, replacing five previous bodies that had competed to control the national game.

## MICHEL PLATINI

Arguably France's greatest ever player, midfielder Michel Platini was European Footballer of the Year for three consecutive years—1983, 1984, and 1985. A club player with Nancy, St. Étienne, and Juventus, he was for many years France's top scorer and managed the national side between 1988 and 1992. He was elected President of UEFA in 2007.

After narrowly failing to reach the World Cup final in 1982, the great French team of the 1980s finally won the trophy it deserved two years later, on home soil. Star players Platini, Jean Tigana, and Alain Giresse helped to secure a 2–0 victory over Spain in the European Championship final in Paris. The goals came from Platini himself (his ninth of the tournament) and Bruno Bellone.

The son of Polish immigrants, Raymond Kopaszewski, or "Kopa" for short (left) was one of the finest players of the post-war era. He was named by Pelé as one of the 125 greatest living players in a list compiled by FIFA in 2004.

## JUST FONTAINE

Striker Just Fontaine's place in soccer history is assured by his remarkable performance during the 1958 World Cup Finals in Sweden. His 13-goal total is still a tournament record for the most scored by a player at a single World Cup. France reached the semi-finals, but was defeated 5–2 by the eventual winner Brazil.

FRANCE DREAM TEAM? 1. Fabien Barthez 2. Lilian Thuram 3. Bixente Lizarazu 4. Patrick Vieira 5. Marius Trésor 6. Marcel Desailly 7. Zinedine Zidane 8. Michel Platini 9. Just Fontaine 10. Raymond Kopa 11. Thierry Henry

## ZINEDINE ZIDANE

is widely acknowledged as one of the greatest players in the history of the game. As an attacking midfielder, his range of passing, ball control, and powerful shooting made him the most influential player in the French World Cup and European Championship winning teams.

*Thierry Henry's pace is complemented by his ability to change position and confuse defenders.*

## THIERRY HENRY

Few attackers have been more feared by defenders in the last ten years than Thierry Henry. Blessed with blistering pace, exceptional skill, and masterful movement both on and off the ball, Henry's grace and elegance disguises an almost clinical ability to punish opponents. From precise passing to spectacular finishing, Henry has it all.

## FACT FILE: FRANCE
### NICKNAME
Les Bleus (The Blues)

### TOP GOAL SCORERS
1. Thierry Henry 44 (1997–present)
2. Michel Platini 41 (1976–1987)
3. David Trézéguet 34 (1998–present)
4. Zinedine Zidane 31 (1994–2006)
5. Just Fontaine 30 (1953–1960)
  = Jean-Pierre Papin 30 (1986–1995)

### MOST APPEARANCES
1. Lilian Thuram 136 (1994–present)
2. Marcel Desailly 116 (1993–2004)
3. Zinedine Zidane 108 (1994–2006)
4. Patrick Vieira 104 (1997–present)
5. Didier Deschamps 103 (1989–2000)

### TROPHIES/HONORS
**FIFA WORLD CUP**
1998 France 3 Brazil 0

**UEFA EUROPEAN CHAMPIONSHIP**
1984 France 2 Spain 0
2000 France 2 Italy 1 (aet)

**OLYMPIC GOLD MEDAL**
1984 France 2 Brazil 0

**FIFA CONFEDERATIONS CUP**
2001 France 1 Japan 0
2003 France 1 Cameroon 0

## FRANCE '98

France's finest sporting hour came on a warm evening in Paris on July 12, 1998. Sixty years after the country had last hosted the World Cup, France made the most of home advantage. Led by captain, Didier Deschamps, and roared on by a passionate crowd at the Stade de France, France beat Brazil 3–0 to win the trophy for the first time.

## DID YOU KNOW?

*Superstitious World Cup-winning defender Laurent Blanc kissed the bald head of goalkeeper Fabien Barthez before every match because he believed it brought good luck.*

# ITALY

*"YOU KNOW, THERE WILL ALWAYS BE A LITTLE BIT OF ITALY IN THIS TROPHY."*

SILVIO GAZZANIGA, MILANESE SCULPTOR OF THE CURRENT WORLD CUP

One of the world's great soccer nations, Italy's success is matched only by the passion of its fans. Italy is the current world champion and, with four World Cups, the second most successful soccer nation after Brazil. Although built on a solid defensive style, the "Azzurri" have nevertheless featured some of soccer's most exciting creative talents, from Giuseppe Meazza and Sandro Mazzola to Roberto Baggio. Containing opponents and then hitting them with swift, skillful counterattacks are the hallmarks of Italian play.

The Federazione Italiana Giuoco Calcio was formed in 1898. The four stars represent each of Italy's World Cup triumphs.

## SPAIN '82

The 1982 World Cup final is regarded as the second best of all time, after Brazil '70. Inspired by the great Paolo Rossi and legendary goalkeeper Dino Zoff, an entertaining Italian team beat West Germany 3–1 in a game they totally dominated.

Italy's team coach Vittorio Pozzo is carried high by his squad after winning the 1934 World Cup against Czechoslovakia—the first time the Italians won the trophy. Four years later, Pozzo's team successfully defended the trophy, after winning Gold at the 1936 Olympics. Between December 1934 and 1939, Pozzo's Italy did not lose a single game.

**LUIGI "GIGI" RIVA** is Italy's all-time leading goal scorer, with 35 goals in 42 games between 1965 to 1974. Gigi was quick and intelligent, with lightning fast reactions and great ability in the air. His powerful shot earned him the nickname "Rombo di Tuono"—or "Sound of Thunder." Here, Gigi is scoring Italy's opening goal against Yugoslavia in the 1968 European Championships final replay.

Roberto Baggio, or "Il Divin Codino" (The Divine Ponytail), on the way to scoring a memorable goal against Czechoslovakia in the 1990 World Cup.

ITALY DREAM TEAM? 1. Dino Zoff 2. Fabio Cannavaro 3. Giacinto Facchetti 4. Gaetano Scirea 5. Franco Baresi 6. Paolo Maldini 7. Roberto Baggio 8. Gianni Rivera 9. Paolo Rossi 10. Giuseppe Meazza 11. Luigi Riva

## PAOLO ROSSI

Paolo Rossi's six goals helped Italy win the 1982 World Cup. He also won the Golden Boot for top scorer and Golden Ball for best player in the tournament and was named 1982 World and European Footballer of the Year.

## 2006 TRIUMPH

Italy beat France to win its fourth World Cup in 2006. It was the first all-European final since Italy last won the tournament in 1982. After extra time the score was 1–1, so for only the second time ever, the final was decided on penalties. The Italians won 5–3.

Ecstatic captain Fabio Cannavaro holds up the 2006 World Cup.

Defender Paolo Maldini is a legend of Italian soccer. The most capped player for club, (AC Milan) and country, he has seven Serie A and five Champions League winners' medals.

**FRANCESCO TOTTI** is a current star of Italian soccer. Winner of the 2006–07 Golden Boot after scoring the most club goals in the whole of Europe, Totti made his national debut in 1998. He was named Man of the Match in the Euro 2000 final, which Italy lost to France, and was selected for the 23-man All-Star Team at the 2006 World Cup Finals. However, in July 2007 Totti retired from international soccer to concentrate on playing for his club, AS Roma.

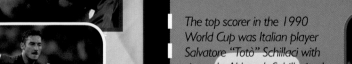

### FACT FILE: ITALY
#### NICKNAME
Azzurri (Blues)

#### TOP GOAL SCORERS
1. Luigi Riva 35 (1965–1974)
2. Giuseppe Meazza 33 (1930–1939)
3. Silvio Piola 30 (1935–1952)
4. Roberto Baggio 27 (1988–2004)
= Alessandro Del Piero 33 (1995–present)

#### MOST APPEARANCES
1. Paolo Maldini 126 (1988–2002)
2. Dino Zoff 112 (1968–1982)
3. Fabio Cannavaro 111 (1997–present)
4. Giacinto Facchetti 94 (1963–1977)
5. Alessandro Del Piero 85 (1995–present)

#### TROPHIES/HONORS
##### FIFA WORLD CUP
1934 Italy 2 Czechoslovakia 1 (aet)
1938 Italy 4 Hungary 2
1982 Italy 3 West Germany 1
2006 Italy 1 France 1 (Italy won 5–3 in a penalty shootout)

##### UEFA EUROPEAN CHAMPIONSHIP
1968 Italy 1 Yugoslavia 1 (aet)
Replay: Italy 2 Yugoslavia 0

##### OLYMPIC GOLD MEDAL
1936 Italy 1 Norway 0 (aet)

### DID YOU KNOW?

The top scorer in the 1990 World Cup was Italian player Salvatore "Totò" Schillaci with six goals. Although Schillaci only played 16 times for his country, many Italian fans still refer to the 1990 World Cup as "Notti Magiche di Totò Schillaci" (magical nights of Totò Schillaci).

# GERMANY

Germany is arguably the most consistent soccer-playing nation in the world. While the national team—playing as either Germany or West Germany—may not have won the World Cup as many times as Brazil or Italy, the team has reached no less than 12 major competition finals and won a total of six tournaments. Teamwork, organization, and skill are the trademarks of "Die Nationalelf," combined with a never-say-die attitude that means no German side ever concedes defeat until the final whistle.

The Deutscher Fussball-Bund (soccer association) was founded in 1900. It was split between 1946 and 1991, when Germany was divided into East Germany and West Germany.

## GREATEST MOMENTS

Perhaps Germany's finest achievement came in the 1954 World Cup Finals. The team was beaten 8–3 in one of the earlier group games by the mighty Hungary. But, amazingly, Germany overcame the same opponents 3–2 with a fantastic comeback in the final. This unlikely victory was known as the "Miracle of Berne," after the Swiss city in which the final was played.

Germany's record goal scorer is Gerd Müller. Nicknamed "Der Bomber," he scored an amazing 68 goals in just 62 international appearances.

## "DER KAISER"

A brilliant leader known as "Der Kaiser" (the Emperor), Franz Beckenbauer also had the ability to switch defense into attack as a sweeper. He captained the 1974 team to World Cup victory at home and in 1990 became only the second man to win the trophy as a player and coach when West Germany triumphed in Italy.

Germany's World Cup triumph of 1990 was not the greatest of games, but the narrow 1–0 win over Argentina enabled West Germany to gain revenge for its defeat by the South Americans four years earlier. Victory was secured with a late penalty scored by Andreas Brehme, pictured holding the trophy aloft.

## LOTHAR MATTHÄUS

was the modern successor to Beckenbauer. A determined, outspoken man off the field, he was just as forthright on it, driving his side to success in the 1990 World Cup. He holds the record for German international appearances with 142 caps won over a 20-year period. Matthäus was able to play as a defender or midfielder but spent most of the later stages of his career as a sweeper.

GERMANY DREAM TEAM?   1. Sepp Maier 2. Karl-Heinz Schnellinger 3. Paul Breitner 4. Wolfgang Overath 5. Lothar Matthäus 6. Franz Beckenbauer 7. Günter Netzer 8. Fritz Walter 9. Gerd Müller 10. Helmut Rahn 11. Uwe Seeler

*Ballack is a perfect example of the modern midfielder—athletic, skillful, and a leader on the field.*

Jürgen Klinsmann was a successful club player across Europe and a World Cup winner in 1990. Although he was often mocked for his exaggerated dives to win free kicks, he was first and foremost a superb all-around striker. He later managed an attacking German team to the semifinals of the 2006 World Cup.

## BALLACK

Current Germany captain Michael Ballack is a dynamic midfielder with an eye for goal and a powerful header of the ball. As a young player he was nicknamed "Little Kaiser" because of comparisons with the great Beckenbauer.

Striker Lukas Podolski is one of the rising stars of German soccer. His impressive performances in the 2006 World Cup led to him to be named as the FIFA Best Young Player of the tournament.

## DID YOU KNOW?

*In the 1974 World Cup final, eventual winners West Germany were 1–0 down before they had even touched the ball! Their Dutch opponents kept the ball for two minutes from kickoff and scored a penalty.*

## FACT FILE: GERMANY

### NICKNAME
Die Nationalelf (The National Eleven)

### TOP GOAL SCORERS
1. Gerd Müller 68 (1966–1974)
2. Jürgen Klinsmann 47 (1987–1998)
= Rudi Völler 47 (1982–1994)
3. Karl-Heinz Rumenigge 45 (1976–1986)
4. Uwe Seeler 43 (1954–1970)

### MOST APPEARANCES
1. Lothar Matthäus 150 (1980–2000)
2. Jürgen Klinsmann 108 (1987–1998)
3. Jürgen Kohler 105 (1986–1998)
4. Franz Beckenbauer 103 (1965–1977)
5. Thomas Hässler 101 (1988–2000)

### TROPHIES/HONORS

#### FIFA WORLD CUP
1954 West Germany 3 Hungary 2
1974 West Germany 2 Netherlands 1
1990 West Germany 1 Argentina 0

#### UEFA EUROPEAN CHAMPIONSHIP
1972 West Germany 3 USSR 0
1980 West Germany 2 Belgium 1
1996 Germany 2 Czech Republic 1 (aet)

#### OLYMPIC GAMES
1976 East Germany 3 Poland 1

### EAST GERMANY
While Germany was split into two nations between 1946 and 1991, East Germany was in the shadow of its more successful neighbor. When Germany became a single nation again, East German players such as Ulf Kirsten, Thomas Doll, and Matthias Sammer played for the new, unified team. Sammer was named European Footballer of the Year in 1996.

East Germany triumphed at the 1976 Olympics in Montreal. The 3–1 victory over Poland was a great moment in East German history, with goals from Hartmut Shade, Martin Hoffman, and Reinhard Häfner.

# NETHERLANDS

## "WE ARE THE BRAZILIANS OF EUROPE."

KEES RIJVERS, DUTCH INTERNATIONAL
1946–1960 AND MANAGER 1981–1984

The Netherlands is the greatest national team never to have won the World Cup. Despite a succession of supremely gifted players, its only major triumph has been the 1988 European Championship. Exciting, talented, and inventive the team undoubtedly is, but too often disagreements between the players or an inability to rise to the occasion have let the talented "Oranje" down.

## KNVB

The Koninklijke Nederlandse Voetbalbond (Royal Dutch Soccer Union) formed in 1889. The lion symbol, used since 1907, is based on the emblem of the country's royal family.

## MOMENT OF GLORY

When captain Ruud Gullit received the European Championship trophy in 1988 victory was made even sweeter because it came on the home soil of their great rivals West Germany, whom they knocked out en route to the final. In the final, Gullit scored a header and Marco van Basten a volley in a convincing victory over the Soviet Union.

## JOHAN CRUYFF

For many the greatest player of all time, Cruyff had superb technical ability. He was quick, a great passer of the ball, a fine goal scorer, and could read the game expertly. He won major honors with all his clubs, Ajax, Barcelona, and Feyenoord, and was European Footballer of the Year three times.

*In 2003 the KNVB named Cruyff Dutch soccer's outstanding player of the last 50 years.*

Gifted midfielder Arie Haan was a member of the 1970s Dutch team and a key exponent of the famous "Total Football" style. During the 1978 World Cup, he scored his most famous goal— a stunning 40-yard strike against Italy in the second group stage.

## SUPER STRIKER

Marco van Basten is widely regarded as one of the best strikers of all time. He scored a total of 276 goals for his clubs Ajax and AC Milan and the Dutch national team. Perhaps Van Basten's most famous goal was his spectacular volley in the Euro '88 final. He was European Footballer of the Year in 1988, 1989, and 1992, and World Player of the Year in 1992. He now manages the Netherlands.

Midfielder Clarence Seedorf has won the Champions League with three different clubs—Ajax, Real Madrid, and AC Milan.

# FACT FILE: NETHERLANDS

### NICKNAMES

Oranje, Clockwork Orange, Orange Crush, The Orangemen

### TOP GOAL SCORERS

1. Patrick Kluivert 40 (1994–2004)
2. Dennis Bergkamp 37 (1990–2000)
3. Faas Wilkes 35 (1946–1961)
4. Johan Cruyff 33 (1966–1977)
= Abe Lenstra 33 (1940–1959)

### MOST APPEARANCES

1. Edwin van der Sar 122 (1995–present)
2. Frank de Boer 112 (1990–2004)
3. Philip Cocu 101 (1996–2006)
4. Marc Overmars 86 (1993–2004)
5. Aron Winter 84 (1987–2000)

### TROPHIES/HONORS

**UEFA EUROPEAN CHAMPIONSHIP**
1988 Netherlands 2 USSR 0

**DENNIS BERGKAMP'S** fine ball control and excellent first touch, combined with quick thinking and vision, made him one of the world's top players. He was nicknamed "The Iceman" because of his calmness and he made a habit of scoring great goals, often from outside the area.

## DID YOU KNOW?

In the 1970s, the Dutch invented "Total Football." Under this system, every player could play in every position, giving the side a fluid formation that opponents found difficult to play against. Although this system was great to watch, it only worked if a team had 11 super-talented players, and many coaches also felt that it gave the players too much responsibility on the field.

Ruud van Nistelrooy is one of the most reliable goal scorers in world soccer. He scored 28 times in 54 games for his country before announcing his retirement from international soccer in 2007. He has also set goalscoring records for two of the world's biggest clubs—Manchester United and Real Madrid. Fortunately for the Netherlands, van Nistelrooy reconsidered his decision to retire.

Rafael van der Vaart and Dirk Kuyt are two of the exciting young talents representing the current generation of Dutch players. Van der Vaart is a skillful attacking midfielder with an eye for goal, and Kuyt is a powerful, hard-working forward. While the national team has yet to find a regular way to use van der Vaart's exceptional talents, Kuyt has become a regular in the side.

**NETHERLANDS DREAM TEAM?** 1. Edwin van der Sar 2. Wim Suurbier 3. Ruud Krol 4. Johan Neeskens 5. Ronald Koeman 6. Wim van Hanegem 7. Johan Cruyff 8. Ruud Gullit 9. Marco van Basten 10. Dennis Bergkamp 11. Johnny Rep

# SPAIN

*"REPUTATIONS DO NOT WIN MATCHES AND TROPHIES, ONLY GOALS CAN DO THAT."* REAL MADRID, ARGENTINA, AND SPAIN LEGEND ALFREDO DI STÉFANO

Spain is the great enigma of world soccer. For a country that has produced so many outstanding players and with a population that has such a passion for the game, the national side has tended to underperform. Despite some of the most distinguished club sides in Europe, the Spanish national team has only the 1964 European Championship title and a couple of World Cup quarter-final placings to show for their extraordinary talents.

The Real Federación Española de Fútbol was formed in 1913. "Real" means royal and is a title of honour given by the monarchy, reflecting the prestige soccer enjoys in Spain.

## FAMOUS VICTORY

When Spain hosted and won the European Championship in 1964, it seemed to promise a dazzling new era for the national side. Goals from Pereda and Marcelino earned a 2–1 win over the Soviet Union and enabled the team to parade the Henri Delaunay cup amid wild celebrations at Real Madrid's Bernabéu stadium. However, just two years later Spain crashed out of the World Cup Finals at the group stage.

1960 European Footballer of the Year, Luis Suárez played in the 1964 final despite injury. The inspirational midfielder set up both goals.

## EMILIO BUTRAGUEÑO

Emilio Butragueño was a prolific scorer for his club Real Madrid. For the national team he scored 26 goals in 69 appearances, including four in a 5–1 thrashing of Denmark at the 1986 World Cup. He was nicknamed "El Buitre" (the Vulture) for his deadly ability to snap up chances.

Spanish hopes for future success rest on the shoulders of young players like Cesc Fàbregas. The outstanding midfielder broke into the national team at the age of 18 in 2006, three years after he had won the Golden Shoe for top goal scorer and Golden Ball for best player at the FIFA U-17 World Championships.

Butragueño slips past a french defender in the 1984 European Championship.

**SPAIN DREAM TEAM?** 1. Ricardo Zamora 2. Marquitos 3. Jose Antonio Camacho 4. Luis Suárez 5. Miguel Ángel Nadal 6. Fernando Hierro 7. Amancio Amaro 8. Alfredo Di Stéfano 9. Emilio Butragueño 10. Raúl 11. Francisco Gento

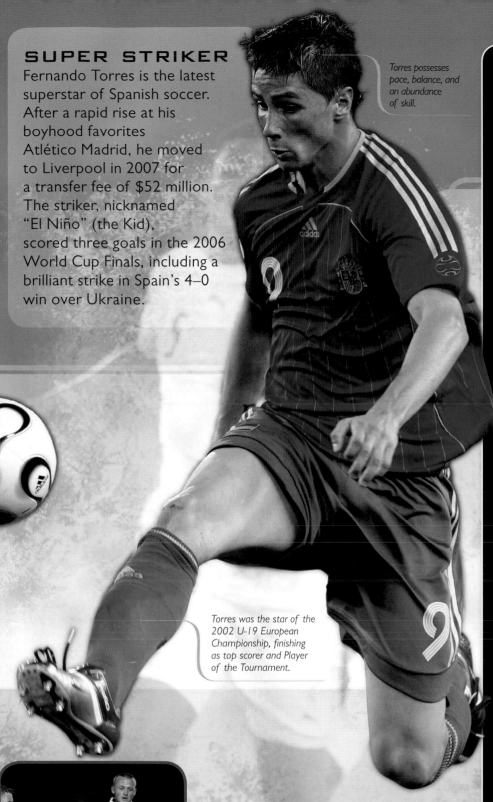

## SUPER STRIKER

Fernando Torres is the latest superstar of Spanish soccer. After a rapid rise at his boyhood favorites Atlético Madrid, he moved to Liverpool in 2007 for a transfer fee of $52 million. The striker, nicknamed "El Niño" (the Kid), scored three goals in the 2006 World Cup Finals, including a brilliant strike in Spain's 4–0 win over Ukraine.

*Torres possesses pace, balance, and an abundance of skill.*

*Torres was the star of the 2002 U-19 European Championship, finishing as top scorer and Player of the Tournament.*

## FACT FILE: SPAIN
### NICKNAMES
La Furia Roja (The Red Fury),
La Selección (The Selection)

### TOP GOAL SCORERS
1. Raúl 44 (1996–2006)
2. Fernando Hierro 29 (1989–2002)
3. Fernando Morientes 27 (1998–present)
4. Emilio Butragueño 26 (1984–1992)
5. Alfredo Di Stéfano 23 (1957–1961)

### MOST APPEARANCES
1. Andoni Zubizaretta 126 (1985–1998)
2. Raúl 102 (1996–2006)
3. Fernando Hierro 89 (1989–2002)
4. José Antonio Camacho 81 (1975–1988)
5. Rafael Gordillo 75 (1978–1988)

### TROPHIES/HONORS

#### UEFA EUROPEAN CHAMPIONSHIP
1964 Spain 2 USSR 1

#### OLYMPIC GOLD MEDAL
1992 Poland 2 Spain 3

### BERNABÉU
Named after a former Real Madrid president, the Santiago Bernabéu was built in 1947 and has a capacity of 75,000. It has hosted many prestigious games, including the 1982 World Cup final. In addition to being Spain's national stadium, it is also the home of Spanish club side Real Madrid.

## RAÚL

Raúl González Blanco, to give him his full name, is Spain's top scorer. By 2006 he had scored 44 goals in 102 appearances and earned a reputation as one of the best European strikers of the last 10 years. With Real Madrid his honors include three Champions League titles.

## DID YOU KNOW?

*Foreign players were banned from playing in the Spanish league from 1963 to 1973. It was felt that the high number of non-Spanish players was affecting the development of homegrown players and thereby having a negative impact on the national team. The ban was lifted when Barcelona signed the talented Dutchman Johan Cruyff.*

# EUROPEAN TEAMS

"THE DIFFERENCES BETWEEN THE BIG TEAMS AND THE SO-CALLED SMALLER TEAMS HAVE BECOME SMALLER."
OTTO REHHAGEL, COACH OF GREECE IN 2004

Soccer is not just the dominant sport in European nations that have already won major trophies. From Portugal in the west to Ukraine in the east, it is the most popular sport in virtually every country and home to many famous national teams and great club sides as well as millions of passionate supporters. Here is a selection of some of the most popular teams in Europe, from up-and-coming nations such as Croatia and Portugal to sleeping giants such as Russia and Poland.

## RUSSIA

Despite a massive population, prestigious domestic clubs, and a rich soccer heritage, Russia has struggled at international tournaments. As the USSR (see "Did You Know?"), the country won the first European Championship in 1960 but so far has consistently failed to make an impression at the World Cup Finals.

Andrey Arshavin is one of Russian soccer's big stars. A creative and dynamic striker, who can also play in midfield, Arshavin was Russian Footballer of the Year in 2005 and 2006.

**FACT FILE**

**TOP GOAL SCORER**
Vladimir Beschastnykh 26 (1992–2003)

**MOST APPEARANCES**
Viktor Onopko 109 (1992–2004)

**TROPHIES/HONORS**
(Competing as the USSR)
**UEFA EUROPEAN CHAMPIONSHIP**
1960 USSR 2 Yugoslavia 1 (aet)
(Competing as Russia)
none

## GREECE

A type of soccer was played in ancient Greece in 200 BCE, but Greece had to wait until 2004 for its first trophy, with an unlikely but deserved victory over Portugal at the European Championship.

**FACT FILE**

**TOP GOAL SCORER**
Nikos Anastopoulos 29 (1977–1988)

**MOST APPEARANCES**
Theodoros Zagorakis 120 (1994–2007)

**TROPHIES/HONORS**
UEFA EUROPEAN CHAMPIONSHIP
2004 Greece 1 Portugal 0

A solid, practical, and defensive approach was the key to Greece's 2004 triumph, with the winning goal scored by Angelos Charisteas in the final against the hosts, Portugal.

## TURKEY

Turkey is an emerging force on the world scene. The team reached the quarterfinals of the European Championships in 2000 and was World Cup semifinalists in 2002.

Hakan Sükür has been one of Turkey's most consistent performers in the last decade. He scored one of the goals that earned Turkey an impressive third place at the 2002 World Cup Finals.

**FACT FILE**

**TOP GOAL SCORER**
Hakan Sükür 51 (1992–present)

**MOST APPEARANCES**
Rüstü Recber 114 (1993–present)

**TROPHIES/HONORS**
none

## SWEDEN

The story of Swedish soccer is one of only moderate success. The team reached the World Cup final when it played host in 1958, and was losing semifinalists in 1994. On both occasions, the victor was Brazil.

**FACT FILE**

**TOP GOAL SCORER**
Sven Rydell 49 (1923–1932)

**MOST APPEARANCES**
Thomas Ravelli 143 (1981–1997)

**TROPHIES/HONORS**
OLYMPIC GOLD MEDAL
1948 Sweden 3 Yugoslavia 1

Three of Sweden's biggest recent stars, Freddie Ljungberg (center), Henrik Larsson (left), and Zlatan Ibrahimovic (right) celebrate Ljungberg's goal in the 5–0 win against Bulgaria during their Group C Euro 2004 qualifying game.

EUROPE DREAM TEAM? 1. Lev Yashin (USSR) 2. Eric Gerets (Belgium) 3. Robert Jarni (Croatia) 4. Dave Mackay (Scotland) 5. John Charles (Wales) 6. Josef Masopust (Czechoslovakia) 7. József Bozsik (Hungary) 8. Ladislao Kubala (Czechoslovakia/Hungary/Spain) 9. Eusébio (Portugal) 10. Ferenc Puskás (Hungary/Spain) 11. George Best (Northern Ireland)

# SCOTLAND

Despite being a nation of just five million people, Scotland has enjoyed some epic international campaigns. Although the team has never won a trophy, it is one of the oldest and best supported national sides.

Founded 1873

Kenny Dalglish was one of the world's finest players during the early 1980s. A skillful and creative forward, he was known as "King Kenny" by the Tartan Army—the name given to Scotland's passionate and devoted fans.

**FACT FILE**

TOP GOAL SCORERS
Kenny Dalglish 30 (1971–1986)
Denis Law 30 (1958–1974)

MOST APPEARANCES
Kenny Dalglish 102 (1971–1986)

TROPHIES/HONORS
none

# POLAND

Poland has never quite lived up to its promise. Its best World Cup showing was third place in the 1982 World Cup after losing 2–0 to eventual champions Italy in the semifinal.

Like many of his countrymen, the Glasgow Celtic striker Maciej Zurawski plays outside of Poland.

**FACT FILE**

TOP GOAL SCORER
Wlodzimierz Lubanski 48 (1963–1980)

MOST APPEARANCES
Grzegorz Lato 100 (1971–1984)

TROPHIES/HONORS
OLYMPIC GOLD MEDAL
1972 Poland 2 Hungary 1

# CROATIA

Founded 1912

Of the countries that emerged from the breakup of Yugoslavia (see "Did You Know"), Croatia has proved the most successful, with third place at France '98.

Davor Šuker was a stylish and prolific striker and won the Golden Boot at the 1998 World Cup Finals.

**FACT FILE**

TOP GOAL SCORER
Davor Šuker 45 (1990–2002)

MOST APPEARANCES
Dario Šimic 95 (1996–present)

TROPHIES/HONORS
none

## DID YOU KNOW?

*Political upheavals have transformed European soccer in the last 20 years. The breakup of the Soviet Union, revolutions in Eastern Europe, and civil war in Yugoslavia have led to the formation of new nations and the reemergence of old ones. The Soviet Union (USSR) was split into Russia and smaller independent countries such as Georgia, Belarus, and Ukraine; Yugoslavia became Serbia, Bosnia-Herezegovina, Croatia, Montenegro, Macedonia, and Slovenia, and Czechoslovakia became the Czech Republic and Slovakia.*

# NORWAY

Norwegian soccer has emerged in recent years thanks to stars such as Morten Gamst Pedersen and John Arne Riise.

Manchester United legend Ole Gunnar Solskjaer is Norway's most famous player of the last decade.

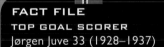

**FACT FILE**

TOP GOAL SCORER
Jørgen Juve 33 (1928–1937)

MOST APPEARANCES
Thorbjørn Svenssen 104 (1947–1962)

TROPHIES/HONORS
none

# ROMANIA

The Romania team of the 1990s was the best so far and made the quarterfinals of US '94 and Euro 2000.

Founded 1909

Romania's Footballer of the Century was Gheorghe Hagi, star of the famous '90s side.

**FACT FILE**

TOP GOAL SCORER
Gheorghe Hagi 35 (1983–2000)

MOST APPEARANCES
Dorinel Munteanu 134 (1991–present)

TROPHIES/HONORS
none

# HUNGARY

Modern soccer owes much to the great Hungarian team of the 1950s. "The Magical Magyars" pioneered a fast and skillful style with imaginative passing and movement. However, Hungary has struggled to make an impact in recent times.

The late Ferenc Puskás is widely regarded as one of the world's best ever players. He scored a phenomenal 84 goals in just six years for Hungary, before changing nationality and appearing for Spain.

**FACT FILE**

TOP GOAL SCORER
Ferenc Puskás 84 (1949–1956)

MOST APPEARANCES
József Bozsik 101 (1947–1962)

TROPHIES/HONORS
OLYMPIC GOLD MEDAL
1952 Hungary 2 Yugoslavia 0
1964 Hungary 2 Czechoslovakia 1
1968 Hungary 4 Bulgaria 1

## REPUBLIC OF IRELAND

Although Gaelic games such as Gaelic football, hurling, handball, and camogie are hugely popular in the Republic of Ireland, football is still the country's most popular team sport. A period of success began in the late 1980s with stars such as Niall Quinn, Ray Houghton, and Roy Keane. Jack Charlton's side reached the World Cup quarterfinals in Italia '90 and the second round four years later. Recent years have seen mixed fortunes for this talented squad.

Striker Robbie Keane made his debut at just 17 and is now his country's captain as well as top goal scorer.

**FACT FILE**

**TOP GOAL SCORER**
Robbie Keane 32 (1998–present)

**MOST APPEARANCES**
Steve Staunton 102 (1988–2002)

**TROPHIES/HONORS**
none

## DENMARK

Traditionally, Denmark was known for producing fine players but had never made much of an international impact as a team. That was until Euro '92, when it caused a major upset by beating West Germany 2–0 in the final in Gothenburg.

Founded 1889

For more than a decade, Peter Schmeichel was regarded as the best goalkeeper in the world. He was a superb shot stopper and dominated his area.

**FACT FILE**

**TOP GOAL SCORER**
Poul "Tist" Nielsen 52 (1910–1925)

**MOST APPEARANCES**
Peter Schmeichel 129 (1987–2001)

**TROPHIES/HONORS**
UEFA EUROPEAN CHAMPIONSHIP
1992 Denmark 2 Germany 0
CONFEDERATIONS CUP
1995 Denmark 2 Argentina 0

## UKRAINE

The modern Ukrainian team only came into existence in 1991 (see "Did You Know?" p. 45). Featuring many players who play for or at least began their careers at the great club side Dinamo Kiev, the national team is one of the strongest in the new-look Eastern Europe.

Star striker Andriy Shevchenko was European Footballer of the Year in 2004.

**FACT FILE**

**TOP GOAL SCORER**
Andriy Shevchenko 36 (1995–present)

**MOST APPEARANCES**
Oleksandr Shovkovskiy 82 (1994–present)

**TROPHIES/HONORS**
none

## PORTUGAL

With a passionate soccer culture and a history of gifted players and great club sides, Portugal has all the ingredients for international success. Yet for all its promise, the team has never quite realized its potential, losing the Euro 2004 final and finishing third in the 1966 World Cup.

A brilliant playmaker and goal scorer, Luis Figo was the star of the so-called "Golden Generation" that won the World Youth Championships in 1989.

Portugal has a new superstar in Cristiano Ronaldo. Lightning quick, blessed with a blistering shot, and famous for his stepovers and tricks, Ronaldo is a modern master.

**FACT FILE**

**TOP GOAL SCORER**
Pauleta 47 (1997–2006)

**MOST APPEARANCES**
Luis Figo 127 (1991–2006)

**TROPHIES/HONORS**
none

## AUSTRIA

Austria could also claim to be sleeping giants of European soccer. It finished third in the 1954 World Cup, but has not gone beyond the second round since. 2008 will be Austria's first time in the European Championships, which they will cohost with Switzerland.

All-time top scorer Toni Polster in action for his country.

**FACT FILE**

**TOP GOAL SCORER**
Anton "Toni" Polster 44 (1988–2000)

**MOST APPEARANCES**
Andreas Herzog 103 (1998–2002)

**TROPHIES/HONORS**
none

## CZECH REPUBLIC

The 1989 "Velvet Revolution" divided Czechoslovakia into two nations (see p. 45) and the Czech Republic emerged as the stronger soccer team. It was runner-up in the 1996 European Championship and qualified for the 2006 World Cup in Germany.

Skilled midfielder Pavel Nedved is regarded as the best Czech player of his generation.

**FACT FILE**

**TOP GOAL SCORER**
Jan Koller 50 (1999–present)

**MOST APPEARANCES**
Karel Poborský 118 (1994–2006)

**TROPHIES/HONORS**
(Competing as Czechoslovakia)
**UEFA EUROPEAN CHAMPIONSHIP**
1976 Czechoslovakia 2 West Germany 2
Czechoslovakia won 5–3 on penalties
(Competing as Czech Republic)
none

## BELGIUM

The Belgian national team's best performance was as runners-up in the 1980 European Championship, when it lost 2–1 to West Germany in the final.

Eric Gerets is one of Belgium's most famous players. A defender who won 86 caps playing for his country, Gerets also won the European Cup in 1988 with PSV Eindhoven.

**FACT FILE**

**TOP GOAL SCORERS**
Paul Van Himst 30 (1960–1974)
Bernard Voorhoof 30 (1928–1940)

**MOST APPEARANCES**
Jan Ceulemans 96 (1977–1990)

**TROPHIES/HONORS**
**OLYMPIC GOLD MEDAL**
1920 Belgium 2 Czechoslovakia 0

## SWITZERLAND

Switzerland reached the quarterfinals of the World Cup in 1934 and 1938 but has enjoyed little success since then. They were knocked out of the 2006 Finals tournament despite not conceding a single goal.

**FACT FILE**

**TOP GOAL SCORERS**
Kubilay Türkyilmaz 34 (1988–2001)
Max Abegglen 34 (1922–1937)

**MOST APPEARANCES**
Heinz Hermann 117 (1978–1991)

**TROPHIES/HONORS**
none

## WALES

Founded 1876

Despite the popularity of rugby, Welsh soccer has enjoyed a recent boom. However, the national side continues to miss out barely on major tournaments and the 1958 World Cup Finals is Wales' only qualification so far.

From John Charles to Ian Rush, Wales has produced many world-class players. The best of recent years has been Ryan Giggs, Manchester United's dazzling winger.

**FACT FILE**

**TOP GOAL SCORER**
Ian Rush 28 (1980–1996)

**MOST APPEARANCES**
Neville Southall 92 (1990–2006)

**TROPHIES/HONORS**
none

## SERBIA

The Serbian team was formed as one of the relics of the old Yugoslavia side that broke up in the 1990s (see p. 45). Striker Savo Milošević holds both appearance and goal scoring records for his country.

**FACT FILE**

**TOP GOAL SCORER**
Savo Milošević 35 (1994–2006)

**MOST APPEARANCES**
Savo Milošević 101 (1994–2006)

**TROPHIES/HONORS**
none

## NORTHERN IRELAND

With just 1.5 million people, Northern Ireland can't compete with the larger nations. However, it can claim to be British champion – it won the British Home Championships in 1984, the last time it was contested. Championships

Founded 1880

Striker David Healy is seen here in action against Spain, whom Northern Ireland also defeated in the Euro 2008 qualifiers.

**FACT FILE**

**TOP GOAL SCORER**
David Healy 33 (2000–present)

**MOST APPEARANCES**
Pat Jennings 119 (1964–1986)

**TROPHIES/HONORS**
none

## BULGARIA

Bulgaria's finest hour came in the 1994 World Cup Finals in the USA. It beat the holders Germany 2–1 in the quarterfinal before losing by the same score to Italy in the semifinal.

Founded 1923

**FACT FILE**

**TOP GOAL SCORER**
Hristo Bonev 47 (1967–1979)

**MOST APPEARANCES**
Borislav Mikhailov 102 (1990–2006)

**TROPHIES/HONORS**
none

# NORTH AMERICA

"FOOTBALL IS FULL OF SURPRISES."

St. Lucia, the Bahamas, the British Virgin Islands… this may sound like a list of dream vacation destinations but, in fact, they are all members of the soccer confederation that unites North and Central America and the Caribbean. In addition to including some of the world's most exotic soccer outposts, it also represents some serious contenders for international glory, such as Mexico and the US. Beach soccer is also popular in this region and an annual tournament is hotly contested with sides from the South American confederation.

The Confederation of North American, Central American and Caribbean Association Football (CONCACAF) came together in 1961. It produced four qualifiers in the 2006 World Cup. The best ever World Cup result for a CONCACAF member is the US's semifinal in 1930.

GREENLAND

CANADA

UNITED STATES OF AMERICA

MEXICO

THE BAHAMAS

DOMINICAN REPUBLIC

BRITISH VIRGIN ISLANDS

PUERTO RICO

ANGUILLA

ANTIGUA AND BARBUDA

GUADELOUPE

DOMINICA

MARTINIQUE

ST LUCIA

BARBADOS

ANTILLES

ST KITTS AND NEVIS

CUBA

JAMAICA

HAITI

ST VINCENT AND

# SOUTH AMERICA

*"NOT MUCH OCCURS IN LATIN AMERICA THAT DOESN'T BEAR DIRECTLY OR INDIRECTLY ON FOOTBALL."*
URUGUAYAN HISTORIAN AND AUTHOR EDUARDO GALEANO

The nations and star names of this region read like a list of reasons to get excited about the beautiful game. Pelé, Ardiles, Maradona, Romário, Ronaldinho, Messi, and a flood of attractive exports have illuminated soccer clubs across the globe. This stronghold of soccer has seen a team within its own federation win the coveted World Cup every time it has hosted the tournament.

The Confederación Sudamericana de Fútbol, (South American Soccer Confederation) is also known as CONMEBOL or CSF. It was founded in 1916 by Argentina, Brazil, Chile, and Uruguay. It has 10 member nations and has produced the World Cup winners on nine occasions. CONMEBOL has four guaranteed World Cup places, plus a chance to playoff with the winners of the Oceania group.

BELIZE
GUATEMALA
EL SALVADOR
HONDURAS
NICARAGUA
COSTA RICA
PANAMA
ECUADOR
COLOMBIA
VENEZUELA
SURINAM
FRENCH GUIANA
GUYANA
BRAZIL
PERU
BOLIVIA
PARAGUAY
ARGENTINA
CHILE
URUGUAY

South American soccer fans have blazed a flamboyant trail for the rest of the world to follow. Traditions like fiesta (street partying) and samba (music and dance), have given them a head start in knowing how to support their heroes in awesome style!

# BRAZIL

## "BEAUTY COMES FIRST. VICTORY IS SECONDARY. WHAT MATTERS IS JOY."

SÓCRATES, BRAZIL MIDFIELDER 1979–1986

Magical, mesmeric, spellbinding—these terms aren't often lavished on soccer teams, except for Brazil. Universally admired for its scintillating style and breathtaking skills, Brazil is the most successful soccer nation of all time and has won the World Cup a record five times. Brazil has also given the game arguably its greatest ever player—the legendary Pelé—and blazed a glorious trail for others to follow. For Brazil soccer really is "the beautiful game"!

The Confederação Brasileira de Futebol (Brazilian Soccer Confederation) was founded in 1914.

*Pelé's real name is Edson Arantes do Nascimento.*

*Victorious captain, Cafu, collects the trophy in 2002.*

## WORLD CUP

Brazil's World Cup triumphs include 1958, when a 17-year-old Pelé scored twice in a 5–2 win over Sweden, and 1970, when victory over Italy allowed Brazil to keep the Jules Rimet trophy. Surprisingly, the 2–0 win over Germany in the 2002 final was the first ever competitive clash between these international heavyweights.

## BEST EVER?

Voted FIFA Footballer of the Century in the year 2000, Pelé is the only player ever to be part of three World Cup-winning squads and he scored 77 goals in 92 appearances for his country. A sensational dribbler with an unstoppable shot, he was also an unselfish and inspired playmaker. Pelé's talent and sportsmanship made him universally loved, even by his opponents.

Many argue that Brazil's finest player was actually Garrincha, not Pelé. Despite a deformed spine and one leg longer than the other, he was a mesmerising dribbler. Garrincha won the World Cup in 1958 and 1962.

Zico is possibly the greatest Brazilian never to have won the World Cup. In 1982 and 1986, teams featuring Zico, Sócrates, Falcão, and Junior were a joy to watch, but lost out. In the 2006 World Cup Finals Zico faced Brazil as manager of Japan.

## DID YOU KNOW?

*Brazil hasn't always played in yellow and blue. The famous uniform was designed by a 19-year-old fan in a competition to give the team a makeover after the nation turned against the unlucky white uniform worn in the 1950 World Cup.*

BRAZIL DREAM TEAM? | 1. Gílmar 2. Cafu 3. Nílton Santos 4. Didi 5. Lúcio 6. Bellini 7. Garrincha 8. Leônidas 9. Ronaldo 10. Pelé 11. Rivelino

**RONALDO** follows in an illustrious tradition of great Brazilian strikers. Although he has been criticized for his weight and for his poor performance in the 1998 World Cup final, his record is undeniable. He is the World Cup Finals' top scorer with 15 goals in four World Cups, and was voted the FIFA World Player of the Year in 1996, 1997, and 2002.

*Kaká got his nickname as a child because he was unable to say his real name, Ricardo.*

## KAKÁ

Midfielder Kaká is regarded as one of the best players in the world today. His vision, range of passing and forceful shooting make him equally comfortable playing deep in midfield or pushing up into attack. He was Brazil's stand-out player in an otherwise disappointing 2006 World Cup Finals.

## RONALDINHO

Ronaldinho was voted FIFA World Player of the Year in 2004 and 2005 and was part of the World Cup winning team in 2002. Famous for his close control and dribbling skills, he is also a powerful and prolific shooter, despite not being an out-and-out striker. However, it is Ronaldinho's mastery of the unexpected—his ability to pull off a pass, move, feint, or shot to stun even the best of defenders—that has won him many fans around the world.

# FACT FILE: BRAZIL

### NICKNAMES
A Seleção (The Selected), Canarinho (Little Canary)

### TOP GOAL SCORERS
1. Pelé 77 (1957–1971)
2. Ronaldo 62 (1994–present)
3. Romário 55 (1987–2005)
4. Zico 52 (1971–1989)
5. Bebeto 39 (1985–1998))

### MOST APPEARANCES
1. Cafu 142 (1990–2006)
2. Roberto Carlos 125 (1992–2006)
3. Rivelino 122 (1965–1978)
4. Émerson Leão 106 (1970–1986)
5. Cláudio Taffarel 101 (1987–1998)

### TROPHIES/HONORS

#### FIFA WORLD CUP
1958 Brazil 5 Sweden 2
1962 Brazil 3 Czechoslovakia 1
1970 Brazil 4 Italy 1
1994 Brazil 3 Italy 2
2002 Brazil 2 Germany 0

#### COPA AMÉRICA
1919 Brazil 1 Uraguay 0
1922 Brazil 3 Paraguay 0
1949 Brazil 7 Paraguay 0
1989 Brazil 1 Uruguay 0
1997 Brazil 3 Bolivia 1
1999 Brazil 3 Uruguay 0
2004 Brazil 4 Argentina 2
2007 Brazil 3 Argentina 0

The Maracanã stadium in Rio de Janeiro is the biggest soccer arena in the world. It hosted the equivalent of a World Cup final when Brazil played Uruguay in the deciding game of the 1950 tournament, in an unusual round-robin system. Brazil lost 2–1 in front of an estimated 210,000 fans.

# ARGENTINA

*"IF YOU PLAY WELL AND SHOW THE ARGENTINIAN PEOPLE WHAT THEY WANT TO SEE, THEY'LL THANK YOU FOR IT ALL YOUR LIFE."*

HÉCTOR ENRIQUE, PART OF ARGENTINA'S '86 TEAM

They may have lost the first ever World Cup 4–2 to Uruguay, but they've made up for it since with two World Cups, 14 Copa Américas, and six victories in Pan American games. Many heroes have played a part in Argentina's dramatic history. "El Gran Capitan," Daniel Passarella, was the first Argentine to touch the World Cup, while Leopoldo Luque lit up the 1978 finals with his sensational long-range efforts on goal. Today, Juan Román Riquelme's playmaking magic gives new hope to a soccer-crazy country.

The first Argentinian soccer association was founded by Glaswegian teacher Alexander Hutton in 1891. It laid the foundations for the modern Argentine Soccer Association.

## HISTORIC MOMENT

Argentina came of age in spectacular style when they hosted and won their first World Cup in 1978. It was a torrid tournament, full of controversy. Argentina beat Brazil to the final on goal difference after beating Peru 6–0 in their final round two match. They then overpowered the Netherlands' "Total Football" in the final.

*Daniel Passarella triumphantly holds the World Cup aloft.*

*Maradona is regarded by many as the greatest player of all time.*

Mario Kempes won the 1978 World Cup for Argentina with two goals in a 3–1 extra time victory over the Netherlands. He scored six goals in the Finals and was South American Player of the Year.

Maradona's talent was epitomized by the 1986 World Cup quarterfinal when he took out the whole England defense with a surging, spellbinding dribble to score the "Goal of the Century."

## MARADONA

Dazzling Diego Maradona scored 34 goals in 91 internationals. His squat, muscular frame gave him a low center of gravity, which made him almost impossible to knock off the ball. He scored five goals in the 1986 World Cup Finals and inspired his side to beat West Germany 3–2 in the final. Despite a career dogged by scandal and controversy both on and off the field, Maradona remains a hero in his native country.

| ARGENTINA DREAM TEAM? | 1. Ubaldo Fillol 2. Javier Zanetti 3. Silvio Marzolini 4. Omar Sívori 5. Daniel Passarella 6. Roberto Ayala 7. José Manuel Moreno 8. Ángel Labruna 9. Alfredo Di Stéfano 10. Diego Maradona 11. Mario Kempes |
|---|---|

## STAR STRIKER

Prolific goal scorer Gabriel Batistuta hit 56 goals in 78 games for Argentina, which earned him the nickname "Batigol." He hit four goals in USA '94, and five in France '98—tournaments in which his team as a whole achieved relatively little success. When Batistuta retired from the national team, Hernán Crespo took over as the main striker. Despite competition from younger players such as Messi, Tévez, and Saviola, Crespo's record of more than a goal every other game speaks for itself.

## NEW MARADONA?

Lionel Messi is a big game player. A visionary passer of the ball and scorer of special goals, he is on the way to fulfilling Maradona's prediction that he has a true successor at last. Messi scored two goals and created more in Argentina's impressive, but ultimately unsuccessful 2007 Copa América campaign. One of a stunning array of strikers at Barcelona, his own legend is just beginning.

### FACT FILE: ARGENTINA
#### NICKNAMES
Albicelestes (White and Sky Blues),
Los Gauchos (The Cowboys)

#### TOP GOAL SCORERS
1. Gabriel Batistuta 56 (1991–2002)
2. Hernán Crespo 35 (1995–present)
3. Diego Maradona 34 (1977–1994)
4. Luis Artime 24 (1961–1967)
5. Leopoldo Luque 22 (1975–1981)
= Daniel Passarella 22 (1976–1986)

#### MOST APPEARANCES
1. Javier Zanetti 117 (1994–present)
2. Roberto Ayala 115 (1994–2007)
3. Diego Simeone 106 (1988–2002)
4. Oscar Ruggeri 97 (1983–1994)
5. Diego Maradona 91 (1977–1994)

#### TROPHIES/HONORS
##### FIFA WORLD CUP
1978 Argentina 3 Netherlands 1 (aet)
1986 Argentina 3 West Germany 2

##### COPA AMÉRICA
1921, 1925, 1927, 1929, 1937, 1941, 1945, 1946, 1947, 1955, 1957, 1959 (round-robin league tournaments) 1991 (round-robin, then final round of four teams in a mini league) 1993 Argentina 2 Mexico 1

##### CONFEDERATIONS CUP
1992 Argentina 3 Saudi Arabia 1

##### OLYMPIC GAMES
2004 Argentina 1 Paraguay 0

### DID YOU KNOW?

*Messi had one of the shortest ever debuts in international soccer, when he was sent off after just forty seconds against Hungary. He came on in the 63rd minute and the referee believed he deliberately used an elbow against Vilmos Vanzcak.*

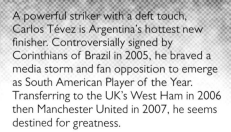

A powerful striker with a deft touch, Carlos Tévez is Argentina's hottest new finisher. Controversially signed by Corinthians of Brazil in 2005, he braved a media storm and fan opposition to emerge as South American Player of the Year. Transferring to the UK's West Ham in 2006 then Manchester United in 2007, he seems destined for greatness.

The Estadio Monumental Antonio V. Liberti is Argentina's national stadium. It is better known as El Monumental or River Plate Stadium and can hold more than 65,000 fans.

# SOUTH AMERICAN TEAMS

**"OUR FOOTBALL COMES FROM THE HEART, THEIRS COME FROM THE MIND."** PELÉ COMPARES THE GAME IN SOUTH AMERICA AND EUROPE

South America has so much more to offer than just Brazil and Argentina. From historically illustrious teams such as Uruguay, to optimistic minnows such as Venezuela, this diverse continent captures everything that is fascinating about the world game. South America often produces a dark horse to illuminate a World Cup.

*Recoba is famous for his dribbling, technique, and strong, accurate left-foot shot.*

## FACT FILE

**TOP GOAL SCORER**
Hector Scarone 31 (unknown–1930)
**MOST APPEARANCES**
Rodolfo Rodriguez 78 (unknown–1994)

### TROPHIES/HONORS
**FIFA WORLD CUP**
1930 Uruguay 4 Argentina 2
1950 Uruguay topped a four-team final group
**COPA AMÉRICA**
1916, 1917, 1920, 1923, 1924, 1926, 1935, 1942, 1956, 1959, 1967, 1959, 1967 (round-robin league tournaments)
1983 Uruguay 3 Brazil 1 (agg)
1987 Uruguay 1 Chile 0
1995 Uruguay 1 Brazil 1 (Uruguay won 5–3 in a penalty shootout.
**OLYMPIC GAMES**
1924 Uruguay 3 Switzerland 0
1928 Uruguay 2 Argentina 1 (replay)

## URUGUAY

The Asociación Uruguaya de Fútbol was founded in 1900 and was one of the original members of CONMEBO.L Although it is one of the few nations to have won the World Cup more than once, Uruguay has been through a lengthy lean spell in recent years that has, unfortunately, coincided with the upsurge of local rivals Argentina. In 2006, Uruguay didn't even qualify for the World Cup Finals, missing out after losing a nail-biting playoff to Australia.

*Victory in the first ever World Cup is not Uruguay fans' fondest memory—securing the trophy in 1950 at the expense of host Brazil was an even sweeter triumph.*

### ÁLVARO RECOBA
has scored 12 goals in 58 internationals. He managed to upstage Brazilian striker Ronaldo on their shared debut for Inter Milan. The Uruguayan scored two late goals, one a 35-meter rocket.

*Chilavert celebrates scoring Paraguay's third goal in a 5–1 win over Bolivia in 2001.*

Founded 1906

## PARAGUAY

Although overshadowed by more glamorous neighbors, Paraguay has come close to causing major World Cup upsets. Making round two in 1998, it was only squeezed out by a "golden goal" in the 114th minute by ultimate winner, France. In 2002 it was a round two exit again, this time 1–0 to eventual finalist Germany.

Inspired, impulsive, and often controversial, José Luis Chilavert combined daring goalkeeping with a talent for scoring free kicks and penalties. He scored eight goals in international matches and an amazing 62 throughout his career.

## FACT FILE

**TOP GOAL SCORER**
José Cardozo 25 (1991–2006)
**MOST APPEARANCES**
Carlos Gamarra 110 (1993–2006)

### TROPHIES/HONORS
**COPA AMÉRICA**
1953 and 1979 (round-robin league tournaments)

---

**REST OF SOUTH AMERICA**
1. José Luis Chilavert (Paraguay) 2. Víctor Rodríguez Andrade (Uruguay) 3. José Nasazzi (Uruguay) 4. Obdulio Varela (Uruguay) 5. Héctor Chumpitaz (Peru) 6. Elías Figueroa (Chile) 7. Carlos Valderrama (Colombia) 8. Juan Alberto Schiaffino (Uruguay) 9. Alberto Spencer (Ecuador/Uruguay) 10. Teófilo Cubillas (Peru) 11. Leonel Sánchez (Chile)

# COLOMBIA

A 1–0 victory over Mexico in the 2001 Copa América is the only major trophy for this underachieving side. Its only World Cup appearance of recent years was in France '98, where it managed just one win, 1–0 against Tunisia. Tragedy struck in 1994, when defender Andrés Escobar scored an own-goal in a 2–1 defeat to the US. He was shot dead a short time later.

**FACT FILE**

**TOP GOAL SCORER**
Arnoldo Iguarán 25 (1979–1993)

**MOST APPEARANCES**
Carlos Valderrama 111 (1983–1998)

**TROPHIES/HONORS**
**COPA AMÉRICA**
2001 Colombia 1 Mexico 0

# VALDERRAMA was a

gifted playmaker with a style all his own, and not just because of his hairstyle! In 111 internationals his unhurried style and classy touch made the toughest game look like a stroll in the park. His Colombia team impressed at Italy '90 and was the only side to avoid defeat against eventual winners Germany.

*Valderrama was instantly recognizable thanks to his hairstyle.*

Fiery striker Faustino Asprilla notched up an impressive 20 goals in 57 caps. Among his memorable displays was Colombia's legendary 5–0 thrashing of Argentina in 1993. Red cards, fights, and great stories for the press were never far away when "Tino" was involved.

# VENEZUELA is the only

side in the South American confederation never to have qualified for a World Cup Finals. Inspired by top players such as Juan Arango, the country hopes to lose its pushover status en route to the 2010 Finals.

**FACT FILE**

**TOP GOAL SCORER**
Juan Arango 23 (2000–present)

**MOST APPEARANCES**
José Manuel Rey 87 (1996–present)

**TROPHIES/ HONORS**
none

# BOLIVIA

participated in the first World Cup in 1930 and again in 1950, but in recent years has had little impact on the tournament, aside from making it to the Finals in the US in 1994.

**FACT FILE**

**TOP GOAL SCORER**
Juan Carlos Arce 18 (2004–present)

**MOST APPEARANCES**
Marco Sandy 93 (unknown–present)

**TROPHIES/ HONORS**
**COPA AMÉRICA**
1963 (round-robin tournament)

# ECUADOR

is traditionally regarded as a South American lightweight, but it impressed at the 2006 finals, beating Poland and Costa Rica before losing to England in the second round.

**FACT FILE**

**TOP GOAL SCORER**
Agustín Delgado 31 (1994–present)

**MOST APPEARANCES**
Iván Hurtado 143 (1993–present)

**TROPHIES/ HONORS**
none

# PERU

Between 1970 and 1982 Peru's flowing ball was admired across the globe. Teófilo Cubillas scored 5 goals in 2 World Cups, but a 1970 quarterfinal was the best result and Peru has not graced the Finals for 24 years.

**FACT FILE**

**TOP GOAL SCORER**
Teófilo Cubillas 30 (1970–1978, 1981–1986)

**MOST APPEARANCES**
Roberto Palacios 118 (1992–present)

**TROPHIES/HONORS**
**COPA AMÉRICA**
1939 (round-robin league tournament)
1975 Peru 3 Colombia 1 (agg)

Héctor Chumpitaz played in two World Cup Finals and helped his side lift the Copa América in 1975.

# CHILE

Established in 1895, the Federación de Fútbol de Chile was also one of the founder members of CONMEBOL. As host of the 1962 World Cup Finals, Chile recorded a best-ever third place. In 1998, Marcelo Salas's goals brightened its World Cup. He scored twice in a 2–2 draw with Italy and in its 4–1 defeat to Brazil in the second round.

Matías Fernández was voted South American Footballer of the Year in 2006. This attacking midfielder is also a free kick specialist.

**FACT FILE**

**TOP GOAL SCORER**
Marcelo Salas 35 (1994–2005)

**MOST APPEARANCES**
Leonel Sánchez 84 (1955–1968)

**TROPHIES/HONORS**

# USA

Once known for bringing razzmatazz, cheerleaders, and big-screen replays to soccer—aka football—the US now boasts a robust national team. Eyebrows were raised when the US was allocated the 1994 World Cup, but qualification for every World Cup since has silenced critics. A "clean sheet" elsewhere may be a "shutout" here, but fresh blood and new ideas from the US have invigorated the world game.

The United States Soccer Federation was formed in 1913 and it was affiliated to FIFA in the same year. It was actually called the US Football Federation until 1945, when it was changed to soccer.

*Bart McGhee (left) and Bert Patenaude (right)*

## HISTORY MAKERS

The US exceeded expectations at the 1930 World Cup and reached the semifinals. American Bart McGhee scored the first-ever goal in a World Cup Finals in a 3–0 win against Belgium and his teammate Bert Patenaude is generally credited with scoring the first-ever World Cup hat trick against Paraguay.

## RECENT SUCCESS

In 2007 the US overcame the rest of North and Central America to triumph in the CONCACAF Gold Cup. Also the host country, the US beat Mexico 2–1 in the final.

| USA DREAM TEAM? | |
|---|---|
| 1. Kasey Keller 2. Eddie Pope 3. Thomas Dooley 4. Tab Ramos 5. Marcelo Balboa 6. Paul Caligiuri 7. Claudio Reyna 8. John Harkes 9. Joe Gaetjens 10. Landon Donovan 11. Walter Bahr | |

## SHUTOUT KINGS

The US has a fine crop of world class goalkeepers. Brad Friedel (top, 82 caps) was nicknamed "The Human Wall" for his performances in the 2002 World Cup, while Kasey Keller (middle, 101 caps) famously kept a "clean sheet" against Brazil in the US's shock 1–0 victory in 1998. Tim Howard (bottom, 22 caps) has won an FA Cup medal with Manchester United in 2004 and currently plays for Everton.

## TEAM LEADER

US captain Landon Donovan has scored 34 goals in 96 appearances. He was MLS Soccer Athlete of the Year in 2003 and 2004, and was honored with a place in the MLS All-Time Best Team. He plays for LA Galaxy club, alongside David Beckham.

*Since Claudio Reyna's retirement, Donovan has been the US's first choice No.10.*

The first American ever to be named in a World Cup All-Tournament team (2002), Claudio Reyna (112 caps) appeared in four US World Cup squads from 1994 to 2006. He preceded Donovan as US captain, and his leadership skills and battling midfield style earned him the nickname "Captain America." Reyna currently plays for Red Bull New York in the MLS.

## FACT FILE: USA

### NICKNAMES
The Stars and Stripes,
The Red, White, and Blue

### TOP GOAL SCORERS
1. Landon Donovan 34 (2000–present)
2. Eric Wynalda 34 (1990–2000)
3. Brian McBride 30 (1993–2006)
4. Joe-Max Moore 24 (1992–2002)
5. Bruce Murray 21 (1985–1993)

### MOST APPEARANCES
1. Cobi Jones 164 (1992–2004)
2. Jeff Agoos 134 (1988–2003)
3. Marcelo Balboa 128 (1988–2000)
4. Claudio Reyna 112 (1994–2006)
5. Paul Caligiuri 110 (1984–1997)

### TROPHIES/HONORS
#### CONCACAF GOLD CUP
1991 USA 0 Honduras 0 (USA won 4–3 in a penalty shootout)
2002 USA 2 Costa Rica 0
2005 USA 0 Panama 0 (USA won 3–1 in a penalty shootout)

Center forward Eric Wynalda (106 caps) joint all-time US top scorer, with 34 goals. He was the first US-born player to play in the German Bundesliga, for Saarbrucken (1992–1994). In 1996 he scored the first-ever goal in the MLS, for San Jose Clash.

## DID YOU KNOW?

*In the 1950 World Cup the US beat England 1–0 in one of the greatest upsets of all time, thanks to keeper Frank Borghi and goal scorer Joe Gaetjens.*

*In 1984 the national side, then known as Team America, played in the North American Soccer League. It was believed that regular competition would improve the side, but it finished bottom of the league.*

## FREDDY ADU

18-year-old Ghana-born Fredua Koranteng Adu looks destined to be a big star for the US. He already holds the unique record of a hat trick in both the U-17 and U-20 World Cups, and has now signed for Portuguese side Benfica.

# CONCACAF TEAMS

The CONCACAF has 40 members and is dominated by Mexico and the USA. The federation also includes three South American nations—Guyana, Surinam, and French Guiana. Since 1991 CONCACAF's showpiece tournament has been the Gold Cup. With seven Gold Cup wins Mexico is the most successful national team, but the USA is catching up fast. The USA hosted the tournament in 2007 and won it for the third time.

*Rafa Márquez is Mexican soccer's modern superstar.*

## MEXICO

Founded 1927

Since the 1990s, Mexico has established itself as a regional and world soccer power. The team combines a direct, physical approach with individual brilliance. Striker Hugo Sánchez is widely regarded as the greatest Mexican player of all time and he is now the national coach.

Goalkeeper Antonio Carbajal made his World Cup Finals debut as a 21-year-old in 1950, and 16 years later became the first player to appear in five consecutive Finals tournaments. He was respected for his safe hands and his leadership, but in all his 11 games at the Finals he ended up on the winning side only once.

## CUBA

With baseball as the national sport, Cuba has never been a major soccer power. However, the national team has shown greater promise in recent times, reaching the last four of the CONCACAF Gold Cup in 2003 and only narrowly missing out on qualification for the 2006 World Cup Finals in Germany.

**FACT FILE**

**TOP GOAL SCORER**
Information unknown

**MOST APPEARANCES**
Information unknown

**TROPHIES/HONORS**
none

Rafael Márquez is Mexico's captain. He plays as a defender or midfielder and made his international debut at 17 years old. He became the first Mexican to win a UEFA Champions League medal when his club, Barcelona, won the title in 2006.

**FACT FILE**

**TOP GOAL SCORER**
Jared Borgetti 43 (1997–present)

**MOST APPEARANCES**
Claudio Suárez 178 (1992–2006)

**TROPHIES/HONORS**
**CONCACAF CHAMPIONSHIP AND GOLD CUP**
1965, 1971, 1977 (round-robin team tournaments)
1977 (top World Cup qualifying team awarded trophy)
1993 Mexico 4 USA 0
1996 Mexico 2 Brazil 0
1998 Mexico 1 USA 0
2003 Mexico 1 Brazil 0

**CONFEDERATIONS CUP**
1999 Mexico 4 Brazil 3

CONCACAF DREAM TEAM? 1. Antonio Carbajal (Mexico) 2. Claudio Suárez (Mexico) 3. Róger Flores (Mexico) 4. Mauricio Solís (Costa Rica) 5. Rafael Márquez (Mexico) 6. Gilberto Yearwood (Honduras) 7. Luis Garcia (Mexico) 8. Dwight Yorke (Trinidad & Tobago) 9. Hugo Sánchez (Mexico) 10. Cuauhtemoc Blanco (Mexico) 11. Emmanuel Sanon (Haiti)

## COSTA RICA

Founded 1921

First successful in the early 1960s, Costa Rica suffered a slump in the 1970s and 1980s. The national side has re-emerged as a force in the 1990s and 2000s and qualified for three World Cups. Costa Rica is currently ranked 56th in the world which makes it Central America's most successful team.

### FACT FILE
**TOP GOAL SCORER**
Rolando Fonseca 47 (1992–present)
**MOST APPEARANCES**
Luis Marin 123 (1993–present)

**TROPHIES/HONORS**
CONCACAF CHAMPIONSHIP
AND GOLD CUP
1963, 1969 (round-robin team tournaments)
1989 (top World Cup qualifying team awarded trophy)

With 45 goals in 72 international matches, Paolo Wanchope is one of Costa Rica's most prolific strikers. He has played club soccer in England, Spain, Japan and the USA.

## HAITI

A golden age in the late 1960s and 1970s saw Haiti reach the World Cup Finals in 1974. However, political and social problems led to a decline in fortune for the national soccer team. Now ranked 83rd by FIFA, and playing home games in Miami, USA, the future looks brighter.

### FACT FILE
**TOP GOAL SCORER**
Emmanuel Sanon 13 (1970–1974)

**MOST APPEARANCES**
Pierre Richard Bruny 54 (1998–present)

**TROPHIES/HONORS**
none

## HONDURAS

Hondurans are passionate about soccer and in 1970 the result of a match led to a war against El Salvador. So far, Honduras has appeared only once in the World Cup Finals, in 1982. However, thanks to stars such as David Suazo, the team could be considered a rising power.

### FACT FILE
**TOP GOAL SCORERS**
Carlos Pavón 47 (1993–present)

**MOST APPEARANCES**
Amado Guevara 104 (1994–present)

**TROPHIES/HONORS**
none

## TRINIDAD AND TOBAGO

Nicknamed the "Soca Warriors", Trinidad and Tobago is the Caribbean's most successful national team. However, a row over bonus payments following Trinidad and Tobago's first ever World Cup in 2006 means that many of the team's stars no longer play for their country.

### FACT FILE
**TOP GOALS CORER**
Stern John 67 (1995–present)
**MOST APPEARANCES**
Angus Eve 118 (1994–present)

**TROPHIES/HONORS**
none

One-time T&T captain Dwight Yorke played in Manchester United's famous 1999 treble-winning side.

## CANADA

Victory in the 2000 CONCACAF Gold Cup was seen to be Canada's big breakthrough, but failure to qualify for the 2006 World Cup was a major setback.

Founded 1912

Canada striker Tomasz Radzinski has played at the top level in England and Belgium.

### FACT FILE
**TOP GOAL SCORERS**
John Catliff 19 (unknown)
Dale Mitchell 19 (1980–1993)
**MOST APPEARANCES**
Randy Samuel 82 (1982–1997)

**TROPHIES/HONORS**
CONCACAF CHAMPIONSHIP
AND GOLD CUP
1985 (top World Cup qualifying team awarded trophy)
2000 Canada 2 Colombia 0

## JAMAICA

Known as the "Reggae Boyz", Jamaica caught the world's attention when the team made it to the 1998 World Cup Finals, its first visit to the tournament. However, the team has struggled recently and is now ranked 94th in the world.

### FACT FILE
**TOP GOAL SCORER**
Theodore Whitmore 24 (1993–2005)
**MOST APPEARANCES**
Durrant Brown 107 (unknown)

**TROPHIES/HONORS**
none

Midfielder Theodore Whitmore is Jamaica's all-time top scorer, and was his country's Footballer of the Year in 1998.

# AFRICA

## "WHEREVER YOU GO THERE [AFRICA], THEY'RE ALL PLAYING FOOTBALL ALL THE TIME. EVERYWHERE"

CARLOS BILARDO, FORMER LIBYA AND ARGENTINA COACH

The Confederation of African Football was formed in 1957, and was allocated its first guaranteed World Cup place in 1970. The first African Cup of Nations took place in the same year but featured only three teams. Today, the CAF has 53 members and Africa has five World Cup Finals places. (This will rise to six in 2010 as South Africa qualifies automatically as hosts.)

When the Brazilian legend Pelé said that an African nation would win the World Cup by the year 2000, his prediction was a little premature. However, his remarks helped to bring African soccer to the world's attention. During the last decade, the soccer world has had to sit up and take notice of Africa. Skillful and entertaining teams such as Ghana, Senegal, and Egypt have emerged, as well as talented individuals such as Ivory Coast's Didier Drogba and Cameroon's Samuel Eto'o. In this diverse continent, soccer has a power beyond politics or religion to unite divided nations and bring a shared sense of identity.

CAPE VERDE ISLAND

## AFRICAN STYLE

Blowing your own horn is common to all soccer fans, but in Africa a deafening bray can often be heard from the passionate supporters who love to make themselves heard. As elsewhere in the world, soccer fanaticism provides an opportunity for celebration that everyday life sometimes fails to deliver.

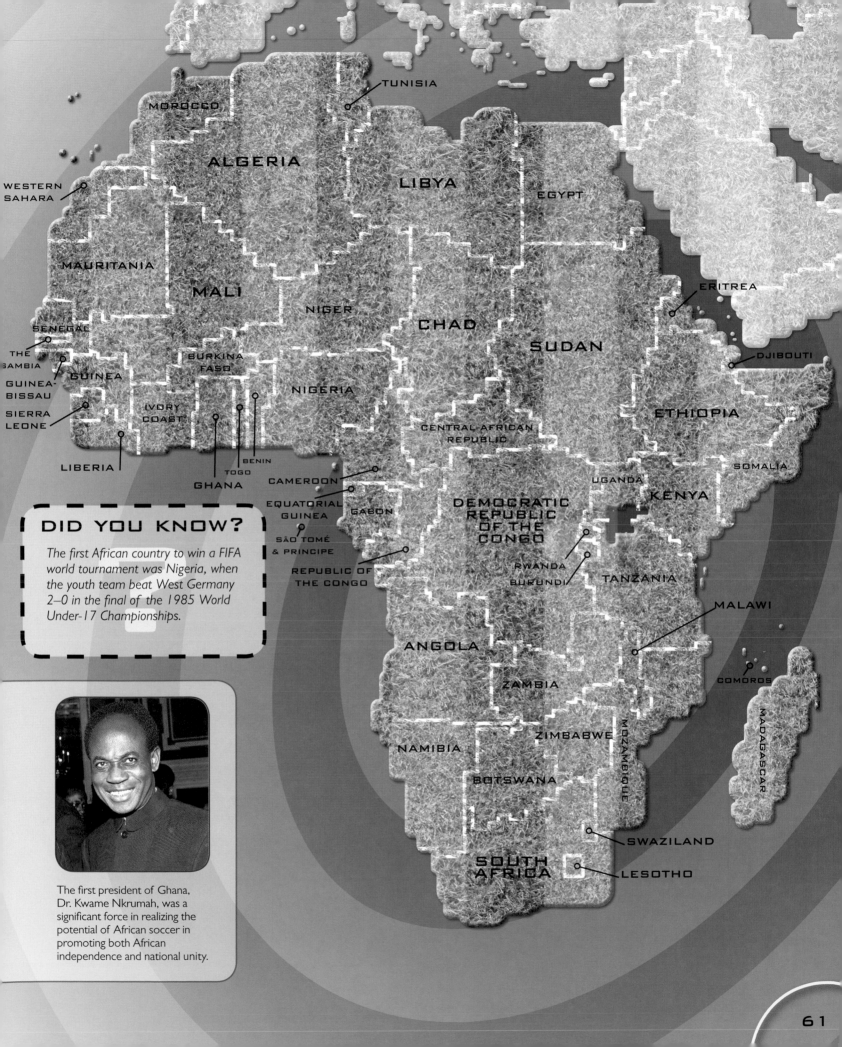

TUNISIA

MOROCCO

ALGERIA

LIBYA

EGYPT

WESTERN
SAHARA

MAURITANIA

MALI

NIGER

CHAD

SUDAN

ERITREA

SENEGAL

THE
GAMBIA

GUINEA

GUINEA-
BISSAU

SIERRA
LEONE

BURKINA
FASO

DJIBOUTI

NIGERIA

ETHIOPIA

IVORY
COAST

LIBERIA

BENIN

TOGO

GHANA

CAMEROON

CENTRAL AFRICAN
REPUBLIC

SOMALIA

UGANDA

KENYA

EQUATORIAL
GUINEA

GABON

DEMOCRATIC
REPUBLIC
OF THE
CONGO

SÃO TOMÉ
& PRINCIPE

RWANDA

BURUNDI

TANZANIA

REPUBLIC OF
THE CONGO

MALAWI

ANGOLA

ZAMBIA

COMOROS

MADAGASCAR

ZIMBABWE

MOZAMBIQUE

NAMIBIA

BOTSWANA

SWAZILAND

SOUTH
AFRICA

LESOTHO

## DID YOU KNOW?

The first African country to win a FIFA
world tournament was Nigeria, when
the youth team beat West Germany
2–0 in the final of the 1985 World
Under-17 Championships.

The first president of Ghana,
Dr. Kwame Nkrumah, was a
significant force in realizing the
potential of African soccer in
promoting both African
independence and national unity.

# SOUTH AFRICA

**"2010 IS ON EVERYONE'S LIPS AND THE PEOPLE OF SOUTH AFRICA ARE LOOKING FORWARD TO GIVING THE WORLD A WARM AFRICAN WELCOME."**

MOLEFI OLIPHANT, PRESIDENT OF THE SOUTH AFRICAN FA

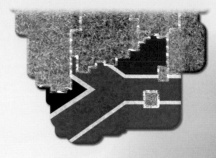

South Africa is proudly pioneering a new era of African soccer, after spending three decades in sporting exile. In 1962 it was expelled by FIFA for refusing to field a mixed-race team and was only allowed back when the apartheid (racial segregation) regime ended in 1992. South Africa celebrated by beating Cameroon 1–0 in its comeback match, thanks to a late penalty by Theophilus "Doctor" Khumalo. Now the "Bafana Bafana" prepare to welcome the World Cup to Africa for the first time.

The South African Football Association was founded in 1991, after a long struggle to rid sports in South Africa of all its past racial division.

## SUCCESS!

For many South Africans, it was enough simply to host the African Cup of Nations in 1996, but to win was unbelievable, especially for the 80,000 home fans. A year later Phil Masinga's winning goal against Congo saw South Africa qualify for their first World Cup.

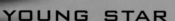
*Aaron Mokoena in action against Ghana in 2006.*

Mark Williams secured a place in South African sports history with the only two goals in the 1996 African Cup of Nations final. Although he traveled widely as a player, his career was overshadowed by that 1996 tournament, where he scored five goals in total—one more than strike partner John "Shoes" Moshoeu.

## YOUNG STAR

Aaron Mokoena is the youngest player ever to play for South Africa. He won his first cap in 1999 against Botswana at the age of 18 years and 56 days. This versatile player, known as "The Ax," can play in defense or midfield and is currently captain of his national team.

## SHAUN BARTLETT

One of South Africa's all-time top scorers is a striker with a tendency to score spectacular goals. Shaun Bartlett's long-range volley for Charlton Athletic was voted England's goal of the season in 2001, and he scored two fiercely struck goals in the 1998 World Cup.

SOUTH AFRICA DREAM TEAM? 1. Andre Arendse 2. Aaron Mokoena 3. Neil Tovey 4. Jomo Sono 5. Lucas Radebe 6. Mark Fish 7. Doctor Khumalo 8. Patrick Ntsoelengoe 9. Steve Mokone 10. Benni McCarthy 11. Kaizer Motaung

## FACT FILE: SOUTH AFRICA

### NICKNAME
Bafana Bafana (The Boys)

### TOP GOAL SCORERS
1. Benni McCarthy 29 (1997–present)
2. Shaun Bartlett 28 (1995–2005)
3. Phil Masinga 19 (1992–2001)
4. Siyabonga Nomvethe 14 (1999–present)
5. Donald Wilson 11 (1947)

### MOST APPEARANCES
1. Shaun Bartlett 74 (1995–2005)
2. John Moshoeu 73 (1993–2004)
3. Lucas Radebe 70 (1992–2003)
4. Andre Arendse 67 (1995–2004)
5. Helman Mkhalele 66 (1994–2001)

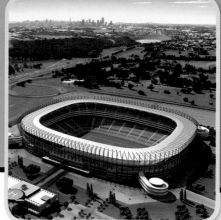

### TROPHIES/HONORS
**AFRICAN NATIONS CUP**
1996 South Africa 2 Tunisia 0

Orlando Pirates and Leeds United supporters admired central defender Lucas Radebe for his inspiring leadership and strength. He captained South Africa's World Cup teams in 1998 and 2002. Since retiring from the game he has become an antiracism campaigner, FIFA Fair Play Award winner, and children's charity worker.

*Benni McCarthy in action in the African Cup of Nations qualifying in 2006.*

## BENNI MCCARTHY

Although South Africa's star striker has enjoyed impressive spells with Ajax Cape Town, Ajax Amsterdam, Celta Vigo, and Porto, his international career has been disrupted by disputes with coaches. Despite quitting the team three times, McCarthy is still a folk hero in his native country.

## 2010

The World Cup Finals are on their way to Africa at last! Just one FIFA delegate's vote denied South Africa the chance to host the 2006 tournament, but now the pressure is on to bring the ambitious plans for 2010 to life. Of the 10 venues, five will be entirely new ones, with more seats promised per match than at any World Cup since 1994.

## SOCCER CITY

The FNB Stadium, built in Johannesburg in 1987 to house 80,000 spectactors, is being demolished for the World Cup Finals. In its place will be the all-new Soccer City Stadium. Its design inspired by traditional African pottery, the new stadium will allow up to 104,000 people to watch the 2010 World Cup final.

# IVORY COAST

> "WHEN WE PLAY, ALL OF IVORY COAST IS HAPPY."
>
> MIDFIELDER YAYA TOURÉ

Ivory Coast's (also known as Côte d'Ivoire) first visit to the World Cup Finals in 2006 earned "the Elephants" many admirers, even if their entertaining football was not quite enough to reach the second round. Since 2006, the Ivory Coast's national team has continued to emerge as a new force in world football, and more and more top-class Ivoirian talents are playing for the world's most prestigious clubs.

The FIF (Fédération Ivoirienne de Football) was founded in 1960.

## FACT FILE: IVORY COAST

### NICKNAME
Les Éléphants (The Elephants)

### TOP GOAL SCORERS
1. Didier Drogba 28 (2002–present)
2. Information not available
3. Information not available
4. Information not available
5. Information not available

### MOST APPEARANCES
1. Cyrille Domoraud 51 (1995–present)
= Bonaventure Kalou 51 (1998–present)
3. Information not available
4. Information not available
5. Information not available

### TROPHIES/HONORS

**AFRICAN CUP OF NATIONS**
1992 Ivory Coast 0 Ghana 0
(Ivory Coast won 11–10 in a penalty shootout)

*Drogba was the top scorer in the English Premier League in 2006–2007 with 20 goals for Chelsea.*

## DROGBA

Didier Drogba is one of the most prolific strikers in the world today. His pace and power terrify defenders, while his finishing is as graceful as it is clinical. Drogba also uses his status as a sporting hero in his work as a UN Goodwill Ambassador.

Feyenoord forward Bonaventure Kalou scored a decisive penalty to give Ivory Coast a much-deserved victory in the 2006 World Cup Finals. Despite the 3–2 win over Serbia, the promising Africans were edged out by Argentina and the Netherlands in a difficult group.

## TOP TALENT

Kolo Touré (right) and his younger brother Yaya are products of the Ivory Coast's flourishing youth academies. Kolo is a versatile defender, while Yaya is a surging midfielder. Watch out for youngest brother Ibrahim, an up-and-coming striker.

## DID YOU KNOW?

*Laurent Pokou has scored more African Cup of Nations goals than any other player. He scored six at the 1968 tournament and then eight more two years later, including five in a single match, a 6–1 victory over Ethiopia. Pokou also played club soccer for Stade Rennais and AS Nancy in France.*

| IVORY COAST DREAM TEAM? | 1. Alain Gouaméné 2. Emmanuel Eboué 3. Dominique Sam Abou 4. Didier Zokora 5. Kolo Touré 6. Cyrille Domoraud 7. Bonaventure Kalou 8. Yaya Touré 9. Laurent Pokou 10. Didier Drogba 11. Youssouf Falikou Fofana |
|---|---|

# GHANA

### "FOOTBALL IS NOT SIMPLY THE MOST POPULAR SPORT IN GHANA, IT'S LIKE A RELIGION."

OTTO PFISTER, COACH OF GHANA'S U-17
WORLD CUP WINNERS IN 1991

The Ghana Football association was founded in 1957.

Over the years, Ghana has acquired a reputation for developing dynamic young teams. It won the Under-17s World Cup in 1991 and 1995 and a bronze medal at the 1992 Olympic Games. Like its neighbor and rival, Ivory Coast, Ghana made its World Cup Finals debut in 2006 but only Egypt has won the African Cup of Nations more times than Ghana's "Black Stars."

## FACT FILE: GHANA
### NICKNAME
The Black Stars

**TOP GOAL SCORERS**
1. Abédi "Pelé" Ayew 33 (1981–1998)
2. Information not available
3. Information not available
4. Information not available
5. Information not available

**MOST APPEARANCES**
1. Abédi "Pelé" Ayew 73 (1981–1998)
2. Information not available
3. Information not available
4. Information not available
5. Information not available

**TROPHIES/HONORS**
**AFRICAN CUP OF NATIONS**
1963 Ghana 3 Sudan 0
1965 Ghana 3 Tunisia 2 (aet)
1978 Ghana 2 Uganda 0
1982 Ghana 1 Libya 1 (Ghana won 7–6 in a penalty shootout)

## YOUNG STAR

Midfielder Sulley Muntari is already a firm favorite with Ghana fans thanks to his dazzling dribbling skills and combative playing style. Despite an often fiery temperament, Muntari is a vital part of the Ghana team.

Muntari scored the first goal in Ghana's 2–0 victory over the Czech Republic in the 2006 World Cup Finals.

Michael Essien (right) and captain Stephen Appiah were the midfield motors as Ghana—the youngest squad at the 2006 World Cup—became the only African side in the second round. The versatile Essien has long been seen as a future African Footballer of the Year—a prize won by flamboyant Ghana midfielders Ibrahim Sunday in 1971 and Karim Abdul Razak in 1978.

## DID YOU KNOW?

The world's first black professional soccer player, Arthur Wharton, was born in what is now Accra, Ghana. He played for various teams in the English leagues from 1885 to 1902.

Three-times African Footballer of the Year Abédi "Pelé" Ayew (left) is arguably one of the greatest ever African soccer players and surely worthy of his illustrious nickname. He is Ghana's most capped player as well as the top scorer and he was one of the first African footballers to enjoy success in Europe, in particular with French side Olympique Marseille.

GHANA DREAM TEAM? 1. Robert Mensah 2. Ofei Ansah 3. Kwasi Appiah 4. Michael Essien 5. Samuel Kuffour 6. Charles Addo Odametey 7. Baba Yara 8. Karim Abdul Razak 9. Opoku "Bayie" Afriyie 10. Abédi "Pelé" Ayew 11. Mohammed "Polo" Ahmed

### TOP GOAL SCORERS
1. Patrick Mboma 33 (1995-2004)
2. Information not available
3. Information not available)
4. Information not available)
5. Information not available

### MOST APPEARANCES
1. Rigobert Song 108 (1993-present)
2. Information not available)
3. Information not available)
4. Information not available
5. Information not available

### TROPHIES/HONORS
**AFRICAN CUP OF NATIONS**
1984 Cameroon 3 Nigeria 1
1988 Cameroon 1 Nigeria 0
2000 Cameroon 2 Nigeria 2 (aet)
(Cameroon won 4–3 on penalties)
2002 Cameroon 0 Senegal 0 (aet)
(Cameroon won 3–2 on penalties)

**OLYMPIC GOLD MEDAL**
2000 Cameroon 2 Spain 2
(Cameroon won 5–3
on penalties)

**NICKNAME**
The Indomitable Lions

Fédération
Camerounaise de
Football was
founded in 1959.

# CAMEROON

## "IT'S THANKS TO FOOTBALL THAT A SMALL COUNTRY COULD BECOME GREAT."

CAMEROON LEGEND ROGER MILLA

Cameroon captivated the world when it opened Italia '90 by defeating reigning champions Argentina. It went on to reach the quarterfinals—becoming the first African side to do so. Although Cameroon surprisingly missed out on the 2006 World Cup; a young side, inspired by the great Samuel Eto'o, is bouncing back confidently.

## STAR STRIKER
Samuel Eto'o has never looked back since making his international debut at the age of 15. The lightning-quick striker has averaged almost a goal per game for his country, and picked up an unprecedented hat trick of African Footballer of the Year prizes in 2003, 2004, and 2005.

*Eto'o is a skilled playmaker and strong in defence.*

Rigobert Song (above) became the youngest player to be red-carded in a World Cup, in 1994, aged 17. He was sent off again four years later but the rugged defender recovered to become Cameroon's most-capped and most reliable player.

Roger Milla (left) came out of semiretirement to become the hero of the 1990 World Cup Finals. At the age of 38, the veteran Cameroon striker scored four times in Italia '90, celebrating each goal in his unique style. Four years later, at USA '94, Milla became the World Cup's oldest scorer, with goal against Russia.

While Samuel Eto'o has created headlines with big-money moves to Real Madrid and Barcelona, it is actually fellow forward Patrick Mboma (left) who is Cameroon's all-time top scorer. Mboma was also the leading scorer in the 2000 and 2002 African Cup of Nations campaigns and African Footballer of the Year in 2000.

**CAMEROON DREAM TEAM?** 1. Thomas Nkono 2. Rigobert Song 3. Lauren 4. Marc-Vivien Foé 5. Stephen Tataw 6. Emmanuel Kundé 7. Geremi 8. Théophile Abega 9. Patrick Mboma 10. Roger Milla 11. Samuel Eto'o

# NIGERIA

**"WE ARE STILL THE TEAM TO BEAT IN AFRICA. EVERY GAME FOR US IS LIKE A FINAL."**

FORMER NIGERIA CAPTAIN "JAY-JAY" OKOCHA

The Nigeria Football Association was founded in 1945.

When the "Super Eagles" are soaring, their blend of exuberant passing and awesome power inspires dreams of a first African World Cup winner. The potential is certainly there: Nigeria's "Golden Eaglets" won the U-17 World Championships in 1985, 1993, and 2007. The senior team won Olympic gold in1996, but, so far, have not gone beyond the second round of the World Cup Finals.

## NWANKWO KANU

As a teenager, striker Nwankwo Kanu (right) was part of Nigeria's 1993 U-17 World Championship winning team. Three years later he added an Olympic gold medal and now, over a decade later, Kanu is Nigeria's captain.

## FACT FILE: NIGERIA
**NICKNAME**
Super Eagles

**TOP GOAL SCORERS**
1. Rashidi Yekini 37 (1984–1998)
2. Segun Odegbami 24 (1976–1981)
3. Sunday Oyarekhua 17 (1971–1975)
4. Samson Siasia 16 (1989–1998)
5. Thompson Usiyan 15 (1976–1978)

**MOST APPEARANCES**
1. Muda Lawal 86 (1975–1985)
2. "Jay-Jay" Okocha 74 (1993–2006)
3. Peter Rufai 68 (1981–1998)
4. Nwankwo Kanu 67 (1994–present)
5. Finidi George 66 (1991–2002)

**TROPHIES/HONORS**
**AFRICAN CUP OF NATIONS**
1980 Nigeria 3 Algeria 0
1994 Nigeria 2 Zambia 1

**OLYMPIC GOLD MEDAL**
1996 Nigeria 3 Argentina 2

Like long-time captain Augustine "Jay-Jay" Okocha, Obafemi Martins (above) not only scores and sets up breath-taking goals, but also celebrates them in acrobatic style. As the Nigerian stars of the 1990s reach retirement, two-time Young African Footballer of the Year Martins is spearheading a Nigerian revival alongside powerful midfield prodigy Mikel Jon Obi.

*Nwankwo Kanu has won more major medals than any other African player.*

All-time top scorer, Rashidi Yekini (left), scored Nigeria's first ever World Cup Finals' goal in USA '94, in a 3–0 win over Bulgaria. Strikers Yekini and Daniel Amokachi, plus wingers Tijani Babandiga and Finidi George, inspired Nigeria to the second round of the tournament.

Nigeria clinched its first major trophy in the year it first hosted the African Cup of Nations, beating Algeria 3–0 in 1980 before 80,000 fans in Lagos. Captain and future coach Christian Chukwu lifted the trophy after two goals from Segun Odegbami and one from Muda Lawal. Further success came 14 years later in Tunisia, when Nigeria beat Zambia in the final and Yekini won the Golden Boot.

NIGERIA DREAM TEAM? 1. Peter Rufai 2. Christian Chukwu 3. Taribo West 4. Augustine "Jay-Jay" Okocha 5. Stephen Keshi 6. Uche Okechukwu 7. Finidi George 8. Segun Odegbami 9. Rashidi Yekini 10. Nwankwo Kanu 11. Emmanuel Amuneke

# AFRICAN TEAMS

"AFRICAN FOOTBALL IS DEVELOPING AND GETTING BETTER ALL THE TIME."

FORMER GHANA COACH FREDERICK OSAM-DUODU

The 2006 World Cup demonstrated African soccer's increasing strength and depth as surprise packages, including Angola and Togo, made their debuts. More widely recognised heavyweights such as Nigeria, Cameroon, and South Africa did not even qualify. So, with the likes of Mali also emerging fast, competition for Africa's five remaining places in 2010 looks set to be more exhilarating than ever.

## SENEGAL

Senegalese soccer seemed to burst from nowhere in 2002 when the team reached its first African Cup of Nations final and then beat holders France 1–0 in the opening game of the World Cup Finals. The "Lions of Teranga" made it as far as the quarterfinals in that tournament.

Two-time African Footballer of the Year El Hadji Diouf has led Senegal's rise from outsiders to contenders.

### FACT FILE

**TOP GOAL SCORERS**
Mamadou Diallo 21 (1994–2000)

**MOST APPEARANCES**
El-Hadji Diouf 41 (2000–present)

**TROPHIES/HONORS**
none

## TUNISIA

Tunisia made history in 1978 when it became the first African country to win a match at a World Cup Finals. The team came from behind to beat Mexico 3–1 in the tournament hosted by Argentina. Tunisia took 20 years to return to the Finals, but was the only African team there in both 2002 and 2006. A first African Cup of Nations triumph came in 2004.

Brazil-born striker Francileudo Santos scored four times for Tunisia at the 2004 African Cup of Nations, including this opener in the final against Morocco.

### FACT FILE

**TOP GOAL SCORER**
Ezzedine Chakroun (unknown)

**MOST APPEARANCES**
Sadok Sassi "Attouga" (unknown)

**TROPHIES/HONORS**
AFRICAN CUP OF NATIONS
2004 Tunisia 2 Morocco 1

## ALGERIA

Despite a shock 2–1 win over West Germany in the 1982 World Cup Finals, Algeria was denied the chance of being the first African team to make it to the second round thanks to Germany's win over Austria in the final group game. Algeria returned to the Finals in 1986, but has not qualified since then.

West German defender Paul Breitner tries to control the ball under pressure from Algerian midfielder Mustapha Dahleb during the 1982 World Cup Finals.

### FACT FILE

**TOP GOAL SCORER**
Rabah Madjer 40 (1978–1992)

**MOST APPEARANCES**
Mahieddine Meftah 107 (unknown)

**TROPHIES/HONORS**
AFRICAN CUP OF NATIONS
1990 Algeria 1 Nigeria 0

## GUINEA

Guinea still awaits a World Cup debut, despite some success in Europe for players including Titi Camara at Marseille and Liverpool and Bobo Baldé at Toulouse and Celtic. It remains to be seen when Guinea will emerge from the shadows of its more famous neighbors Mali, Senegal, and Ivory Coast.

### FACT FILE

**TOP GOAL SCORERS**
Information not available

**MOST APPEARANCES**
Information not available

**TROPHIES/HONORS**

# EGYPT

Predictably nicknamed "The Pharaohs," Egypt has reigned supreme a record five times in the African Cup of Nations and given African soccer some of its most revered names – from 1928 Olympics semi-finals star Mukhtar Al-Tetsh to Hossam Hassan in the modern era.

**FACT FILE**

**TOP GOAL SCORERS**
Hossam Hassan 80 (1985–2006)

**MOST APPEARANCES**
Hossam Hassan 170 (1985–2006)

**TROPHIES/HONORS**
**AFRICAN CUP OF NATIONS**
1957 Egypt 4 Ethiopia 0
1959 Egypt 2 Sudan 1
1986 Egypt 0 Cameroon 0 (Egypt won 5–4 in a penalty shootout)
1998 Egypt 2 South Africa 0
2006 Egypt 0 Ivory Coast 0 (Egypt won 4–2 in a penalty shootout)

Host Egypt became the first country to win the African Cup of Nations five times when it beat Ivory Coast on penalties in front of an ecstatic Cairo crowd in February 2006.

# MOROCCO

In 1986 Morocco became the first African team to top a World Cup first round group. It finished ahead of England, Poland and Portugal to qualify for the second round, but lost 1–0 to eventual tournament runner-up West Germany.

**FACT FILE**

**TOP GOAL SCORERS**
Salaheddine Bassir 43 (unknown–2005)

**MOST APPEARANCES**
Noureddine Naybet 115 (1990–2006)

**TROPHIES/HONORS**
**AFRICAN CUP OF NATIONS**
1976 (round-robin league tournament)

# ANGOLA

Angola made its World Cup Finals debut in 2006 and earned creditable draws with Mexico and Iran, but lost 1–0 to former colonial rulers Portugal and did not progress beyond the group stage.

**FACT FILE**

**TOP GOAL SCORERS**
Fabrice "Akwá" Maieco 36 (1995–present)

**MOST APPEARANCES**
Fabrice "Akwá" Maieco 80 (1995–present)

**TROPHIES/HONORS**
none

# MALI

Mali played its first World Cup qualifier in 2000 and looks like a force for the future thanks to stars such as Fredi Kanouté and Mahamadou Diarra.

**FACT FILE**

**TOP GOAL SCORERS**
Information not available

**MOST APPEARANCES**
Information not available

**TROPHIES/HONORS**
none

# TOGO

Togo's first World Cup Finals in 2006 involved three defeats and a threatened strike by the players. However, just reaching the Finals tournament was a positive sign for the tiny West African nation.

**FACT FILE**

**TOP GOAL SCORERS**
Emmanuel Adebayor 16 (2000–present)

**MOST APPEARANCES**
Mohamed Kader 49 (1995–present)

**TROPHIES/HONORS**
none

# LIBERIA

Although the team has never reached the World Cup Finals, George Weah put Liberian soccer on the world map. He also coached and funded Liberia, or "The Lone Stars."

Founded 1936

Striker George Weah is the only African so far to become FIFA World Footballer. In 2005 Weah, unsuccessfully, ran for president in Liberia.

**FACT FILE**

**TOP GOAL SCORERS**
Information not available

**MOST APPEARANCES**
Information not available

**TROPHIES/HONORS**
none

# DEMOCRATIC REPUBLIC OF CONGO

DR Congo's golden age was 1974. Under its former name, Zaire, it won a second African Cup of Nations and made its only World Cup Finals appearance so far.

**FACT FILE**

**TOP GOAL SCORERS**
Information not available

**MOST APPEARANCES**
Information not available

**TROPHIES/HONORS**
**AFRICAN CUP OF NATIONS**
1968 Congo-Kinshasa (now DR Congo) 1 Ghana 0
1974 Zaire (now DR Congo) 2 Zambia 0

AFRICA DREAM TEAM? 1. Badou Zaki (Morocco) 2. Hatem Trabelsi (Tunisia) 3. Pierre Kalala (DR Congo) 4. Lakhdar Belloumi (Algeria) 5. Ibrahim Youssef (Egypt) 6. Noureddine Naybet (Morocco) 7. Mahmoud El-Khatib (Egypt) 8. Kalusha Bwalya (Zambia) 9. George Weah (Liberia) 10. Hossam Hassan (Egypt) 11. Salif Keita (Mali)

MONGOLIA

UZBEKISTAN

KYRGYZSTAN

TURKMENISTAN    TAJIKISTAN

SYRIA
LEBANON
JORDAN

IRAQ    IRAN    AFGHANISTAN

DEMOCRATIC
PEOPLES
REPUBLIC OF
KOREA

CHINA

REPUBLIC
OF KOREA

KUWAIT

QATAR

PAKISTAN

BHUTAN

NEPAL

SAUDIA
ARABIA

UNITED
ARAB
EMIRATES

INDIA

OMAN

BANGLADESH

LAOS

YEMEN

BURMA

VIETNAM

THAILAND

CAMBODIA

BRUNEI

SRI LANKA

MALAYSIA

SINGAPORE

INDONESIA

# ASIA

## "THE FUTURE IS ASIA"

AFC MOTTO

When cohosts the Republic of Korea
(also known as South Korea) lined up to
play Germany in the semifinal of the
2002 World Cup Finals it was the first time an
Asian side had reached that stage of the
tournament. Although Korea lost the match
1–0, they proved that Asian teams were
serious international contenders. Making a
bigger impact on the world stage is a prime
objective for this region, and a major plan is
under way to revitalize the domestic leagues in
ambitious countries such as China, Japan, Iran,
and, of course, the Republic of Korea.

Founded in 1954, the AFC (Asian
Football Confederation) is divided
into four subgroups: East Asia,
containing the Rebublic of Korea,
Democratic People's Republic of
Korea, China, and Japan; West Asia,
covering the Middle East; Central
and South Asia, including India and
Pakistan; and the ASEAN,
representing Southeast Asia and,
since 2006, Australia.

# OCEANIA

**"WE HAVE SHOWN THAT THE SOUTH PACIFIC CAN PRODUCE EXCEPTIONAL FOOTBALL TALENT."**
OFC PRESIDENT REYNALD TEMARII

Formed in 1966, by Australia, New Zealand, and Fiji, the OFC (Oceania Football Confederation) is the smallest and also the weakest of the world's soccer confederations. Of its current eleven members, only one has ever qualified for the World Cup Finals—New Zealand, which failed to get past the group stage in 1982.

Beautiful tropical paradises are not generally noted for their soccer success, but places like the Solomon Islands, Tahiti, and Fiji provide stunning locations for the beautiful game to thrive in. Since the departure of Australia in 2006, many of the Oceania federation national teams hover dangerously close to the bottom of FIFA's rankings. However, even in this success-starved region, the game of soccer can boast many passionate followers.

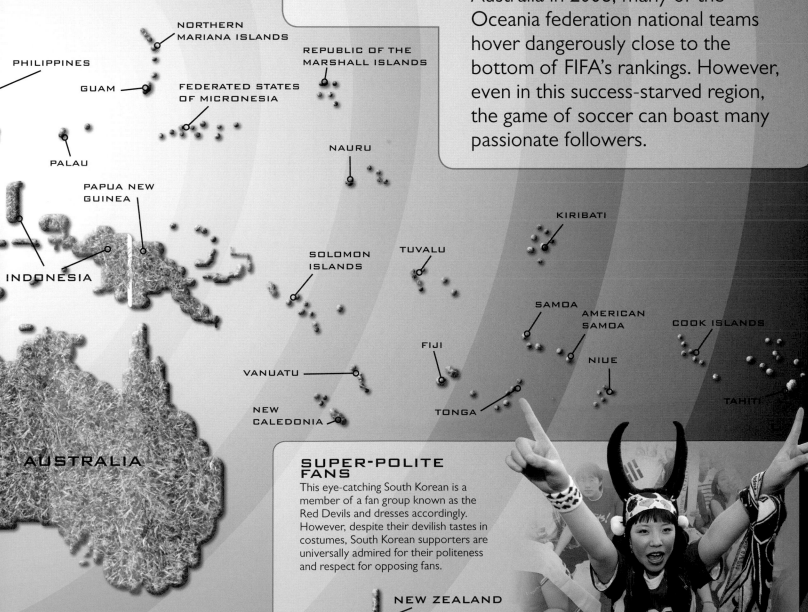

JAPAN

PHILIPPINES

NORTHERN MARIANA ISLANDS

GUAM

FEDERATED STATES OF MICRONESIA

REPUBLIC OF THE MARSHALL ISLANDS

PALAU

NAURU

PAPUA NEW GUINEA

KIRIBATI

INDONESIA

SOLOMON ISLANDS

TUVALU

SAMOA

AMERICAN SAMOA

COOK ISLANDS

FIJI

NIUE

VANUATU

TAHITI

NEW CALEDONIA

TONGA

AUSTRALIA

## SUPER-POLITE FANS

This eye-catching South Korean is a member of a fan group known as the Red Devils and dresses accordingly. However, despite their devilish tastes in costumes, South Korean supporters are universally admired for their politeness and respect for opposing fans.

NEW ZEALAND

# THE MIDDLE EAST

"SPORT IS THE SHORTEST ROUTE TO PEACE. WE WILL DO WHAT WE CAN AND WE HOPE THAT THE POLITICIANS WILL DO THE REST OF THE JOB."

ARAB ISRAEL INTERNATIONAL ABBAS SUAN

Middle East soccer has known mixed fortunes over the years. However, in this often turbulent region, soccer is widely welcomed as a force for peace, unity, and hope. Iraq's 2007 Asian Cup victory was a major boost not only for the war-torn country but also for the Middle East region as a whole.

## IRAN

Iranian soccer entered a golden age in 1968 with three consecutive Asian Cups, gold at the 1974 Asian Games, and a draw with Scotland at the 1978 World Cup Finals. Modern day heroes Ali Daei, Mehdi Mahdavikia, and Ali Karimi hope to emulate that success.

Striker Ali Daei (above) has scored more international goals than any man on Earth—109 in 149 games since his international debut in 1993.

## ISRAEL

Israel was runner-up in the first two AFC Asian Cups in 1956 and 1960 and eventually won the tournament in 1964. All-time top scorer Mordechai Spiegler skippered the side at its first World Cup Finals in 1970. While Israel hasn't yet returned to the Finals, it ran France and Switzerland close in the 2006 qualifiers. Israel left the AFC in 1994 to join UEFA and Israeli club sides also participate in European competitions.

Founded 1928

### FACT FILE
**TOP GOAL SCORER**
Mordechai Spiegler 32 (1963–1977)
**MOST APPEARANCES**
Arik Benado 95 (1998–present)

**TROPHIES/HONORS**
**AFC ASIAN CUP**
1964 (round-robin league tournament)

When Iran faced the USA at the 1998 World Cup Finals, the two teams symbolically exchanged flowers before kickoff. Iran won 2–1 thanks to goals from Hamid Reza Estili and Mehdi Mahdavikia.

### FACT FILE
**TOP GOAL SCORER**
Ali Daei 109 (1993–2006)
**MOST APPEARANCES**
Ali Daei 149 (1993–2006)

**TROPHIES/HONORS**
**AFC ASIAN CUP**
1968 (round-robin league tournament)
1972 Iran 2 Korea Republic 2 (aet)
1976 Iran 1 Kuwait 0

## SAUDI ARABIA

Saudi Arabia has won the Asian Cup three times. It first visited the World Cup Finals in 1994, reaching the second round and has qualified for every Finals since.

Founded 1959

### FACT FILE
**TOP GOAL SCORER**
Majed Abdullah 67 (1977–1994)
**MOST APPEARANCES**
Mohammed Al-Deayea 181 (1990–2006)

**TROPHIES/HONORS**
**AFC ASIAN CUP**
1984 Saudi Arabia 2 China 1
1988 Saudi Arabia 0 Korea Republic 0 (Saudi Arabia won 4–3 in a penalty shootout)
1996 Saudi Arabia 0 United Arab Emirates 0 (Saudi Arabia won 4–2 in a penalty shootout)

Saeed Al-Owairan's surging 70-yard solo effort against Belgium in 1998 was one of the World Cup's greatest-ever goals.

## IRAQ

Iraqi players, officials and fans were happy just to reach the 2007 AFC Asian Cup, after years of repression under the B'ath regime. But in one of soccer's biggest upsets, it beat Saudi Arabia 1–0 in the final. Perhaps it should not have been a complete surprise—Iraq was also semifinalist at the 2004 Olympic Games in Athens.

Iraq captain Younis Mahmoud scored the winning goal in the 2007 Asian Cup final. Goalkeepr Noor Sabri also put in a match-winning performance.

### FACT FILE
**TOP GOAL SCORER**
Hussein Saeed 63 (1976–1990)
**MOST APPEARANCES**
Hussein Saeed 126 (1976–1990)

**TROPHIES/HONORS**
**AFC ASIAN CUP**
2007 Iraq 1 Saudi Arabia 0

---

MIDDLE EAST DREAM TEAM? 1. Mohammed Al-Deayea (Saudi Arabia) 2. Mehdi Mahdavikia (Iran) 3. Bassim Abbas (Iraq) 4. Avi Nimni (Israel) 5. Rahman Rezaei (Iran) 6. Tal Ben-Haim (Israel) 7. Ali Karimi (Iran) 8. Saeed Al-Owairan (Saudi Arabia) 9. Ali Daei (Iran) 10. Majed Abdullah (Saudi Arabia) 11. Mordechai Spiegler (Israel)

## UNITED ARAB EMIRATES

Although nearly 85 percent of the United Arab Emirates' population are foreign citizens, the national team still managed to reach the 1990 World Cup Finals. However, Brazilan coach Mario Zagalo was fired just before the tournament and the UAE lost all three games. The UAE also lost the 1996 Asian Cup final to Saudi Arabia in a penalty shootout.

**FACT FILE**

**TOP GOAL SCORER**
Adnan Al-Talyani 53 (1983–1997)

**MOST APPEARANCES**
Adnan Al-Talyani 164 (1983–1997)

**TROPHIES/HONORS**
none

Adnan Al-Talyani is UAE's most prolific scorer and most capped player. In fact, only four men in the world have won more international caps than the UAE striker.

## LEBANON

Lebanon became a member of FIFA as early as 1935 but has had little to cheer about since then, aside from a successful hosting of the 2000 AFC Asian Cup Finals.

**FACT FILE**

**TOP GOAL SCORER**
Information not available

**MOST APPEARANCES**
Information not available

**TROPHIES/HONORS**
none

## PALESTINE

FIFA recognized Palestine as an independent soccer association in 1998. A troubled homeland means that the team plays in Qatar and trains in Egypt.

**FACT FILE**

**TOP GOAL SCORER**
Fahed Attal 12 (unknown)

**MOST APPEARANCES**
Information not available

**TROPHIES/HONORS**
none

## QATAR'S

long-awaited emergence seemed to be underway when striker Khalfan Ibrahim was named the 2006 Asian Footballer of the Year. In the same year Qatar triumphed in both the Asian Games and the Arab world's Gulf Cup.

**FACT FILE**

**TOP GOAL SCORER**
Information not available

**MOST APPEARANCES**
Information not available

**TROPHIES/HONORS**
none

## KUWAIT

won the Asian Cup in 1980 and also created one of the World Cup's most bizarre moments in 1982, when the team stormed off the field until a French "goal" was disallowed for offside.

**FACT FILE**

**TOP GOAL SCORER**
Jassem Al Houwaidi 63 (unknown)

**MOST APPEARANCES**
Wail Sulaiman Al Habashi 109 (unknown)

**TROPHIES/HONORS**
AFC ASIAN CUP 1980
Kuwait 3 Korea Republic 0

## BAHRAIN

was FIFA's most improved side in 2004, after rising 95 places to 44th in the rankings in four years. It also achieved its best-ever fourth in that year's Asian Cup.

**FACT FILE**

**TOP GOAL SCORER**
A'ala Hubail 30 (unknown)

**MOST APPEARANCES**
Abdulrazzaq Mohamed 102 (unknown)

**TROPHIES/HONORS**
none

## SYRIA

Syria's finest hour came when it won the 1994 AFC Youth Championship by beating Japan 2–1 in the final.

**FACT FILE**

**TOP GOAL SCORER**
Information not available

**MOST APPEARANCES**
Information not available

**TROPHIES/HONORS**
none

## JORDAN

Jordan achieved its highest FIFA ranking of 37 in 2004, after qualifying for its first-ever Asian Cup and then reaching the quarterfinals.

**FACT FILE**

**TOP GOAL SCORER**
Information not available

**MOST APPEARANCES**
Information not available

**TROPHIES/HONORS**
none

## OMAN

Although Oman is still yet to reach the World Cup Finals or get through the Asian Cup's first round, it is ranked in FIFA's top 100 teams.

**FACT FILE**

**TOP GOAL SCORER**
Imad Al-Hosni (unknown)

**MOST APPEARANCES**
Information not available

**TROPHIES/HONORS**
none

## YEMEN

South Yemen played in the 1976 Asian Cup, where it lost heavily to Iran, before the creation of a united Yemen side in 1990.

**FACT FILE**

**TOP GOAL SCORER**
Information not available

**MOST APPEARANCES**
Information not available

**TROPHIES/HONORS**

# SOUTH KOREA

**"KOREAN PEOPLE LOVE THE NATIONAL TEAM AND THEIR SUPPORT... IS INCREDIBLE."** AFSHIN GHOTBI, ASSISTANT COACH AT THE 2002 AND 2006 WORLD CUPS

## KFA

The Korea Football Association was founded in 1928.

South Korea experienced unexpected glory in 2002 when it cohosted the World Cup Finals. Thanks to manager Guus Hiddink's astute leadership, some exciting young players, and passionate fans the team reached the semifinals. Life since then has been a bit of an anticlimax, but South Korean soccer continues to draw some well-earned respect worldwide.

## FACT FILE: SOUTH KOREA

### NICKNAMES
Taeguk Warriors, Tigers, Red Devils

### TOP GOAL SCORERS
1. Cha Bum-Kun 55 (1972–1986)
2. Information not available
3. Information not available
4. Information not available
5. Information not available

### MOST APPEARANCES
1. Hong Myung-Bo 135 (1990–2002)
2. Information not available
3. Information not available
4. Information not available
5. Information not available

### TROPHIES/HONORS
#### AFC ASIAN CUP
1956 South Korea 4 Taiwan 1 (agg)
1960 South Korea 1 China 0

Park Ji-Sung was a hero when his volley beat Portugal in the 2002 World Cup.

## CHA BUM-KUN
Cha Bum-Kun was nicknamed "Cha Boom," and any goalkeeper who tried to stop one of his shots knew why. The striker's move to Germany in 1977 paved the way for other Asian players to move to Europe, but few could emulate Cha's ability and his achievements. Many young Germans grew up idolizing him, including Michael Ballack, Jürgen Klinsmann, and Oliver Kahn.

## PARK JI-SUNG
Manchester United's Park Ji-Sung played under manager Guus Hiddink for both South Korea and PSV Eindhoven. In fact, it was Hiddink who made the wise decision to switch Park from a defensive midfield role to the wing.

### DID YOU KNOW?
In the 1977 Park's Cup, Korea was losing 4–1 to Malaysia before Cha Bum-Kun scored an amazing seven-minute hat trick to level the score.

As a classy center-back and rallying captain, Hong Myung-Bo provided a firm foundation for the 2002 World Cup team. He was voted the tournament's third best player before retiring with a record 135 caps.

Ahn Jung-Hwan paid a high price for the greatest moment of his soccer career—the golden goal that knocked Italy out of the 2002 World Cup in the second round. His Italian employers Perugia fired the striker, saying he had "ruined Italian soccer."

**SOUTH KOREA DREAM TEAM?**
1. Lee Woon-Jae 2. Choi Jin-Cheul 3. Lee Young-Pyo 4. Song Chong-Gug 5. Hong Myung-Bo 6. Kim Tae-Young 7. Park Ji-Sung 8. Kim Nam-Il 9. Cha Bum-Kun 10. Kim Joo-Sung 11. Seol Ki-Hyeon

# JAPAN

**"OUR FANS ARE AMONG THE BEST IN THE WORLD."** TAKESHI OKADA, JAPAN MANAGER AT THE 1998 WORLD CUP

The Japan Football Association was formed in 1921. Its symbol is a mythical three-legged raven.

After decades living in the shadow of sports such as baseball, table tennis, and martial arts, Japanese soccer came of age when the new professional J-League was launched in 1993. A successful cohosting of the World Cup followed in 2002. This, combined with AFC Asian Cup triumphs in 2000 and 2004, has elevated soccer to the second most popular sport in Japan.

## FACT FILE: JAPAN

**NICKNAMES**
Nihon Daihyo (Japanese Representatives), Blues, Blue Samurai

**TOP GOAL SCORERS**
1. Kunishige Kamamoto 74 (1964–1977)
2. Kazuyoshi Miura 55 (1990–2000)
3. Hiromi Hara 37 (1978–1988)
4. Takuya Takagi 27 (1992–1997)
5. Kazushi Kimura 26 (1979–1986)

**MOST APPEARANCES**
1. Masami Ihara 122 (1988–1999)
2. Yoshikatsu Kawaguchi 110 (1997–present)
3. Kazuyoshi Miura 89 (1990–2000)
4. Alessandro Dos Santos 82 (2002–present)
5. Satoshi Tsunami 80 (1980–1995)

**TROPHIES/HONORS**
**AFC ASIAN CUP**
1992 Japan 1 Saudi Arabia 0
2000 Japan 1 Saudi Arabia 0
2004 Japan 3 China 1

## KAZU

After leaving for Brazil at age 15 and playing for Pelé's old team Santos, Kazuyoshi Miura returned to Japan in 1990. Known as "Kazu," the super striker (left) won the first two J-League Championships with Verdy Kawasaki before becoming 1993 Asian Footballer of the Year and then joining Genoa in Italy. Kazu famously performed a unique dance when he scored a great goal.

Shunsuke Nakamura (right) is a midfield playmaker and free-kick specialist who has played for both Reggina in Italy and Celtic in Scotland. Although he did not feature in Japan's 2002 World Cup squad, he later returned to the team. He was Japan's star performer in its 2004 Asian Cup victory and scored Japan's opening goal against Australia in the 2006 World Cup.

## TAKAHARA

Japan and Eintracht Frankfurt striker Naohiro Takahara was joint top scorer at the 2007 Asian Cup. In 2001 he became the first Japanese player in the Argentine first division when he was loaned to Boca Juniors.

*Takahara previously played for Japanese club Júbilo Iwata.*

Central midfielder Hidetoshi Nakata (left) was a key part of Japan's soccer boom. Although Junichi Inamoto scored more goals and Kazuyuki Toda had even brighter dyed hair, it was Nakata who captured the hearts of the Japanese people. His 2001 Serie A title with AS Roma was celebrated across Japan, but his decision to retire after the 2006 World Cup at the age of 29 was a major shock.

## DID YOU KNOW?

*Kunishige Kamamoto's seven goals made him the top scorer at the 1968 Summer Olympics in Mexico City, where Japan won the bronze medal. Kamamoto is Japan's all-time top scorer and has now swapped soccer for politics.*

**JAPAN DREAM TEAM?** 1. Yoshikatsu Kawaguchi 2. Akira Kaji 3. Koji Nakata 4. Hidetoshi Nakata 5. Tsuneyasu Miyamoto 6. Masami Ihara 7. Junichi Inamoto 8. Shunsuke Nakamura 9. Kunshige Kamamoto 10. Kazuyoshi Miura 11. Yasuhiko Okudera

# CHINA

The Chinese Football Association was originally founded in 1924, but it was replaced by a new body in 1949 after the country became the People's Republic of China.

**"FOOTBALL IS VERY MUCH IN THE HEARTS OF THE CHINESE PEOPLE."**

ARIE HAAN, CHINA MANAGER 2002–2004

Over the years, China has struggled to make a significant impact on the world of soccer. However, recent years have brought encouraging signs such as qualifying for its first World Cup in 2002—although it lost all three games without scoring. A professional domestic league is also gaining ground and soccer is rapidly becoming a popular sport among a population of 1.3 billion.

In 2004 Dong Fangzhuo moved from Dalian Shide to Manchester United, but the young striker and winger had to wait three years for his United debut.

## HAO HAIDONG

Talented striker Hao Haidong (far left) scored a record 41 goals in 115 appearances for his country. His status as China's greatest soccer figure is challenged only by fellow forward Lee Wei Tong, captain of the country's 1936 Olympic team and later a vice-president of FIFA.

China has twice finished AFC Asian Cup runner-up, but perhaps the country's finest achievement was to hold then world champions Brazil to a 0–0 draw in 2002. Ronaldo, Ronaldinho, and Rivaldo could find no way past inspired goalkeeper Liu Yunfei, while Sun Jihai came agonizingly close to a glorious winner.

## FACT FILE: CHINA
### NICKNAMES
Team China, Guozu (National Foot), Guojia Dui (National Team)

### TOP GOAL SCORERS
1. Hao Haidong 41 (1992–2004)
2. Liu Haiguang 36 (1983–1990)
3. Ma Lin 33 (1984–1990)
4. Li Hui 28 (1983–1988)
5. Su Maozhen 26 (1992–2002)

### MOST APPEARANCES
1. Li Ming 141 (1992–2004)
2. Jia Xiuquan 136 (1983–1992)
3. Fan Zhiyi 132 (1992–2002)
4. Xie Yuxin 120 (1987–1996)
5. Li Fusheng 119 (1976–1984)

### TROPHIES/HONORS
none

## ZHENG ZHI

He calls himself the best Chinese player of his generation, and Zheng Zhi's confidence is matched by his versatility. Although he is best known as a goalscoring midfielder and occasional forward, he began his international career as a defender.

*Zheng Zhi's work rate makes him an ideal captain.*

### DID YOU KNOW?

*In China an estimated TV audience of 250 million people watched their team lose 3–1 to Japan in the 2004 Asian Cup final, a Chinese record for a sporting event.*

CHINA DREAM TEAM? 1. Ou Chuliang 2. Zheng Zhi 3. Sun Jihai 4. Li Ming 5. Fan Zhiyi 6. Jia Xiuquan 7. Li Tie 8. Shao Jia Yi 9. Hao Haidong 10. Lee Wei Tong 11. Yang Chen

# AUSTRALIA

## "THE FUTURE IS ALWAYS BRIGHT FOR AUSTRALIAN FOOTBALL."

HARRY KEWELL

The Australian Soccer Association was founded in 1961 and is now called Football Federation Australia.

Like the US, Australia is not yet as dominant in soccer as it is in other sports. The team failed to score in its first World Cup in 1974, but after a long wait returned in 2006 and only an injury-time penalty for Italy denied it a place in the quarterfinals. After years of record wins in Oceania, Australia left to join the more competitive AFC in 2006.

### FACT FILE: AUSTRALIA

NICKNAME
Socceroos

**TOP GOAL SCORERS**
1. Damian Mori 29 (1992–2002)
2. John Aloisi 27 (1997–present)
3. John Kosmina 25 (1977–1988)
= Attila Abonyi 25 (1967–1977)
5. Archie Thompson 21 (2001–present)
= David Zdrilic 21 (1997–present)

**MOST APPEARANCES**
1. Alex Tobin 87 (1988–1998)
2. Paul Wade 84 (1986–1996)
3. Tony Vidmar 76 (1991–2006)
4. Peter Wilson 64 (1970–1977)
5. Attila Abonyi 61 (1967–1977)
= Brett Emerton 61 (1998–present)

**TROPHIES/HONORS**
OFC NATIONS CUP
1980 Australia 4 Tahiti 2
1996 Australia 11 Tahiti 0 (agg)
2000 Australia 2 New Zealand 0
2004 Australia 11 Solomon Islands 1 (agg)

As a 17-year-old, Harry Kewell left the Australian Academy of Sport to join England's Leeds United. A nimble and dangerous striker and Australia's youngest international, Kewell moved to Liverpool in 2003, where he has most often played on the left wing. Although Kewell's career has been hampered by injury in recent years, his reputation as perhaps the most talented Australian player of all time remains.

Australia captain Mark Viduka hugs coach Guus Hiddink during his nation's impressive 2006 World Cup Finals. Often criticized for his physique, Viduka is a deft finisher and even the strongest defenders struggle to battle him off the ball.

Tim Cahill scored Australia's first World Cup Finals goal in a dramatic 3–1 win over Japan. The tough-tackling midfielder also has a welcome knack for scoring.

*The Australia team before its second round game against Italy in the 2006 World Cup Finals.*

## SOCCEROOS

Australia lost World Cup playoffs to Argentina in 1993, Iran in 1997, and Uruguay in 2001. When it finally beat Uruguay in 2005 to qualify for the 2006 World Cup Finals, its long-suffering fans were ecstatic.

## DID YOU KNOW?

*Australia claimed a world record for the highest score in an international when it beat American Samoa 31–0 in April 2001. Striker Archie Thompson scored a record 13 goals but was not picked for the Socceroos' next game.*

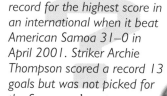

AUSTRALIA DREAM TEAM?
1. Mark Bosnich 2. Joe Marston 3. Tony Vidmar 4. Ned Zelic 5. Peter Wilson 6. Craig Moore
7. Mark Bresciano 8. Johnny Warren 9. Frank Farina 10. Mark Viduka 11. Harry Kewell

# ASIA AND OCEANIA

"THIS IS A FOOTBALL CONTINENT. I CAN'T THINK OF ONE
COUNTRY IN ASIA THAT IS NOT INTERESTED IN FOOTBALL."
PETER VELAPPAN, AFC GENERAL SECRETARY UNTIL 2007

Soccer has a long-standing tradition in many parts of Asia, In fact, early-20th century Philippines striker Paulino Alcántara still holds the scoring record for Spanish club Barcelona with 357 goals in as many games. Staging the 2007 Asian Cup in four countries—Indonesia, Malaysia, Thailand, and Vietnam—showed just how important soccer is across the whole continent. In Oceania, New Zealand is the likeliest candidate for international glory.

## THAILAND

Thailand has been Southeast Asian Games soccer champions 12 times but it is still striving for its big international breakthrough, despite the firepower of strikers Piyapong Piew-on and Kiatisuk Senamuang.

Kiatisuk "Zico" Senamuang is nicknamed after the legendary Brazilian player and manager as a tribute to his lethal finishing and South American-style flamboyance. He worked as a policeman before becoming a professional player and has played in Malaysia, Singapore, and Vietnam.

**FACT FILE**
**TOP GOAL SCORER**
Piyapong Piew-on 103 (1981–1997)
**MOST APPEARANCES**
Kiatisuk Senamuang 130 (1993–present)

**TROPHIES/HONORS**
none

After beating Cambodia in 1972, Thailand waited 35 years for its next win in an Asian Cup Finals match. Victory came in front of its home fans in Bangkok, as Oman had no answer to Pipat Thonkanya's two goals in the 2007 group match.

## NEW ZEALAND

NEW ZEALAND FOOTBALL

Founded 1891

Australia's transfer to the AFC leaves New Zealand as Oceania's dominant team and has boosted its chances of representing the region at a World Cup Finals, as it did in 1982. The "All Whites" may lack the prestige of the country's cricket and rugby teams, but players such as Blackburn Rovers defender Ryan Nelsen hope to change that.

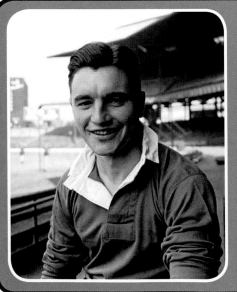

New Zealand soccer owes much to the 1957 emigration of England international Ken Armstrong (left). The ex-Chelsea midfielder helped the game gain popularity while also playing for several clubs. He made 13 appearances for his adopted country.

**FACT FILE**
**TOP GOAL SCORER**
Vaughan Coveny 30 (1992–present)
**MOST APPEARANCES**
Steve Sumner 105 (1976–1988)

**TROPHIES/HONORS**
OFC NATIONS CUP
1973 (round-robin league tournament)
1998 New Zealand 1 Australia 0
2002 New Zealand 1 Australia 0

ASIA'S DREAM TEAM? 1. R Arumugam (Malaysia) 2. Ryan Nelsen (New Zealand) 3. Adrian Elrick (New Zealand) 4. Steve Sumner (New Zealand) 5. Ku Kam Fai (Hong Kong) 6. Soh Chin Aun (Malaysia) 7. Pak Doo-Ik (Korea DPR) 8. Mirjalol Kasymov (Uzbekistan) 9. Paulino Alcántara (Philippines) 10. Mokhtar Dahari (Malaysia) 11. Wynton Rufer (New Zealand)

## DPR KOREA

North Korea had an astounding 1966 World Cup Finals. Its all-out attacking style knocked out Italy and it raced into a 3–0 lead against Portugal, only to lose 5–3. However, international obscurity has followed since then.

**FACT FILE**

**TOP GOAL SCORER**
Information not available

**MOST APPEARANCES**
Information not available

**TROPHIES/HONORS**
none

Pak Doo-Ik's goal beat Italy in the 1966 World Cup Finals.

## HONG KONG

Although Hong Kong has been reunified with China since 1997, it has a separate national team. Playing as Hong Kong China, the team's biggest win was 15–0 against Guam in 2005.

**FACT FILE**

**TOP GOAL SCORER**
Information not available

**MOST APPEARANCES**
Information not available

**TROPHIES/HONORS**
none

## VIETNAM

Reaching the quarterfinals of its first Asian Cup in 2007 was a boost for cohosts Vietnam. A unified Vietnam team—combining South and North—only began playing toegther in 1991 and hopes are high for future success.

**FACT FILE**

**TOP GOAL SCORER**
Le Huynh Duc 30 (unknown)

**MOST APPEARANCES**
Le Huynh Duc 60+ (unknown)

**TROPHIES/HONORS**
none

## UZBEKISTAN

is Asia's strongest ex-Soviet state and the team was quarterfinalist in the 2004 and 2007 Asian Cups. Star striker Maksim Shatskikh has proved a worthy successor to Andriy Shevchenko at Ukraine's Dinamo Kiev.

**FACT FILE**

**TOP GOAL SCORER**
Mirjalol Kasymov 29 (unknown)

**MOST APPEARANCES**
Mirjalol Kasymov 65 (unknown)

**TROPHIES/HONORS**
none

## INDONESIA

As Dutch East Indies, Indonesia was the World Cup Finals' first Asian competitors, losing 6–0 to Hungary in 1938. With a five million playing population, Indonesia has the potential to be "the Brazil of Asia."

Founded 1930

**FACT FILE**

**TOP GOAL SCORER**
Kurniawan Dwi Yulianto 33 (1995–2006)

**MOST APPEARANCES**
Kurniawan Dwi Yulianto 60 33 (1995–2006)

**TROPHIES/HONORS**
none

## MALAYSIA

Malaysian soccer had its heyday in the 1970s and early 1980s, with Mokhtar Dahari dynamic up front and R Arumugam often unbeatable in goal. They beat the USA 3–0 at the 1972 Olympics, but have struggled internationally since then.

**FACT FILE**

**TOP GOAL SCORER**
Mokhtar Dahari 125 (unknown)

**MOST APPEARANCES**
R Arumugam 196 (unknown)

**TROPHIES/HONORS**
none

## PAKISTAN

Soccer fever is strong in Pakistan, despite the sport being overshadowed by cricket. Gradual progress is aided by the likes of ex-Premiership defender Zesh Rehman and captain and playmaker Muhammad Essa (right).

**FACT FILE**

**TOP GOAL SCORER**
Information not available

**MOST APPEARANCES**
Information not available

**TROPHIES/HONORS**
none

Muhammad Essa is a free-kick specialist as well as a talented and creative passer of the ball.

## INDIA

Soccer was brought to India by British army officers in the mid-19th century and the Durand Cup, established in 1888, is the third-oldest soccer competition in the world. The World Cup remains a distant prospect for India. Although it qualified in 1950, the team later withdrew after refusing to wear cleats.

Founded 1937

Despite his short stature, Baichung Bhutia is a giant of Indian football—his country's captain, top scorer, and ambassador abroad.

**FACT FILE**

**TOP GOAL SCORER**
Information not available

**MOST APPEARANCES**
Information not available

**TROPHIES/HONORS**

German soccer fans watch a penalty shootout in their quarter-final match against Argentina in the 2006 World Cup Finals. Germany won the shootout 4–2.

# FAMOUS COMPETITIONS

**"IF YOU DON'T WANT SUCCESS IT'S NOT WORTH PLAYING – WINNING TROPHIES IS THE MAIN THING."** ENGLAND AND LIVERPOOL MIDFIELDER STEVEN GERRARD

From the FIFA World Cup to the African Cup of Nations, each international competition has its own special magic. Agonizing months, even years, of nail-biting qualifying matches played in far-flung stadia all seem worth it when you realize your team has a shot at the big prize. That's the best thing about cup soccer—it gives lesser-known teams a chance to step up and show the world who they are and allows the big teams to dazzle and delight a worldwide audience. Unfortunately, there can only ever be one winner. Until next time, of course.

# FIFA WORLD CUP™

> ## "FIRST AND FOREMOST, THE WORLD CUP SHOULD BE A FESTIVAL OF FOOTBALL."
> FRANZ BECKENBAUER

The World Cup is seen by many as the greatest sporting event on Earth. Held every four years, it brings together the top international teams after three years of qualifying games. The last final, in Germany in 2006, was watched by a global audience of 715 million. In the 18 tournaments played, only seven nations have ever won the title: Argentina, Brazil, England, France, Germany, Italy, and Uruguay.

## FACT FILE:
## FIFA WORLD CUP™ FINALS

### TOP GOAL SCORERS
1. Ronaldo (Brazil) 15 (1994–2006)
2. Gerd Müller (West Germany) 14 (1966–74)
3. Just Fontaine (France) 13 (1958)
4. Pelé (Brazil) 12 (1958–70)
5. Jürgen Klinsmann (Germany) 11 (1990–98)
= Sándor Kocsis (Hungary) 11 (1954)

### FASTEST GOALS
1. Hakan Sükür (Turkey) vs. South Korea 2002—11 seconds
2. Václav Mašek (Czechoslovakia) vs. Mexico 1962—15 seconds
3. Pak Seung-Zin (North Korea) vs. Portugal 1966—23 seconds
4. Ernst Lehner (Germany) vs. Austria 1934—24 seconds
5. Bryan Robson (England) vs. France 1982—27 seconds

*Ronaldo beat Gerd Müller's record with a goal against Ghana in the 2006 Finals. Former Brazil captain Cafu also holds the record for most appearances in the World Cup final with three, and Brazil are the only team to be present at every World Cup Finals.*

## JULES RIMET

**JULES RIMET** was president of FIFA for an incredible 33 years—from 1921 to 1954—and was instrumental in making soccer the world game. It was thanks to this Frenchman that the first Finals were held in 1930. In 1946 the original trophy was renamed the Jules Rimet Trophy in his honor.

*The trophy was stolen in 1983 and has never been recovered. It is thought to have been melted down by the thieves.*

## THE CUP

The current FIFA World Cup trophy was first awarded in 1974. It replaced the Jules Rimet trophy, which Brazil was allowed to keep after its third tournament win in 1970. The bottom of the trophy bears the name and year of every winner since West Germany in 1974. The trophy will need to be replaced in 2038 because there will be no more space!

*Designed by Italian Silvio Gazzaniga, the trophy is 14 in (36 cm) high, weighs just over 13 lb (6 kg), and is made of 18-carat gold.*

## GREATEST GOALS

The World Cup Finals have been blessed with many amazing goals, from 17-year-old Pelé's stunning volley against Sweden in 1958 to the Netherlands' Arie Haan's long-range strike against West Germany in 1978. Here are two of the very best of all time:

In one glorious minute of the 1986 quarterfinal, Argentina's Diego Maradona dribbled 55 yards (50 meters), passing four England players, to score the goal voted FIFA's Greatest World Cup Goal in a 2002 poll.

Carlos Alberto's goal in the 1970 final epitomizes Brazil's extraordinary skill. Nine players dribbled and passed the ball the length of the field before defender Alberto charged into space and powered home Pelé's pass from the edge of the area.

## CONTROVERSY

Since the very beginning, World Cup Finals have never been short of talking points both on and off the field. From arguments over the choice of hosts to controversial goals, disputed decisions and violent tackles, the World Cup has seen it all.

In the 1966 final, a close-range shot from England's Geoff Hurst hit the bar, bounced down and back into play. The linesman ruled that it was a goal and England went on to win the match. However, many people argue that the whole of the ball did not cross the line—meaning it wasn't a goal.

Italy versus Chile in the 1962 Finals was one of the dirtiest games ever as players fought and police had to break up mass brawls. It became known as the "Battle of Santiago."

In 1986, Maradona claimed his first goal against England was due "a little to the head of Maradona, a little to the hand of God." Other people just say it was handball!

This is the actual size of the World Cup trophy.

## 1930 URUGUAY

**FINAL:**
Uruguay 4 Argentina 2
**THIRD PLACE:**
Not awarded
**GOLDEN BOOT:**
Guillermo Stábile 8 (Argentina)
**GOLDEN BALL:** Guillermo Stábile (Argentina)

**ALL STAR TEAM**
1. Enrique Ballesteros (Uruguay) 2. José Nasazzi (Uruguay) 3. Milutin Ivkovic (Yugoslavia) 4. Luis Monti (Argentina) 5. Álvaro Gestido (Uruguay) 6. José Andrade (Uruguay) 7. Pedro Cea (Uruguay) 8. Héctor Castro (Uruguay) 9. Héctor Scarone (Uruguay)10. Guillermo Stábile (Uruguay) 11. Bert Patenaude (USA)

## 1934 ITALY

**FINAL:**
Italy 2 Czechoslovakia 1 (aet)
**THIRD PLACE:**
Germany
**GOLDEN BOOT:**
Oldrich Nejedlý 5 (Czechoslovakia)
**GOLDEN BALL:** Giuseppe Meazza (Italy)

**ALL STAR TEAM**
1. Ricardo Zamora (Spain) 2. Jacinto Quincoces (Spain) 3. Eraldo Monzeglio (Italy) 4. Luiz Monti (Italy) 5. Attilio Ferraris (Italy) 6. Leonardo Cilaurren (Spain) 7. Giussepe Meazza (Italy) 8. Raimundo Orsi (Italy) 9. Enrique Guaita (Italy) 10. Matthias Sindelar (Austria) 11. Oldrich Nejedlý (Czechoslovakia)

## 1938 FRANCE

**FINAL:**
Italy 4 Hungary 2
**THIRD PLACE:**
Brazil
**GOLDEN BOOT:**
Leônidas da Silva 7 (Brazil)
**GOLDEN BALL:** Leônidas da Silva (Brazil)

**ALL STAR TEAM**
1. František Plánicka (Czechoslovakia) 2. Pietro Rava (Italy) 3. Alfredo Foni (Italy) 4.Domingos da Guia (Brazil) 5. Michele Andreolo (Italy) 6. Ugo Locatelli (Italy) 7. Silvio Piola (Italy) 8. Gino Colaussi (Italy) 9. György Sárosi (Hungary) 10. Gyula Zsengellér (Hungaryl) 11. Leônidas da Silva (Brazil)

## 1950 BRAZIL

**FINAL:**
Uruguay 2 Brazil 1
**THIRD PLACE:**
Sweden
**GOLDEN BOOT:**
Ademir 9 (Brazil)
**GOLDEN BALL:** Zizinho (Brazil)

**ALL STAR TEAM**
1. Roque Máspoli (Uruguay) 2. Erik Nilsson (Sweden) 3. José Parra (Spain) 4. Schubert Gambetta (Uruguay) 5. Obdulio Varela (Uruguay) 6. Walter Bahr (USA) 7. Alcides Ghiggia (Uruguay) 8. Zizinho (Brazil) 9.Ademir (Brazil) 10. Jair (Brazil) 11. Schiaffino (Uruguay)

## 1954 SWITZERLAND

**FINAL:**
West Germany 3 Hungary 2
**THIRD PLACE:**
Austria
**GOLDEN BOOT:**
Sándor Kocsis 11 (Hungary)
**GOLDEN BALL:** Sándor Kocsis (Hungary)

**ALL STAR TEAM**
1. Gyula Grosics (Hungary) 2. Ernst Ocwirk (Austria) 3. József Bozsik (Hungary) 4. José Santamaria (Uruguay) 5. Fritz Walter (West Germany) 6. Bauer (Brazil) 7. Helmut Rahn (West Germany) 8. Nándor Hidegkuti (Hungary) 9. Ferenc Puskás (Hungary) 10. Sándor Kocsis (Hungary) 11. Zoltán Czibor (Hungary)

## 1958 SWEDEN

**FINAL:**
Brazil 5 Sweden 2
**THIRD PLACE:**
France
**GOLDEN BOOT:**
Just Fontaine 13 (France)
**GOLDEN BALL:** Raymond Kopa (France)

**ALL STAR TEAM**
1. Lev Yashin (USSR) 2. Djalma Santos (Brazil) 3. Bellini (Brazil) 4. Nílton Santos (Brazil) 5. Danny Blanchflower (Northern Ireland) 6. Didi (Brazil) 7. Pelé (Brazil) 8. Garrincha (Brazil) 9. Just Fontaine (France) 10. Raymond Kopa (France) 11. Gunnar Gren (Sweden)

## 1962 CHILE

**FINAL**
Brazil 3 Czechoslovakia 1
**THIRD PLACE:**
Germany
**GOLDEN BOOT:**
Garrincha 4 (Brazil), Vavá 4 (Brazil), Leonel Sánchez 4 (Chile), Dražan Jerkovic 4 (Yugoslavia), Valentin Ivanov 4 (USSR), Flórián Albert 4 (Hungary)
**GOLDEN BALL:** Garrincha (Brazil)

**ALL STAR TEAM**
1. Antonio Carbajal (Mexico) 2. Djalma Santos (Brazil) 3. Cesare Maldini (Italy) 4. Valeriy Voronin (USSR) 5. Karl-Heinz Schnellinger (West Germany) 6. Zagallo (Brazil) 7. Zito (Brazil) 8. Josef Masopust (Czechoslovakia) 9. Vavá (Brazil) 10. Garrincha (Brazil) 11. Leonel Sánchez (Brazil)

## 1966 ENGLAND

**FINAL:**
England 4 West Germany 2
**THIRD PLACE:**
Portugal
**GOLDEN BOOT:**
Eusébio 9 (Portugal)
**GOLDEN BALL:** Bobby Charlton (England)

**ALL STAR TEAM**
1. Gordon Banks (England) 2. George Cohen (England) 3. Bobby Moore (England) 4. Valeriy Voronin (USSR) 5. Silvio Marzolini (Argentina) 6. Franz Beckenbauer (West Germany) 7. Mário Coluna (Portugal) 8. Bobby Charlton (England) 9. Flórián Albert (Hungary) 10. Uwe Seeler (West Germany) 11. Eusébio (Portugal)

## 1970 MEXICO

**FINAL:**
Brazil 4 Italy 1
**THIRD PLACE:**
West Germany
**GOLDEN BOOT:**
Gerd Müller 10 (West Germany)
**GOLDEN BALL:** Pelé (Brazil)

**ALL STAR TEAM**
1. Ladislao Mazurkiewicz (Uruguay) 2. Carlos Alberto Torres (Brazil) 3. Piazza (Brazil) 4. Franz Beckenbauer (West Germany) 5. Giacinto Facchetti (Italy) 6. Gérson (Brazil) 7. Gianni Rivera (Italy) 8. Bobby Charlton (England) 9. Pelé (Brazil) 10. Gerd Müller (West Germany) 11. Jairzinho (Brazil)

## 1974 WEST GERMANY

**FINAL:**
West Germany 2 Netherlands 1

**THIRD PLACE:**
Poland

**GOLDEN BOOT:**
Grzegorz Lato 7 (Poland)

**GOLDEN BALL:** Johan Cruyff (Netherlands)

**ALL STAR TEAM**
1. Jan Tomaszewski (Poland) 2. Berti Vogts (West Germany) 3. Wim Suurbier (Netherlands) 4. Franz Beckenbauer (West Germany) 5. Marinho Chagas (Brazil) 6. Wolfgang Overath (West Germany) 7. Kazimierz Deyna (Poland) 8. Johan Neeskens (Netherlands) 9. Rob Rensenbrink (Netherlands) 10. Johan Cruyff (Netherlands) 11. Grzegorz Lato (Poland)

## 1978 ARGENTINA

**FINAL:**
Argentina 3 Netherlands 1

**THIRD PLACE:**
Brazil

**GOLDEN BOOT:**
Mario Kempes 6 (Argentina)

**GOLDEN BALL:** Mario Kempes (Argentina)

**ALL STAR TEAM**
1. Ubaldo Fillol (Argentina) 2. Berti Vogts (West Germany) 3. Ruud Krol (Netherlands) 4. Daniel Passarella (Argentina) 5. Alberto Tarantini (Argentina) 6. Dirceu ( Brazil) 7. Franco Causio (Italy) 8. Rob Rensenbrink (Netherlands) 9. Teófilo Cubillas (Peru) 10. Daniel Bertoni (Argentina) 11. Mario Kempes (Argentina)

## 1982 SPAIN

**FINAL:**
Italy 3 West Germany 1

**THIRD PLACE:**
Poland

**GOLDEN BOOT:**
Paolo Rossi 6 (Italy)

**GOLDEN BALL:** Paolo Rossi (Italy)

**ALL STAR TEAM**
1. Dino Zoff (Italy) 2. Claudio Gentile (Italy) 3. Luizinho (Brazil) 4. Fulvio Collovati (Italy) 5. Júnior (Brazil) 6. Zbigniew Boniek (Poland) 7. Falcão (Brazil) 8. Michel Platini (France) 9. Zico (Brazil) 10. Paolo Rossi (Italy) 11. Karl-Heinz Rummenigge (Brazil)

## 1986 MEXICO

**FINAL:**
Argentina 3 West Germany 2

**THIRD PLACE:**
France

**GOLDEN BOOT:**
Gary Lineker 6 (England)

**GOLDEN BALL:** Diego Maradona (Argentina)

**ALL STAR TEAM**
1. Harald Schumacher (West Germany) 2. Josimar (Brazil) 3. Manuel Amoros (France) 4. Maxime Bossis (France) 5. Jan Ceulemans (Belgium) 6. Felix Magath (West Germany) 7. Michel Platini (France) 8. Diego Maradona (Argentina) 9. Preben Elkjær-Larsen (Denmark) 10. Emilio Butragueño (Spain) 11. Gary Lineker (England)

## 1990 ITALY

**FINAL:**
West Germany 1 Argentina 0

**THIRD PLACE:**
Italy

**GOLDEN BOOT:**
Salvatore Schillaci 6 (Italy)

**GOLDEN BALL:** Salvatore Schillaci (Italy)

**ALL STAR TEAM**
1. Sergio Goycochea (Argentina) 2. Andreas Brehme (West Germany) 3. Paolo Maldini (Italy) 4. Franco Baresi (Italy) 5. Diego Maradona (Argentina) 6. Lothar Matthäus (West Germany) 7. Roberto Donadoni (Italy) 8. Paul Gascoigne (England) 9. Salvatore Schillaci (Italy) 10. Roger Milla (Cameroon) 11. Tomáš Skuhravý (Czechoslovakia)

## 1994 USA

**FINAL:**
Brazil 0 Italy 0 (aet)
Brazil won 3–2 on penalties

**THIRD PLACE:**
Sweden

**GOLDEN BOOT:**
Hristo Stoichkov 6 (Bulgaria), Oleg Salenko 6 (Russia)

**GOLDEN BALL:** Romário (Brazil)

**ALL STAR TEAM**
1. Michel Preud'homme (Belgium) 2. Jorginho (Brazil) 3. Márcio Santos (Brazil) 4. Paulo Maldini (Italy) 5. Dunga (Brazil) 6. Krasimir Balakov (Bulgaria) 7. Gheorghe Hagi (Romania) 8. Thomas Brolin (Sweden) 9. Romário (Brazil) 10. Hristo Stoichkov (Bulgaria) 11. Roberto Baggio (Italy)

## 1998 FRANCE

**FINAL:**
France 3 Brazil 0

**THIRD PLACE:**
Croatia

**GOLDEN BOOT:**
Davor Šuker 6 (Croatia)

**GOLDEN BALL:** Ronaldo (Brazil)

**STAR PLAYERS**
**Goalkeepers:** Fabien Barthez (France), José Luis Chilavert (Paraguay) **Defenders:** Roberto Carlos da Silva (Brazil), Marcel Desailly (France), Lilian Thuram (France), Frank de Boer (Netherlands), Carlos Gamarra (Paraguay) **Midfielders:** Dunga (Brazil), Rivaldo (Brazil), Michael Laudrup (Denmark), Zinedine Zidane (France), Edgar Davids (Netherlands) **Forwards:** Ronaldo (Brazil), Davor Šuker (Croatia) Brian Laudrup (Denmark), Dennis Bergkamp (Netherlands)

## 2002 SOUTH KOREA & JAPAN

**FINAL:**
Brazil 2 Germany 0

**THIRD PLACE:**
Turkey

**GOLDEN BOOT:**
Ronaldo 8 (Brazil)

**GOLDEN BALL:** Oliver Kahn (Germany)

**STAR PLAYERS**
**Goalkeepers:** Oliver Kahn (Germany), Rüstü Reçber (Turkey) **Defenders:** Roberto Carlos (Brazil), Sol Campbell (England), Fernando Hierro (Spain), Hong Myung-Bo (South Korea), Alpay Özalan (Turkey) **Midfielders:** Rivaldo (Brazil), Ronaldinho (Brazil), Michael Ballack (Germany), Yoo Sang-Chul (South Korea) **Forwards:** Ronaldo (Brazil), Miroslav Klose (Germany), El Hadji Diouf (Senegal), Hasan Sas (Turkey)

## 2006 GERMANY

**FINAL:**
Italy 1 France 1 (aet)
Italy won 5–3 on penalties

**THIRD PLACE:**
Germany

**GOLDEN BOOT:**
Miroslav Klose 5 (Germany)

**GOLDEN BALL:** Zinedine Zidane (France)

**STAR PLAYERS**
**Goalkeepers:** Gianluigi Buffon (Italy), Jens Lehmann (Germany), Ricardo (Portugal) **Defenders:** Roberto Ayala (Argentina), John Terry (England), Lilian Thuram (France), Philipp Lahm (Germany), Fabio Cannavaro (Italy), Gianluca Zambrotta (Italy), Ricardo Carvalho (Portugal) **Midfielders:** Zé Roberto (Brazil), Patrick Vieira (France), Zinedine Zidane (France), Michael Ballack (Germany), Andrea Pirlo (Italy), Gennaro Gattuso (Italy), Luis Figo (Portugal), Cristiano Ronaldo (Portugal), **Forwards:** Hernán Crespo (Argentina), Thierry Henry (France), Miroslav Klose (Germany), Francesco Totti (Italy), Luca Toni (Italy)

# UEFA EUROPEAN CHAMPIONSHIP

## "FOOTBALL UNITES AND TRANSCENDS EUROPE"

UEFA PRESIDENT AND EUROPEAN CHAMPIONSHIP-
WINNING FRANCE MIDFIELDER MICHEL PLATINI

The UEFA European Championship ranks second only to the World Cup for prestige and popularity in international soccer. More than 50 countries enter the qualifying stages, while the major nations of the continent vie for supremacy. Held every four years, the tournament began in 1960 with a four-team competition, but has grown to become a month-long contest involving 16 teams.

### AN IDEA

Henri Delaunay, former secretary of the French FA, first suggested the idea of a European Championship in 1927, but the first tournament did not take place until 1960.

### 2008

The European Championship trophy was named in Henri Delaunay's honor. A new, larger trophy has been created for the 2008 tournament in Austria and Switzerland; it has a sturdier base and more space for the winners' names. However, the trophy looks very similar to the old one.

*Jürgen Klinsmann celebrates scoring a goal against Russia during Euro '96 in England.*

### FIRST CHAMPIONSHIPS

The USSR defeated Yugoslavia 2–1 in the first European Championship final in Paris. Led by the legendary goalkeeper Lev Yashin, the Soviets needed extra time to complete their victory, with the winning goal scored by Viktor Ponedelnik.

### GERMAN SKILL

Germany is the most successful team in the European Championship. As West Germany and the reunified side, its has won the tournament three times and been runner-up twice. The last triumph in 1996 came when the Germans beat favored hosts England in a thrilling semifinal, before a 2–1 overtime victory over the Czech Republic in the final.

### DID YOU KNOW?

*Germany's Oliver Bierhoff's 94th minute winner in the 1996 final was the first time a major international tournament was decided by a "golden goal." The rule stated that in overtime, the game would end if one team scored a goal. This way of deciding the outcome of a match came to be known as a "golden goal."*

One of the most famous tournaments was in 1992, when outsiders Denmark beat favorites Germany 2–0 in Gothenburg's Ullevi stadium, thanks to goals from John Jensen and Kim Vilfort. The Danes were only at the finals because of the late withdrawal of Yugoslavia, which had to pull out of the competition due to civil war.

## FACT FILE: UEFA EUROPEAN CHAMPIONSHIP
(See p.128 for a complete list of winners)

**TOP GOAL SCORERS**
1. Michel Platini (France) 9
2. Alan Shearer (England) 7
3. Patrick Kluivert (Netherlands) 6
4. Milan Baroš (Czech Republic) 5
= Thierry Henry (France) 5
= Zinedine Zidane (France) 5
= Jürgen Klinsmann (Germany) 5
= Marco Van Basten (Netherlands) 5
= Nuno Gomes (Portugal) 5
= Savo Miloševic (Serbia) 5

**MOST SUCCESSFUL TEAMS**
1. Germany (3 wins)
2. France (2 wins)
3. USSR (1 win)
= Czechoslovakia (1 win)
= Italy (1 win)
= Spain (1 win)
= Netherlands (1 win)
= Denmark (1 win)
= Greece (1 win)

*Before Euro 2004 Greece had never won a game at an international tournament!*

## GOAL KING
Michel Platini holds the record for the most goals scored by one player in a European Championship. He scored nine on the way to France's triumph in 1984, including the opener in the 2–0 defeat of Spain in the final. This total also makes him the Championship's all-time top scorer.

## SURPRISE WIN
When Greece took to the field for the opening group game in Euro 2004 against the hosts Portugal, no one would have predicted that three weeks later both sides would be contesting the final. Greece won that game 2–1 and the final 1–0, thanks to a goal from Angelos Charisteas.

# AFRICAN CUP OF NATIONS

**"A WARNING TO YOU EUROPEANS: ONE DAY WE'LL BEAT YOU TO BECOME WORLD CHAMPIONS!"**
CONFEDERATION OF AFRICAN FOOTBALL PRESIDENT ISSA HAYATOU

## FACT FILE: AFRICAN CUP OF NATIONS
(See p.128 for complete list of winners)

### TOP GOAL SCORERS
1. Laurent Pokou (Ivory Coast) 14
2. Rashidi Yekini (Nigeria) 13
3. Hassan El-Shazly (Egypt) 12
4. Patrick Mboma (Cameroon) 11
= Samuel Eto'o (Cameroon) 11
= Hossam Hassan (Egypt) 11

### MOST SUCCESSFUL TEAMS
1. Egypt (5 wins)
2. Ghana (4 wins)
= Cameroon (4 wins)
3. Congo DR (2 wins)
= Nigeria (2 wins)

Just three teams (Egypt, Sudan, and Ethiopia) took part in the first CAF African Cup of Nations in Sudan in 1957. However, it is now a prestigious biennial event with 16 teams participating in the 2008 tournament in Ghana. The competition is usually held in January, but with many African players playing in European leagues, pressure is growing to move it to the summer.

## CAMEROON
Although much of the world first discovered the delights of Cameroon's football at the 1990 World Cup Finals, the seeds of the team's success were sown in the early 1980s. The "Indomitable Lions" made three consecutive finals that decade and won two of them, most notably beating Nigeria 3–1 in the 1984 final. Cameroon also captured the first two titles of the 21st century thanks to its calmness in penalty shootouts. The country's third victory in 2000 earned it the right to keep the trophy.

The current ACN trophy (left) is the third. Ghana was allowed to keep the original Abdelaziz Abdallah Salem Trophy after its third triumph in 1978, and the African Unity Cup was kept by Cameroon in 2000.

## DID YOU KNOW?

*No player has scored more goals in one African Cup of Nations than Ndaya Mulamba's nine for Zaire (now DPR Congo) in 1974.*

## EGYPT
The "Pharaohs" won the first two ACN titles. Raafat Ateya scored the first-ever ACN goal in 1957 and Al-Diba hit all four goals in that year's final. Egypt has won the title five times, including a penalty shootout victory over Ivory Coast in 2006.

*Mohamed Aboutreika scored Egypt's decisive penalty in the 2006 final.*

## GHANA
Ghana's "Black Stars" put African soccer on the map by winning the 1963 and 1965 tournaments in irresistible style. A third win in 1978 entitled it to keep the trophy, but there have been lengthy, impatient waits between victories since then. Abédi "Pelé" Ayew announced himself as a 17-year-old wonder in Ghana's fourth success in 1982. However, he was suspended for the epic 11–10 shootout defeat to Ivory Coast 10 years later.

# AFC ASIAN CUP

## "THIS IS NOT JUST ABOUT FOOTBALL... THIS HAS BROUGHT GREAT HAPPINESS TO A WHOLE COUNTRY."

JORVAN VIEIRA, BRAZILIAN COACH OF 2007 AFC ASIAN CUP WINNERS IRAQ

The AFC Asian Cup was first held in 1956 in Hong Kong and won by the Republic of Korea. The competition was then held every four years until 2007, when the AFC brought the tournament forward a year to avoid clashing with the Olympics and the European Championship. For the first time, the competition was cohosted by four nations (Indonesia, Malaysia, Vietnam, and Thailand)—and AFC new boys Australia made their debut.

## FACT FILE: AFC ASIAN CUP
(See p 128 for complete list of winners)

### TOP GOAL SCORERS
1. Ali Daei (Iran) 14
2. Lee Dong-Gook (Republic of Korea) 10
3. Naohiro Takahara (Japan) 9
4. Jassem Al Houwaidi (Kuwait) 8
5. Choi Soon-Ho (Republic of Korea) 7
= Behtash Fariba (Iran) 7
= Hossein Kalani (Iran) 7

### MOST SUCCESSFUL TEAMS
1. Saudi Arabia (3 wins)
= Iran (3 wins)
= Japan (3 wins)
2. Republic of Korea (2 wins)
3. Israel (1 win)
= Kuwait (1 win)
= Iraq (1 win)

### IRAN
Iran won every game in the 1968, 1972, and 1976 tournaments to take three consecutive trophies. However, in recent years it has struggled to rediscover this form, despite the goal-scoring efforts of Javad Nekounam (right, center) in 2007.

### SAUDI ARABIA
Saudi Arabia won the tournament in 1984 and 1988. It was runner-up to Japan in 1992, but reclaimed the trophy in 1996 (above) when Mohammed Al-Deayea was the penalty-saving hero.

### JAPAN
In 2004 Shunsuke Nakamura's man-of-the-match display helped Japan to its third win since 1992. Japan beat China 3–1 in the final, and captain Tsuneyasu Miyamoto proudly lifted the trophy (right).

Younis Mahmoud lifts the Asian Cup after Iraq's 2007 victory in Jakarta, Indonesia.

### IRAQ
Australia was the favorite in 2007, but outsiders Iraq, led by captain and crucial goal-scorer Younis Mahmoud, were the surprise winners. Iraq's coach, Jorvan Vieira, had been in charge for just two months.

### DID YOU KNOW?
Iran's Ali Daei is the all-time Asian Cup top scorer, netting 14 goals at the 1996, 2000, and 2004 tournaments.

# COPA AMÉRICA

**"THE COPA AMÉRICA IS MORE DIFFICULT THAN THE WORLD CUP BECAUSE OF THE RIVALRY THAT EXISTS IN SOUTH AMERICA."** DUNGA, WHO WON THE COPA WITH BRAZIL AS A PLAYER AND AS COACH

The Copa América is the oldest—and most fiercely contested—international tournament. It was introduced in 1916 to mark a century of Argentina's independence from Spain. The format, name, and frequency of the competition have varied greatly over the years but it is now established as a 12-team tournament held every four years, with hosting rights rotated between the 10 CONMEBOL countries.

Two or three CONCACAF guest nations are invited to the Copa América tournament. In 2001 guests Honduras (left) stunned Brazil 2–0 in the quarterfinal. Mexico also finished runner-up in that year.

Victory in 2007 meant that Brazil retained the trophy it had also won in 2004.

Joint record-holder Uruguay won the first ever Copa América in 1916 and has won it 13 times since then. Enzo Francescoli (above, pictured in 1995) was the architect of the 1983, 1987, and 1995 victories.

## ARGENTINA

Victory in 1993 brought Argentina its 14th Copa América, and its last international trophy to date. Oscar Ruggeri (right) captained the side and two goals from Gabriel Batistuta proved too much for guests Mexico in the final. Argentina was runner-up to Brazil in 2004 and 2007 and is still chasing a 15th Copa América to take it ahead of Uruguay.

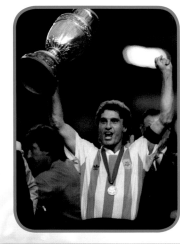

## BRAZIL

In 2007, the result seemed a foregone conclusion. Brazilian stars such as Kaká and Ronaldinho were absent while Riquelme and Messi lit up a majestic Argentina side. However, Brazil outmuscled its old rivals 3–0 in the final to win the Copa for the eighth time.

Robinho's six goals made him the tournament's top scorer.

### DID YOU KNOW?

Argentina striker Martín Palermo missed three penalties during Colombia's 3–0 win in the 1999 Copa América—an international record.

# CONCACAF GOLD CUP

**"THE GOLD CUP IS STILL THE MOST IMPORTANT EVENT FOR US."** BOB BRADLEY, US COACH SINCE 2006.

CONCACAF's showpiece has had a varied history and throughout the 1980s it was chiefly used to decide World Cup places. In 1990 it was rebranded as the CONCACAF Gold Cup and since then the tournament has enjoyed greater prestige. Although the competition is dominated by Mexico and the USA, the 2007 event brought encouraging displays from Canada, Honduras, and Guadeloupe.

## FACT FILE: CONCACAF GOLD CUP
(See p.128 for complete list of winners)

**TOP GOAL SCORERS**
1. Zaguinho (Mexico) 13
2. Landon Donovan (USA) 12
3. Carlos Pavón (Honduras) 9
= Eric Wynalda (USA) 9
4. Paulo Wanchope (Costa Rica) 8
= Walter Centeno (Costa Rica) 8
= Brian McBride (USA) 8

**MOST SUCCESSFUL TEAMS**
1. Mexico (7 wins)
2. USA (4 wins)
3. Costa Rica (3 wins)
4. Canada (2 wins)

### MEXICO
In 1993, striker Zaguinho inspired Mexico to a famous victory. Zaguinho (right, real name Luis Roberto Alves) hit 12 goals and the USA was thrashed 4–0 in the final. Mexico has won the tournament three times since 1993, giving it a record seven wins.

### CANADA 2000
Jason de Vos and Carlo Corazzin got the goals to conquer Colombia in the final, but Canada's victory in 2000 owed much to trusty goalkeeper Craig Forrest (above,).

### USA
In 2007, new coach Bob Bradley helped the USA to continue its good form against rivals Mexico by winning the final 2–1. The USA first entered the tournament in 1989, but lost to Costa Rica in the final. Nevertheless, this secured the USA a place at the 1990 World Cup Finals.

Guests from other federations were invited to the Gold Cup between 1996 to 2005. Brazil was runner-up twice and the Republic of Korea reached the semifinals in 2002.

*The USA retained the trophy against Mexico thanks to goals from Landon Donovan and Benny Feilhaber.*

### DID YOU KNOW?
*In 2003, USA striker Landon Donovan scored four of his team's goals in its 5–0 victory over Cuba in the quarterfinal.*

*In 2007, USA goalkeeper Kasey Keller appeared in his sixth CONCACAF Gold Cup—a tournament record.*

# WOMEN'S COMPETITIONS

"WOMEN'S SOCCER HAS GONE THROUGH AN UNBELIEVABLE DEVELOPMENT IN RECENT YEARS AND THAT WILL CONTINUE, I AM SURE."

NADINE ANGERER, GERMANY'S 2007 WORLD CUP-WINNING GOALKEEPER

The female game's flagship competition, the Women's World Cup was only staged for the first time in 1991 but is already attracting strong challenges from five continents. The 2007 contest enjoyed a higher profile than ever before as Brazil's path to the final upset the usual USA/European dominance. Interest in the women's game is growing and with 26 million female players around the world, the sky is the limit for women's soccer.

In 2007 Birgit Prinz proudly holds the World Cup trophy as Germany retain the title it won in 2003.

## THE WORLD CUP

China welcomed the world in 2007, four years after an outbreak of the SARS disease forced the World Cup Finals to be relocated to the US. Shanghai's Hongkou Stadium staged the spectacular opening ceremony and the tournament enjoyed unprecedented levels of support.

### 2007 FINAL

Germany was a worthy champion in 2007 and did not concede a goal in the entire tournament. It started its campaign with an 11–0 thrashing of Argentina. Striker and team captain Birgit Prinz scored a hat trick in that match and she also scored in the final. Brazil was beaten 2–0 in the final, during which German goalkeeper Nadine Angerer saved a penalty.

### OLYMPICS

Women's soccer debuted at the Olympic Games in 1996. The USA have won gold twice, but in 2000 Norway made them settle for the silver medal (above).

## AFC WOMEN'S ASIAN CUP

The AFC Women's Asian Cup is one of the longest-running international women's competitions. It was introduced in 1975 and first won by New Zealand. China has largely dominated the competition since then—it has triumphed eight times, including a 2006 win over hosts Australia on penalties (celebrated right).

## OTHER WOMEN'S COMPETITIONS

Beginning in 1991, the first four Sudamericano Femenino contests were won by Brazil. However, Argentina finally turned the tables on Brazil in 2006, despite a talented team that included the legendary Marta. Argentina beat its old rivals 2–0 in the final, thanks to goals from Eva Nadia González and María Belén Potassa.

At the other end of the world, in the Oceania region, the OFC Women's Championship has been shared between New Zealand and Australia, with three wins apiece. Chinese Taipei is following close behind with two trophies, in 1986 and 1989. New Zealand won the tournament in 2007, scoring 21 goals in three games.

## EUROPEAN CHAMPIONSHIP

Germany won the first UEFA Women's Championship in 1991, beating Norway 3–1 in the final. The same sides played out the same scoreline in England in 2005 (celebrated above, by Germany's Inka Grings, Conny Pohlers, and Britta Carlson). Amazingly, Norway's narrow victory over Italy in 1993 is the only time Germany has failed to take the title.

## CONCACAF WOMEN'S GOLD CUP

The USA has enjoyed a secure grip on the CONCACAF Women's Gold Cup, winning six out of seven contests. 1998 champion Canada was beaten in the 2006 final by Kristine Lilly's (pictured right, player on the left) last-minute penalty.

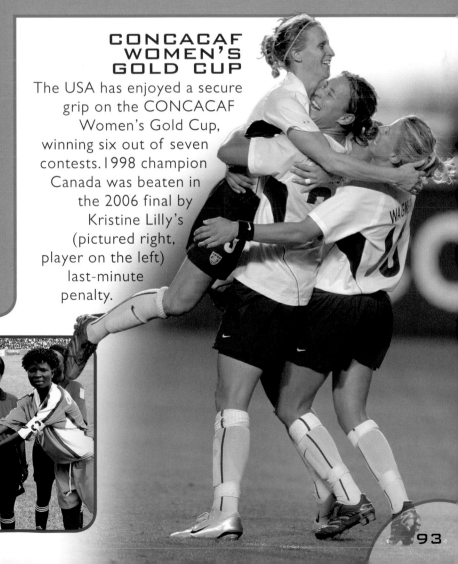

## CAF WOMEN'S CHAMPIONSHIP

Nigeria and Ghana have competed in three CAF Women's Championship finals and all of them have been won by Nigeria. In fact, Nigeria has won all seven CAF tournaments. In the 2006 final (pictured right) Nigeria beat Ghana 1–0, thanks to Perpetua Nkwocha's early goal. Success in the CAF Championships meant that both countries qualified for the 2007 Women's World Cup.

Players from rival English teams Chelsea and Manchester United sportingly shake hands before a Premier League match.

# CLUB SOCCER

"IN HIS LIFE, A MAN CAN CHANGE WIVES, POLITICAL PARTIES, OR RELIGIONS, BUT HE CANNOT CHANGE HIS FAVORITE FOOTBALL TEAM."

URUGUAYAN AUTHOR EDUARDO GALLEANO

Supporting your favorite team can be tough. When results are bad, the weather is foul, and your local rivals have inflicted yet another painful defeat, you might wonder why you ever chose them in the first place. But somehow you just can't stop yourself from caring—once you've given your heart to a team, that's it. For life. After all, there's always next season...

# UEFA CHAMPIONS LEAGUE

**"THE CHAMPIONS LEAGUE IS THE COMPETITION EVERYONE WANTS TO BE IN."** STEVEN GERRARD, LIVERPOOL'S TROPHY-WINNING CAPTAIN IN 2005.

The Champions League is possibly the most prestigious club competition in the world. Originally called the European Cup, it changed its name in 1992 and adopted a league-and-knockout format. The spectacular season-long competition features the best club sides from Europe and many of the world's finest players, and generates huge television and sponsorship deals.

### AJAX
The great Ajax side of Johan Cruyff, Johnny Rep, Arie Haan, and co. reigned supreme during the early 1970s, winning three European Cups in a row thanks to victories over Panathinaikos (1971), Inter (1972), and Juventus (1973). Opponents had no answer to Ajax's philosophy of "Total Football" (see p. 41).

### BAYERN MUNICH
Bayern Munich also achieved three consecutive triumphs, between 1974 and 1976. Great players such as Franz Beckenbauer, Uli Hoeness (right), Georg Schwarzenbeck, Sepp Maier, Paul Breitner, and Gerd Müller were key to the team's success. Bayern secured its fourth trophy in 2001.

*Captain Paolo Maldini lifts the trophy after Milan's 2–1 defeat of Liverpool in 2007.*

### AC MILAN
Italy's most successful European Cup/Champions League club is AC Milan, with seven victories, most recently in 2007. Arguably Milan's finest win was the 4–0 humiliation of Barcelona in 1994. The team, managed by Fabio Capello, produced a performance viewed by some as the best-ever by a club team.

### FAMOUS COMEBACK
Losing 3–0 to AC Milan at half time during the 2005 final in Istanbul, four-time winner Liverpool looked doomed. But the English team launched an unforgettable comeback, inspired by skipper Steven Gerrard (right, scoring Liverpool's first goal). Unbelievably, Liverpool drew level with Milan and then earned its fifth trophy thanks to a nail-biting 3–2 win in the penalty shootout. However, two years later Milan had its revenge and defeated Liverpool 2–1 in a much more straightforward final.

### REAL MADRID
Real Madrid is the most successful team in Europe's top competition with nine wins. It won the first five European Cups (1956–1960), lifted the trophy again in 1966, and has brought the Champions League title back to Spain on a further three occasions (1998, 2000, and 2002). Here Manuel Sanchís and his teammates celebrate the club's 2000 victory (right).

# UEFA CUP

**"WINNING THE UEFA CUP WAS THE HIGHLIGHT OF MY CAREER."** HAKAN SÜKÜR, WINNER WITH GALATASARAY IN 2000

Europe's second most important club competition began in 1955 as the Inter-Cities Fairs Cup. It was renamed the UEFA Cup in 1971, and teams qualified on the basis of domestic league position. In 1999 the competition was merged with the UEFA Cup Winners' Cup to include winners of domestic cup competitions. Today, losing sides from the qualifying rounds of the Champions League are also eligible for the UEFA Cup.

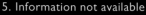

## FACT FILE: UEFA CUP
(See p.131 for complete list of winners)

### TOP GOALSCORERS
1. Information not available
2. Information not available
3. Information not available
4. Information not available
5. Information not available

### MOST SUCCESSFUL TEAMS
**3 WINS**
Internazionale (Italy)
Juventus (Italy)
Liverpool (England)
**2 WINS**
Borussia Mönchengladbach (Germany)
Feyenoord (Netherlands)
IFK Gothenburg (Sweden)
Parma (Italy)
Real Madrid (Spain)
Sevilla (Spain)
Tottenham Hotspur (England)

## FAMOUS VICTORY
Porto's Deco (right) and Nuno Valente (left) hold the UEFA Cup aloft after their side won a wonderfully exciting 2003 final 3–2 against Celtic in Seville. Porto triumphed after scoring a "silver goal" (see p.149) in overtime. A year later it went one better and won the Champions League.

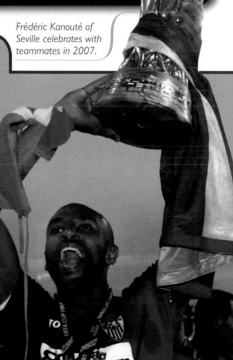

Frédéric Kanouté of Seville celebrates with teammates in 2007.

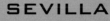

## SEVILLA
Sevilla's 3–1 win on penalties over its countrymen Espanyol in the 2007 UEFA Cup final meant the Spanish side became the first club to retain the trophy since Real Madrid in 1986. Sevilla had thrashed Middlesbrough 4–0 in 2006.

Italian giant Juventus has won the trophy a record three times. Its first triumph was in 1977 against Athletic Bilbao and victory in 1990 (celebrated left) came when it defeated fellow Italians Fiorentina 3–1 on aggregate. Juventus last won the trophy in 1993.

## CUP WINNERS' CUP
Italian team Lazio has held the European Cup Winners' Cup for more than nine years. However, this is because the Roman side got to keep the trophy after winning the last competition in 1999. The ECWC had run for 38 seasons, but came to an end when it was absorbed into the UEFA Cup. Lazio beat Mallorca 2–1, thanks to goals from Christian Vieri (right, center) and Pavel Nedved (far right).

# COPA LIBERTADORES

**"WHEN I ARRIVED AT RIVER [PLATE] MY DREAM WAS TO WIN THE COPA LIBERTADORES"**

ARGENTINA STRIKER HERNÁN CRESPO, WHO WON
THE TROPHY WITH RIVER PLATE IN 1996

## FACT FILE: COPA LIBERTADORES

### TOP GOAL SCORERS

1. Alberto Spencer (Peñarol, Barcelona) 54
2. Fernando Morena (Peñarol) 37
3. Pedro Virgílio Rocha (Peñarol, São Paulo, Palmeiras) 36
4. Daniel Onega (Club Atlético River Plate) 31
5. Julio Morales (Nacional) 30

### MOST SUCCESSFUL TEAMS

1. Independiente (Argentina) 7 wins
2. Boca Juniors (Argentina) 6 wins
3. Peñarol (Uruguay) 5 wins
4. National (Uruguay) 3 wins
= São Paulo (Brazil) 3 wins
= Olimpia (Paraguay) 3 wins
= Estuadiantes LP (Argentina) 3 wins

The Copa Libertadores was introduced in 1960 as South America's challenge to the European Cup (now Champions League), and this exciting annual contest certainly seems to guarantee more goals per game than its European counterpart. The format is similar to the Champions League, with the top teams from each country competing for the trophy. It began with just nine clubs, but now 38 clubs compete for the Copa.

## TOP SCORER

Ecuador's Alberto Spencer was the Libertadores' most lethal striker, with 54 goals in 77 games between 1960 and 1972. He earned three winners' medals with Peñarol of Uruguay.

## BOCA JUNIORS

Argentina's Boca Juniors have dominated the Copa in the 21st century. In 2007 Juan Román Riquelme (on loan from Spain's Villareal) inspired a 5–0 two-leg triumph over Brazil's Grêmio, netting three goals himself.

## INDEPENDIENTE

Argentinian teams have dominated the competition at times, especially Independiente. Its 4–1 playoff victory over Peñarol in 1965 (left) was the second of seven wins, the last of which came in 1984.

A 2004 rule-change permitted clubs from the same country to compete in the final. This resulted in two all-Brazil showdowns in a row. In 2005 São Paulo beat Atlético Paranaense 5–1 over two legs (pictured above) but the following year it could only only finish runner-up, after losing 4–3 on aggregate to fellow Brazilians Internacional.

# CONCACAF CHAMPIONS' CUP

**"CONCACAF HAS BECOME BETTER AND BETTER EACH AND EVERY YEAR, AT ALL LEVELS."**

CHIVAS USA SPORTING DIRECTOR THOMAS RONGEN

The CONCACAF Champions' Cup was first introduced in 1962, but the USA did not participate until 1997, when CONCACAF granted the recently-formed MLS (Major League Soccer) two places in the tournament. The cup is vied for by the leading club sides in the region, and has so far been dominated by clubs from Mexico. From 2009 onward, CONCACAF hope to expand the Champions' Cup to bring a European-style Champions League competition to North and Central America.

## FACT FILE: CONCACAF CHAMPIONS CUP

**TOP GOAL SCORERS**
1. Information not known
2. Information not known
3. Information not known
4. Information not known
5. Information not known

**MOST SUCCESSFUL TEAMS**
1. Club América (Mexico) 5 wins
= Cruz Azul (Mexico) 5 wins
2. Saprissa (Costa Rica) 3 wins
= UNAM Pumas (Mexico) 3 wins

### LA GALAXY

In 2000, Los Angeles Galaxy became only the second US side to take the trophy, beating Honduran side Olimpia 3–2 in the final. Defender Ezra Hendrickson was the surprise two-goal hero, with Cobi Jones (far left) adding a third. DC United had been the first North American winner in 1998, only a year after US teams first entered the competition.

### MEXICO

Mexican teams Club América and Cruz Azul have both won the competition a record five times. Mexican star striker Cuauhtémoc Blanco (right) and defender Duilio Davino (left) helped Club América to ther last victory in 2006.

*Colombian keeper Miguel Calero has lifted the trophy twice with Pachuca, in 2002 and 2007.*

### PACHUCA

In 2007 Mexican side CF Pachuca beat compatriots Chivas de Guadalajara 7–6 in a penalty shootout. Pachuca goalkeeper and captain Miguel "El Condor" Calero did not make a save in the shootout—instead, Chivas forward Alberto Medina hit the post.

### NECAXA

Ecuadorian midfielder Álex Aguinaga (second left) was opening scorer and player of the tournament when Mexico's Necaxa won its first CONCACAF Champions' Cup in 1999. Necaxa beat LD Alajuelense of Costa Rica 2–1 in the final, three years after it had finished runner-up to Cruz Azul in a mini-league final system.

### DEPORTIVO SAPRISSA

Costa Rica's Saprissa recorded its third CONCACAF victory as Rónald Gómez and Christian Bolaños helped defeat UNAM Pumas of Mexico 3–2 in a two leg final. Saprissa is nicknamed "El Monstruo Morado" (The Purple Monster) because of its purple uniform, which is said to be the result of the original red shirts and blue shorts mixing in the wash in 1937.

# ENGLISH CLUBS

*"THANK YOU FOR LETTING ME PLAY IN YOUR BEAUTIFUL FOOTBALL."* FRENCHMAN ERIC CANTONA, FORMER MANCHESTER UNITED STRIKER

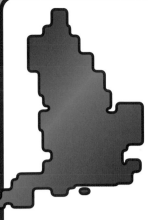

England is often seen as the home of soccer. It has the oldest soccer association (1863), the oldest professional league (1888), and what borders on a national obsession with the game. English soccer is famous for its fast and physical style, and the arrival of foreign players has helped raise the standard of technical skill. In 1992 the top 20 clubs formed the Premier League, which brought major changes to the English game. Factors such as new stadiums, bigger crowds, and rich foreign owners have brought huge financial success, particularly for the biggest clubs such as Manchester United and Arsenal. Every team is desperate to remain in the Premier League, but each season three clubs are promoted from the division below and three are relegated.

There are 92 senior clubs in the English Football League. The Premier League is the top division and is made up of 20 teams.

## ARSENAL
EMIRATES STADIUM, LONDON
Arsenal is by far London's most successful club, with 13 league titles and 10 FA Cups. The modern team has been transformed under Frenchman Arsene Wenger (left center), with young stars like Cesc Fabregas (left, center) producing entertaining and free-flowing soccer.

## CHELSEA
STAMFORD BRIDGE, LONDON
Billionaire Roman Abramovich has helped Chelsea to become one of England's most successful sides. Since he bought the club in 2003 it has won the league twice (2005 and 2006), the League Cup twice (2005 and 2007), and the FA Cup once in 2007, with Didier Drogba (above) scoring the winning goal.

## TOTTENHAM HOTSPUR
WHITE HART LANE, LONDON
Spurs have struggled in recent years but they are famous for being the only "non-league" side to win the FA Cup (1901), the first British side to win a European trophy (1963), and the first to win the "Double" (the league title and the FA Cup) in the 20th century (1961, right).

## FAMOUS CLUBS

Portsmouth FC

Fulham

Bolton Wanderers

Middlesborough

Arsenal

Nottingham Forest

## PRESTON NORTH END

**DEEPDALE, PRESTON, LANCASHIRE**

Preston North End was the first winner of the Football League in 1889 and by winning the FA Cup the same year became the only club to secure the prestigious "Double" for more than 70 years.

## NEWCASTLE UNITED

**ST. JAMES' PARK, NEWCASTLE**

Newcastle United has been one of England's top clubs since the early 1900s, winning four league titles and six FA Cups. Nicknamed the Magpies because of their famous black and white uniform, United has not won a major trophy since the 1969 Inter Cities Fairs Cup, despite coming close.

## EVERTON

**GOODISON PARK, LIVERPOOL**

With nine league titles and five FA Cup wins, Everton is one of England's most successful clubs of all time and fierce local rivals of Liverpool. Despite a lack of recent glory, Goodison Park is still one of the best grounds in England for atmosphere.

## LIVERPOOL

**ANFIELD, LIVERPOOL**

"The Mighty Reds" are England's most successful club side, with 18 league titles, five European Cups, and 17 other major trophies. The 1984 team (above) almost won every competition they played in. They won the European Cup, the League title, and the League Cup, but lost in the fourth round of the FA Cup.

*The Premier League has been won by just four clubs—Man Utd., Chelsea, Arsenal, and Blackburn.*

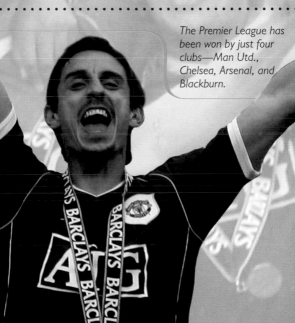

## MANCHESTER UNITED

**OLD TRAFFORD, MANCHESTER**

With millions of fans across the globe, Man Utd. is one of the world's biggest clubs. Current boss Sir Alex Ferguson is the most successful British manager of all time, with 18 major trophies won by his team, which includes homegrown stars Ryan Giggs (left) and Gary Neville (right).

Everton

Newcastle United

Chelsea

Blackpool

Wolverhampton Wanderers

# FRENCH CLUBS

*"FOOTBALL IS A FANTASTIC AND INTELLIGENT GAME THAT TEACHES US HOW TO LIVE TOGETHER."*

MICHEL PLATINI

The French league (Le Championnat) has produced legends such as Just Fontaine, Michel Platini, and Zinedine Zidane. Attacking flair and technical ability are features of the French game, and coaches such as Aimé Jacquet, Gérard Houllier, and Guy Roux have built strong youth development systems. However, despite their undeniable talent, French teams have underachieved in European competitions.

The French League began in 1932, and is split into two divisions, Ligues 1 and 2, each with 20 teams.

## FC SOCHAUX

STADE AUGUSTE BONAL, MONTBÉLIARD

FC Sochaux was France's first professional club. Formed in 1928, it enjoyed early success and won the league in 1935 and 1938. After years of underachievement, a young, talented team has reemerged, winning the French Cup in 2007 (above).

## OLYMPIQUE LYONNAIS

STADE GERLAND, LYON

Lyon is the most successful French club of modern times, winning all six Ligue 1 titles between 2002 and 2007—a French record. Despite domestic success "Les Gones" have never gotten past the quarterfinal of any European competition.

*Lyon's Brazilian free-kick master Juninho Pernambucano in action for Lyon against Bordeaux in the 2007 French Cup final.*

### LEAGUE TROPHY

The Ligue 1 trophy was first contested in 1932–1933, when it was won by Olympique Lillois (now Lille). St. Étienne, with 10 titles, is the most successful club.

# FAMOUS CLUBS

SM Caen

Le Mans UC72

RC Lens

AS Monaco

AS Nancy-Lorraine

OGC Nice

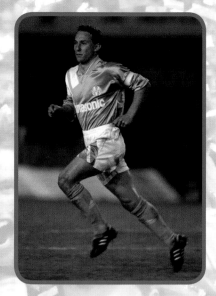

## OLYMPIQUE MARSEILLE

### STADE VÉLODROME, MARSEILLE

France's best-supported club, Marseille has won eight league titles, a record 10 French Cups, and in 1993 became the only ever French Champions League winners. A corruption scandal saw OM relegated in 1994 but it has bounced back in recent years. Legendary players include Jean-Pierre Papin (left) and Didier Deschamps.

## FC GIRONDINS DE BORDEAUX

### STADE CHABAN DELMAS, BORDEAUX

Some of the biggest names in modern French soccer has played for the five-times champions Bordeaux, including Alain Giresse, Christophe Dugarry, Eric Cantona, Jean Tigana, and Zinedine Zidane. After a slump in the early 1990s, Bordeaux are slowly reestablishing its place near the top of Ligue 1.

## AS MONACO

### STADE LOUIS II, MONACO

The club from the tiny country of Monaco is one of the most successful teams in French soccer. It has won seven French titles and reached the final of the UEFA Champions League in 2004.

## AS ST. ÉTIENNE

### STADE GEOFFROY-GUICHARD, ST ÉTIENNE

"Les Verts" (the Greens) dominated French soccer in the 1960s and 70s thanks to great players such as Michel Platini (right), but did not achieve the same success in Europe.

## FC NANTES ATLANTIQUE

### LA BEAUJOIRE-LOUIS FONTENEAU, NANTES

Now languishing in Ligue 2, Nantes has won eight league titles since 1965. The Canaries are famed for their one-touch soccer, and for a youth system that produced players of the quality of Desailly and Deschamps.

## PARIS ST-GERMAIN

### PARC DES PRINCES, PARIS

Formed in 1970 by the merger of two Paris clubs, Paris FC and Stade Saint-Germain, PSG rapidly established a reputation as a cup team, winning the French Cup seven times. The club has featured such stars as David Ginola (above), Youri Djorkaeff, and George Weah.

Paris St-Germain

FC Girondins de Bordeaux

Toulouse FC

FC Lorient

RC Strasbourg

# ITALIAN CLUBS

### "FOOTBALL IS A PHENOMENON IN ITALY. IT'S ALL THEY TALK ABOUT. IT'S CRAZY!"

DAVID TRÉZÉGUET, FRANCE AND JUVENTUS STRIKER

Italian league soccer is split into four divisions with a total of 78 clubs.

Italian soccer, or "calcio," has few rivals when it comes to passion, intensity, and success. Big clubs like AC Milan, Internazionale, Roma, and Juventus play in famous stadiums, field many of the world's finest players, and enjoy fanatical support. Italian teams are famed for an organized, defensive style combined with exciting individual flair. In the 1980s and 1990s Serie A could claim to be the best division in the world as foreign stars such as Maradona, van Basten, Papin, and Gullit, plus homegrown talents such as Franco Baresi, Roberto Mancini and Gianluca Vialli lit up the Italian game. Recent corruption scandals and crowd trouble have tarnished the reputation of Italian soccer, but Italian clubs still rank among the greats.

## GENOA

### STADIO LUIGI FERRARIS, GENOA

Recent years may have been a struggle for the modern Genoa side, but the club can lay claim to being the first of Italy's great teams, winning nine league titles or "scudetti" between 1898 and 1924.

## AS ROMA

### STADIO OLIMPICA, ROME

Proudly wearing their city's ancient wolf symbol on their shirts, the "Giallorossi" (the Yellow-Reds) have won a total of three titles and eight Italian Cups. Their 2007 cup win is celebrated above.

## AC MILAN

### SAN SIRO, MILAN

Mighty AC Milan has won the European Cup no less than seven times and the scudetto (league) on 17 occasions. Pictured above is the club's legendary defender Paolo Maldini, still playing at the age of 39.

# FAMOUS CLUBS

- AC MILAN
- AFC FIORENTINA
- AS LIVORNO CALCIO
- AS ROMA
- ATALANTA BC

- BOLOGNA FC 1909
- CAGLIARI CALCIO
- EMPOLI FC
- FC MESSINA PELORO
- GENOA

## TORINO
STADIO OLIMPICO DE TORINO, TURIN

Torino was the finest Italian side of the 1940s. It won four consecutive league titles 1946–49, before tragedy struck in the Mount Superga disaster of 1949, when a plane carrying the team crashed near Turin, killing 18 players.

## JUVENTUS
STADIO OLIMPICO DE TORINO, TURIN

Italy's most popular club are followed by supporters from Sicily to the Alps. Nicknamed "La Vecchia Signora" (the Old Lady) the club has won two European Cups and 27 scudetti, and has a fine history for producing brilliant players like Alessandro del Piero (left).

### LAZIO
STADIO OLIMPICO, ROME

Lazio has won two league titles (1974 and 2000), four Italian cups, and one European Cup Winners' Cup (1999). Its shares its grounds with fierce local rivals Roma.

Inter players celebrate winning the 2007 Serie A title.

## INTERNAZIONALE
SAN SIRO, MILAN

Internazionale, also known as Inter and Inter Milan, was founded when some members split away from AC Milan in 1908. Pioneering the defensive style known as "catenaccio" (translated as door bolt), Inter was dominant during the 1960s, winning the European Cup twice.

- HELLAS VERONA FC
- JUVENTUS
- INTERNAZIONALE
- LAZIO
- NAPOLI
- PARMA FC
- TORINO
- UC SAMPDORIA
- UDINESE
- US CITTA DI PALERMO

# GERMAN CLUBS

*"THERE ARE NO RIGHT OR WRONG, OR FAIR RESULTS. THERE'S JUST THE FINAL SCORE."*
OTTO REHHAGEL

The modern Bundesliga formed in 1963, for teams in what was then West Germany. After the country's unification in 1991, the East and West German leagues were merged, but the top tier is still dominated by clubs from the former West Germany. Soccer is hugely popular in Germany, and German club sides attract some of the largest crowds in the world. Germany's two professional divisions, the Bundesliga and the 2. Bundesliga, each have 18 teams.

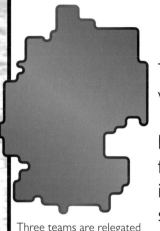

Three teams are relegated from the Bundesliga and three promoted each season.

## HAMBURGER SV

### HSH NORDBANK ARENA

The only club never to have been relegated from the top division, Hamburg has won seven national titles, and was European Champions in 1983.

Matthias Sammer played for Borussia Dortmund from 1993 to 1998 and later managed the club.

## BAYERN MUNICH

### ALLIANZ ARENA, MUNICH

Not only Germany's most successful club, with 20 national championships and four European Cups to its name, Bayern Munich is also the world's third biggest, after Real Madrid and Barcelona of Spain. In 2006–2007 Bayern finished a disappointing fourth in the Bundesliga and has spent millions on new players to reestablish its dominance.

## BORUSSIA DORTMUND

### WESTFALENSTADION, DORTMUND

After initial success in the 1950s and 1960s, Dortmund reemerged as a major club in the 1990s. Winners of six German titles and the Champions League in 1997, its average home attendance of 80,000 is the highest in Europe.

Bayern hopes striker Miroslav Klose will fire it back to the top of the Bundesliga.

## FAMOUS CLUBS

Eintracht Frankfurt

Hertha BSC Berlin

Werder Bremen

Bayer Leverkusen

FC Bayern Munich

Hannover 96

Hamburger SV

## SCHALKE 04

### VELTINS-ARENA, GELSENKIRCHEN

Founded in 1904, Schalke won the league six times between 1934 and 1942 and was a significant force in German soccer. Aside from its seventh league win in 1958 (the last to date) major success eluded Schalke for most of the second half of the 20th century. However, victory in the 1997 UEFA Cup final—its first in Europe—signaled the start of Schalke's revival. So far in the 21st century, Schalke has been Bundesliga runner-up three times and won the German Cup twice.

## VFB STUTTGART

### GOTTLIEB-DAIMLER-STADION, STUTTGART

2007 league champions Stuttgart has won a total of five national titles, but is yet to enjoy sustained European success. The club has one of the most successful youth development programs in Germany and has also featured world-class names such as Jürgen Klinsmann, Denmark's Jon Dahl Tomasson, and Brazil's Giovane Élber.

## WERDER BREMEN

### WESERSTADION, BREMEN

Four-time German champion Werder Bremen established itself as a soccer powerhouse under coach Otto Rehhagel in the 1980s. Now a regular Champions League competitor, it has a reputation for attractive soccer. Werder hopes that German internationals such as Per Mertesacker, Torsten Frings (above left), and Tim Borowski will give it the edge over long-time rivals, Bayern Munich.

## BAYER LEVERKUSEN

### BAYARENA, LEVERKUSEN

Bayer emerged as a force in the late 1980s, but so far has won only one German Cup and a UEFA Cup. Former players include Rudi Völler and Michael Ballack and the club is known for its family-friendly image.

## FC NÜRNBERG

### EASYCREDIT-STADION, NUREMBERG

In the 1920's, nine-time champion Nürnberg was Germany's most popular and successful team. Since then, it has endured lean times, but a German Cup win in 2007 (left) may signal the club's reemergence.

- BORUSSIA DORTMUND
- DSC ARMINIA BIELEFELD
- ENERGIE COTTBUS
- FC DYNAMO DRESDEN
- FC HANSA ROSTOCK
- FC NÜRNBERG
- KARLSRUHER FC
- MSV DUISBURG
- SCHALKE 04
- VFB STUTTGART
- VFL BOCHUM
- VFL WOLFSBURG

# DUTCH CLUBS

### "FOOTBALL IS SIMPLE. BUT THE HARDEST THING IS TO PLAY FOOTBALL IN A SIMPLE WAY." JOHAN CRUYFF

Dutch soccer is dominated by three clubs, Ajax, PSV Eindhoven, and Feyenoord. Since 1965 only one team outside this big three has taken the league title, although in recent years smaller teams such as AZ Alkmaar, FC Twente, and SC Herenveen have shown themselves to be an increasing threat. The Dutch game is traditionally played in an open, attacking style, which brought Dutch sides their greatest success in Europe in the 1970s. But the country's small size means its clubs can't compete financially with the big leagues of Spain, Italy, Germany, and England, and top players now rarely spend more than two or three seasons in the Netherlands before transferring abroad.

The Netherlands' top Dutch league, the Eredivisie, has 18 clubs; the second tier, the Eerste Divisie, has 20.

*Ajax players (right) celebrate after their thrilling penalty shootout victory over AZ Alkmaar in the 2007 KNVB Cup final in Rotterdam.*

## PSV EINDHOVEN
### PHILIPS STADION, EINDHOVEN

PSV was the 2007 League champion (above), and in 1988 became one of only three Dutch teams to win the European Cup (now the Champions League). Dutch champions 20 times, PSV has featured famous players such as the van de Kerkhof brothers, Ruud van Nistelrooy, Philip Cocu, and Ronaldo.

*Ronald Koeman (above) played for PSV between 1986 and 1989 and managed the club in the 2006–2007 season.*

## AJAX
### AMSTERDAM ARENA, AMSTERDAM

Ajax has won a record 29 titles and four European cups. The great Ajax team of the 1966–73 era pioneered the concept of "Total Football" under coach Rinus Michels. The number 14 shirt has been retired in honor of the club's most famous player, the great Johan Cruyff.

## FAMOUS CLUBS

FC Twente

Go Ahead Eagles

Vitesse

N.E.C

Ajax

ADO Den Haag

Klaas-Jan Huntelaar scored 36 goals in his first full season for Ajax in 2006–2007.

Huntelaar can use both feet, and is strong in the air—a classic striker.

## SPARTA ROTTERDAM

### HET KASTEEL, ROTTERDAM

The Netherlands' oldest club was formed in 1888 and, inspired by England's Sunderland FC, adopted a red and white striped uniform in 1889. League champions six times before 1960, Sparta has recently regained its place in the top division after a three year absence.

## WILLEM II

### WILLEM II STADION, TILBURG

Named after a 19th century Dutch king, Willem II has not been league champion since 1955 but is now establishing a presence in European competition for the first time. Famous former players include Marc Overmars, Jaap Stam, and Finland's Sami Hyypiä.

## AZ ALKMAAR

### DSB STADION, ALKMAAR

Founded in 1967, AZ is the only side outside the big three (Ajax, PSV, and Feyenoord) to win the League since 1964. It won it in 1981 but was relegated from the Eredivisie in 1988. Since its return in 1998 it has undergone a remarkable revival, finishing third in the league in 2004–5 and runner-up in the KNVB cup in 2007.

## FEYENOORD

### FEYENOORD STADION, ROTTERDAM

League champion 14 times and European Cup winner once, Feyenoord hopes to repeat past triumphs under captain Giovanni van Bronckhorst (right).

Sparta Rotterdam

Willem II

AZ Alkmaar

FC Groningen

VVV-Venlo

# SPANISH CLUBS

## "FOOTBALL IS AN EXCUSE TO MAKE US HAPPY."

JORGE VALDANO, FORMER REAL ZARAGOZA AND REAL MADRID STRIKER

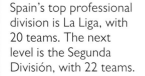

Spain's La Liga is one of the world's top three leagues, alongside those in England and Italy, and it has a reputation for thrilling, attacking soccer. First contested in 1928, it has only ever been won by nine clubs. For years the big two—Real Madrid (30 titles) and Barcelona (18 titles)—dominated, but recently the league has become more competitive with teams such as Sevilla FC, Real Sociedad, and Valencia CF challenging for the title.

Spain's top professional division is La Liga, with 20 teams. The next level is the Segunda División, with 22 teams.

## FC BARCELONA

### CAMP NOU, BARCELONA

Founded in 1899, winners of 18 Spanish titles, 31 Spanish cups, and two European Cups, and never relegated, Barcelona is one of the biggest clubs in the world. With a reputation for flamboyant, entertaining soccer, Barça has nearly 2,000 supporter clubs worldwide and is an integral part of the Catalan region of Spain. Its motto is "Més que un club" (More than a club).

Barcelona's Camp Nou, or "new field" (left) is Europe's biggest stadium, holding 98,772 spectators who fill the ground to watch superstar players such as Samuel Eto'o, Lionel Messi, and Thierry Henry.

Barcelona's Ronaldinho takes a penalty during a 2007 La Liga match against Athletic Bilbao at the Camp Nou Stadium.

## REAL SOCIEDAD

### ANOETA, SAN SEBASTIÁN

Twice league champions in the early 1980s, Real Sociedad has fluctuated between the top two divisions for most of its history and currently plays in the second tier.

## FAMOUS CLUBS

Real Zaragoza

Recreativo de Huelva

Racing Santander

CA Osasuna

Murcia

Real Madrid

## ATHLETIC BILBAO

SAN MAMÉS, BILBAO

Eight-time champion Bilbao is one of only three Spanish sides never to be relegated from La Liga, and it has won the Spanish Cup more times than any other club except Barcelona. Bilbao has a long-standing policy known as "cantera," where it only signs players from the Basque region. In recent years, it has drifted into the midtable, putting the cantera policy under pressure.

## SEVILLA FC

RAMÓN SÁNCHEZ PIZJUÁN, SEVILLE

Champion only once (in 1946), Sevilla returned to La Liga in 2000. It won the Spanish Cup (left) in 2007 and back-to-back UEFA Cups in 2006 and 2007 with a skillful, high-tempo game.

## VALENCIA CF

ESTADIO MESTELLA, VALENCIA

Champions in the 1940s, 1970s, and twice since 2000, Valencia attracts passionate support bettered only by the big two. Its current success has been based on a defensive style at odds with Spanish league tradition, but the emergence of lethal striker David Villa (right) has injected a touch of flair.

## ATLÉTICO MADRID

VICENTE CALDERÓN, MADRID

In the 1960s and 1970s, only Atlético challenged the dominance of city neighbor Real. (Above, Atlético as champions in 1973.) It remains Spain's third most successful club, although it has struggled in recent years.

## REAL MADRID

SANTIAGO BERNABÉU, MADRID

True giants of world soccer, Real has won a record nine European Cups and 30 La Liga titles, including a dramatic last day victory in 2007. Over the years, legendary names such as Alfredo di Stéfano, Ferenc Puskás, Emilio Butragueño, David Beckham, and Ronaldo have worn the famous white shirt and they are the richest club in the world. Spain star Raúl (far right) has also made more than 450 appearances for Madrid.

Real Valladolid

Levante UD

- DEPORTIVO LA CORUNA
- GETAFE CF
- RC CELTA DE VIGO
- RCD ESPANYOL
- REAL BETIS
- VILLAREAL CF

# EUROPEAN CLUBS

"LET FOOTBALL REMAIN THE GAME THAT HAS BEEN THE DREAM OF GENERATIONS, THAT FILLS CHILDREN WITH WONDER AND UNITES EUROPEANS." MICHEL PLATINI

Although European club competition, particularly the Champions League, is dominated by the big sides from the major nations, the rest of Europe nevertheless provides some famous clubs. Portugal, Scotland, Greece, and Turkey, for example, all boast a fiercely contested domestic league system, with passionate rivalries between clubs that enjoy huge support. Other countries such as Ukraine and Sweden have also produced club sides that have fared well in European competition.

## RANGERS

IBROX, GLASGOW, SCOTLAND

Rangers are one half of the "Old Firm"—the name given to Scotland's two biggest clubs, which have enjoyed a long and often bitter rivalry. Rangers have won a phenomenal 51 Scottish league titles, 31 Scottish Cups, and won the European Cup Winners' Cup in 1972.

USA international DaMarcus Beasley is a current Rangers' star.

## DINAMO KIEV

LOBANOVSKY DYNAMO STADIUM, KIEV, UKRAINE

Since Ukraine became an independent country in 1991, Dinamo Kiev has dominated domestic soccer and won the first nine league titles.

Vladislav Vashchuk (front, left) and Valentin Belkevich (front, right) celebrate winning the 2007 Ukrainian Cup.

## CELTIC

CELTIC PARK, GLASGOW, SCOTLAND

The other half of Glasgow's "Old Firm," Celtic has won 41 league titles and 34 Scottish Cups. It was the first British side to win the European Cup, when the "Lisbon Lions" defeated Italian side Internazionale 2–1 in Portugal in 1967.

## FENERBAHÇE

SÜCRÜ SARACOGLU, STADYUMU, ISTANBUL, TURKEY

Fenerbahçe is one of Turkey's biggest clubs, and the best supported. Based in the Asian east of Istanbul, the club has won the league title 17 times and been runner-up 15 times.

A new recruit in 2006 was Brazilian former Real Madrid star, Roberto Carlos.

# FAMOUS CLUBS

FC Steaua Bucharesti (Romania)

SK Slavia Prague (Czech Republic)

Standard Liège (Belgium)

Anderlecht (Belgium)

Dinamo Kiev (Ukraine)

FC Basel 1893 (Switzerland)

## SPORTING LISBON
ESTÁDIO JOSÉ ALVALADE, LISBON, PORTUGAL

Sporting is one of the most successful clubs in Portugal, with 22 league titles, and enjoys a strong rivalry with its Lisbon neighbor, Benfica. In 2003 the club moved to its impressive new home, the 52,000 capacity Estádio José Alvalade.

## ANDERLECHT
CONSTANT VANDEN STOCK STADIUM, BRUSSELS, BELGIUM

Anderlecht is the biggest club side in Belgium by some margin, with 29 domestic titles and three victories in European competition—twice in the Cup Winners' Cup (1976 and 1978) and once in the UEFA Cup (1983).

## BENFICA
ESTÁDIO DA LUZ, LISBON, PORTUGAL

Benfica is the most successful club in Portugal, with a total of 31 league titles and 27 Portuguese Cups. It has also won the UEFA Champions League twice (1961 and 1962, when it was known as the European Cup) and is Portugal's best-supported team, with an estimated 14 million fans worldwide.

Striker Nuno Gomes has had two spells at Benfica, from 1997 to 2000 and from 2002 to the present time.

## OLYMPIACOS
GEORGIOS KARAISKÁKIS STADIUM, ATHENS, GREECE

Olympiacos is the best supported and most successful of the three major Athens sides. The team has won the Greek national championship a record 35 times.

Raul Bravo celebrates Olympiacos' 3–1 victory over Werder Bremen in the Champions League in 2007.

## IFK GOTHENBURG
ULLEVI STADIUM, GOTHENBURG, SWEDEN

IFK Gothenburg is one of the biggest clubs in Sweden, and certainly the most successful, with 17 league titles. It is also the only Swedish side ever to lift a trophy in European competition, with two UEFA Cup triumphs in 1982 and 1987.

## CSKA MOSCOW
DINAMO STADIUM, MOSCOW, RUSSIA

Formerly the team of the Soviet Red Army, CSKA has enjoyed a revival in recent years, winning the Russian league title in 2003, 2005, and 2006. It also won the UEFA Cup in 2005, becoming the first Russian side to win a major European competition.

## SPARTA PRAGUE
AXA ARENA, PRAGUE, CZECH REPUBLIC

Sparta was a successful team in the old Czechoslavakian league. It has also dominated the new Czech Republic premier league since its formation in 1993, with 10 victories in 14 seasons.

Sparta Prague players celebrate winning the Czech league in 2007.

Panathinaikos FC (Greece)

Galatasaray (Turkey)

- AEK ATHENS (GREECE)
- CSKA SOFIA (BULGARIA)
- FC PORTO (PORTUGAL)
- PARTIZAN BELGRADE (SERBIA)
- SHAKHTAR DONETSK (UKRAINE)
- STANDARD LIEGE (BELGIUM)

# SOUTH AMERICA

"FOOTBALL IS PASSION, MULTITUDE, THE JOY OF LIVING."

FORMER ARGENTINA FOOTBALLER AND PLAYERS' UNION
GENERAL SECRETARY JORGE DOMINGUEZ

Although lack of financial muscle means many top stars leave for Europe, there is no doubting the flair and excitement of the region's game or the passion of South American soccer fans. The top sides from each country (38 altogether) qualify for the annual Copa Libertadores (see p. 98) to find the South American champions and, predictably, teams from Argentina and Brazil have dominated the competition.

## COLO COLO

ESTADIO MONUMENTAL
DAVID ARELLANO,
SANTIAGO, CHILE

Chilean champion Colo Colo has won more national cups (26) than any other team, and is the only Chilean team ever to win the Copa Libertadores (in 1991).

Alexis Sánchez celebrates scoring a hat trick for Colo Colo against Venezuela's Caracas during its Libertadores Cup match in March 2007. Sánchez is nicknamed "El Niño Maravilla" (the Wonder Kid).

## CLUB NACIONAL DE FOOTBALL

PARQUE CENTRAL, MONTEVIDEO, URUGUAY

Uruguayan giant Nacional has won 41 domestic titles and is three-time world-club champion. The first World Cup Finals game was played at its stadium in 1930.

Forward Andrés Márquez of Nacional (right) competes for the ball with Elvis González (left) of Colombia's Cúcuta Deportivo.

## CLUB BOLÍVAR

ESTADIO LIBERTADOR
SIMON BOLÍVAR, LA PAZ,
BOLIVIA

Named after the country's founder, Simon Bolívar, the La Paz team has won 15 titles, making it the most successful team in the professional league era (1977 onward).

## SAO PAULO

MORUMBI, SAO PAULO, BRAZIL

A record of five league titles (one more than Corinthians), 21 state championships, and three World Club crowns make Sao Paolo Brazil's most successful club. Its stadium holds 80,000 spectators.

São Paulo's Aloísio celebrates a goal against Boca Juniors in September 2007.

# FAMOUS CLUBS

- BARCELONA SPORTING CLUB (ECUADOR)
- BOTAFOGO (BRAZIL)
- CA PENAROL (URUGUAY)
- CIENCIANO DEL CUZCO (PERU)
- ESTUDIANTES (ARGENTINA)
- FLAMENGO (BRAZIL)
- GREMIO (BRAZIL)
- INDEPENDIENTE (ARGENTINA)
- INTERNACIONAL (BRAZIL)

## BOCA JUNIORS

ESTADIO ALBERTO J. ARMANDO, BUENOS AIRES, ARGENTINA

True giants of the world game, Boca Juniors hold a world record 17 international titles, alongside AC Milan. The legendary Diego Maradona is a fan and the club enjoys a fierce local rivalry with River Plate.

Boca Juniors celebrate winning the Copa Libertadores in 2007.

## ATLÉTICO NACIONAL

ATANASIO GIRARDOT, MEDELLIN, COLOMBIA

The first Columbian winner of the Copa Libertadores (in 1989), Nacional has won nine league titles, the third most successful haul in professional league history. The green and white shirt has been worn by many international stars, including Faustino Asprilla and Juan Pablo Ángel.

## CLUB DEPORTIVO EL NACIONAL

ESTADIO OLIMPICO ATAHUALPA, QUITO, ECUADOR

Owned by the country's military, El Nacional only fields players with Ecuadorian nationality. The team colors represent the three branches of the military. With 13 domestic titles, it is jointly Ecuador's most successful team, an honor shared with Barcelona Sporting Club of Guayaquil.

## ALIANZA LIMA

ESTADIO ALEJANDRO VILLANUEVA, LIMA, PERU

Universitario de Deportes has won more league titles (24) than Alianza (22), but Alianza has only recently recovered after losing its entire team in a plane crash in 1987.

## RIVER PLATE

EL MONUMENTAL, BUENOS AIRES, ARGENTINA

With 32 championships, River Plate is Argentina's most successful club. As local rivals, River vs. Boca is one of the great games.

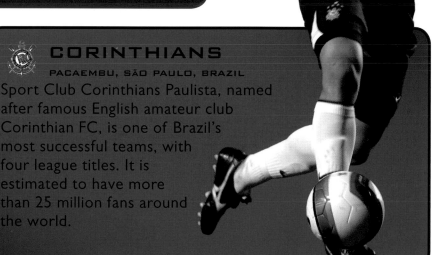

*Midfielder Marcelo Mattos was part of the great 2005 Corinthians team that included Carlos Tévez and Javier Mascherano.*

## CARACAS FC

COCODRILOS SPORTS PARK, CARACAS, VENEZUELA

The nine-time domestic league champion is the most successful team in Venzuelan history, with all nine titles coming in the last 15 years. Its nickname is "Los Rojos" (the Reds). Amazingly, the club only turned professional in 1984.

## CORINTHIANS

PACAEMBU, SÃO PAULO, BRAZIL

Sport Club Corinthians Paulista, named after famous English amateur club Corinthian FC, is one of Brazil's most successful teams, with four league titles. It is estimated to have more than 25 million fans around the world.

- MILLIONARIOS (COLOMBIA)
- NEWELL'S OLD BOYS (ARGENTINA)
- OLIMPIA ASUNCION (PARAGUAY)
- ONCE CALDAS (COLOMBIA)
- PALMEIRAS (BRAZIL)
- SAN LORENZO (ARGENTINA)
- SANTOS (BRAZIL)
- THE STRONGEST (BOLIVIA)
- UNIVERSITARIO DE DEPORTES (PERU)

# NORTH AMERICA

**"WE HAVE COMPETITIVE TEAMS, COMPETITIVE INDIVIDUAL PLAYERS, AND A VERY GOOD AND GROWING LEAGUE."**

LA GALAXY GENERAL MANAGER AND FORMER USA INTERNATIONAL ALEXEI LALAS

The USA first launched a professional soccer league in 1968. Known as the NASL (North American Soccer League) it boasted star signings such as Pelé, Franz Beckenbauer, and George Best. Although the NASL folded in 1984, it helped to raise soccer's profile in North America, particularly among young people. Ten years after the demise of the NASL the US successfully hosted the World Cup Finals, and in 1996 a new MLS ( Major League Soccer) was launched. Over the years, the MLS has flourished, attracting big-money sponsorship and world-class players.

## LA GALAXY

HOME DEPOT CENTER, CARSON, CALIFORNIA, USA

LA Galaxy mixes Hollywood glamour with good, old fashioned successful soccer. It has won the MLS Championship twice and the CONCACAF Champions' Cup once, in 2000. LA Galaxy was the first MLS club to record a profit.

## D.C. UNITED

RFK STADIUM, WASHINGTON DC, USA

The team from the US capital quickly became a power base of the MLS. D.C. United has won four League Championships, including a 1996 league and cup double under coach Bruce Arena and captain John Harkes.

D.C. United's Luciano Emilio celebrates a goal against New England Revolution in 2007.

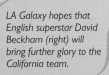

*LA Galaxy hopes that English superstar David Beckham (right) will bring further glory to the California team.*

## TORONTO FC

BMO FIELD, TORONTO, ONTARIO, CANADA

Toronto was the first Canadian entrant to the MLS in 2007. It has, arguably, the most intense fans in the league and enjoys sellout crowds at almost every game.

Toronto FC players celebrate their late 2nd half goal, also against New England Revolution, in October 2007.

# CLUB BADGES

Houston Dynamo

Chivas USA

FC Dallas

DC United

Toronto FC

LA Galaxy

Real Salt Lake

# FC DALLAS

PIZZA HUT PARK, FRISCO, TEXAS

Under its former name Dallas Burn, the Texas team beat D.C. United to the US Open Cup in 1997. In 2007 Dallas signed Brazilian winger Denílson, once the most expensive soccer player in the world.

Guatemala's all-time top scorer Carlos Ruíz (above) has been FC Dallas' skipper and inspiration since signing from LA Galaxy in 2005.

# HOUSTON DYNAMO

ROBERTSON STADIUM, HOUSTON, TEXAS

MLS new boys Houston Dynamo won the 2006 MLS Cup in their first season and then won it again in 2007. The club took over the San Jose Earthquakes franchise, which meant it kept the same players, but changed the team's name and moved to a different state (Texas, from California).

*Midfielder Corey Ashe heads the ball during a match between Houston Dynamo and Real Salt Lake in September 2007.*

# CONCACAF CLUBS

## CF PACHUCA

ESTADIO HIDALGO, PACHUCA, MEXICO

In the last decade Mexico's oldest club CF Pachuca has outshone rivals Cruz Azul and Club América to win five national championships and two CONCACAF Champions' Cups.

## SAPRISSA

ESTADIO RICARDO SAPRISSA AYMÁ, SAN JOSÉ, COSTA RICA

Saprissa has a record haul of 25 domestic titles as well as four CONCACAF Champions' Cups.

Pachuca captain Gabriel Caballero raises the SuperLiga trophy after his team's victory in the 2007 final.

## CLUB DEPORTIVO GUADALAJARA

ESTADIO JALISCO, GUADALAJARA, MEXICO

Commonly known as the "Chivas" (Goats), Guadalajara is the best-supported side in Mexico. A spinoff team, Chivas USA, joined the MLS in 2005.

## SV TRANSVAAL

ANDRÉ KAMPERVEEN STADIUM, PARAMARIBO, SURINAM

Transvaal has won the Surinam league 19 times and the CONCACAF Champions Cup twice. SV Robinhood has 23 league titles.

## CLUB DEPORTIVO OLIMPIA

ESTADIO MANUEL FERREIRA, ASUNCIÓN, PARAGUAY

Paraguay's oldest club celebrated its centenary in 2002 with a third Copa Libertadores. Cerro Porteño and Libertad have dominated the league so far this century.

Red Bull New York

New England Revolution

Colorado Rapids

Chicago Fire

Kansas City Wizards

Columbus Crew

San Jose Earthquakes

# AFRICAN CLUBS

"IT'S ALL ABOUT FOOTBALL, FOOTBALL, FOOTBALL, FOOTBALL—THE WHOLE OF AFRICA, WE LOVE FOOTBALL." NIGERIA CAPTAIN AND STRIKER NWANKWO KANU

Despite some of the greatest talents being tempted away by rich European clubs, Africa has an impressive soccer culture. Rowdy rivalries, noble histories, and some of the loudest, proudest fans on the planet—African club soccer has all the right ingredients. The African Cup of Champions kicked off in 1964 and became the CAF Champions League in 1997.

## RAJA CASABLANCA
STADE MOHAMED V, CASABLANCA, MOROCCO

Founded in 1949, the "people's club" took 26 years to win a trophy. However, it won the CAF Champions League in 1989, 1997, and 1999. Along with local rivals Wydad Casablanca, it is Morocco's most powerful club.

Defender Abdellatif Jrindou is the current Raja Casablanca captain.

## MAMELODI SUNDOWNS
LOFTUS VERSFIELD STADIUM, PRETORIA, SOUTH AFRICA

Having a billionaire owner helps, but Mamelodi Sundowns were already a rising power in South Africa before Patrice Mosepe's 2003 takeover. The club has won five league titles since 1998.

## CANON YAOUNDÉ
STADE OMNISPORTS, YAOUNDÉ, CAMEROON

Canon Yaoundé is one of the most successful clubs in Cameroon. It has won nine league titles, three CAF Champions Leagues (1971, 1978, 1980) and one CAF Cup Winners' Cup.

## EL-AHLY
CAIRO INTERNATIONAL STADIUM, CAIRO, EGYPT

Named the CAF's "Club of the Century" in 2000, El-Ahly's record of five CAF Champions League titles and 32 Egyptian titles is unrivaled. It did not lose a game from 1974 to 1977.

The Sundowns beat Orlando Pirates to South Africa's Supa 8 cup in 2007.

*Goalkeeper Essam Al Hadari (left) and skipper Shady Mohamed (right) celebrate El-Ahly's 32nd league title in July 2007.*

# FAMOUS CLUBS

Kaizer Chiefs (South Africa)

Cotonsport Garoua (Cameroon)

Invincible Eleven (Liberia)

ASEC Mimosas (Cote D'Ivoire)

Accra Hearts of Oak Sporting Club (Ghana)

## ENYIMBA

ENYIMBA INTERNATIONAL STADIUM, ABA, NIGERIA

In 2003 Enyimba, whose name means "Elephant," brought the CAF Champions League trophy to Nigeria for the first time, 13 years after turning professional.

Goalkeeper Dele Aiyenugba secured Enyimba's first Nigerian FA Cup in 2005.

## ÉTOILE SPORTIVE DU SAHEL

STADE OLYMPIQUE DE SOUSSE, SOUSSE, TUNISIA

Tunisia's oldest club, Sahel has won an array of CAF trophies to add to 11 domestic league titles, thanks to Tunisian heroes such as midfielder Kaies Ghodhbane and Brazil-born striker Francileudo Santos, backed by big-name imports such as Ivory Coast forward Kader Keïta.

## ASEC MIMOSAS

STADE FÉLIX HOUPHOUËT-BOIGNY, ABIDJAN, IVORY COAST

ASEC Mimosas' 22 league titles to 2007 is an awesome record, but just as impressive is the youth academy created by Jean-Marc Guillou that has produced Emmanuel Eboué, Bonaventure and Salomon Kalou, and Kolo and Yaya Touré.

## ACCRA HEARTS OF OAK SPORTING CLUB

OHENE DJAN STADIUM, ACCRA, GHANA

Along with Asante Kotoko, Hearts of Oak has dominated soccer in Ghana. Although rival Asante has won 20 league titles, Hearts can boast of being Ghana's oldest club. It has won 19 league titles (including 2006–2007) and one CAF Champions League (2000).

Hearts of Oak defender Charles Vadis beats Enyimba attacker Sunday Mba to the ball during a 2006 CAF Champions League match.

## HAFIA FC

STADE 28 SEPTEMBRE, CONAKRY, GUINEA

Guinea's greatest got to keep the first African championship trophy after its third win in 1977, and it won the Guinean league 15 times (including titles won under its previous name, Conakry II). However, success has eluded Hafia in recent years, with clubs such as Horoya AC and AS Kaloum Star rising to the top instead.

## EL ZAMALEK

CAIRO STADIUM, CAIRO

El Zamalek and El-Ahly are Egypt's answer to the Glasgow "Old Firm" (see p. 112–113), and foreign referees are brought in to oversee their fierce derby matches. Zamalek shares El-Ahly's record of five CAF Champions League titles and has won the league 11 times. It topped FIFA's club rankings in 2003.

Striker Walid Abdel–Latif in action for El Zamelek in a CAF Champions League match in 2005.

- ASANTE KOTOKO (GHANA)
- AS DOUANES (SENEGAL)
- DC MOTEMA PEMBE (PR CONGO)
- JS KABYLIE (ALGERIA)
- FAR RABAT (MOROCCO)
- ORLANDO PIRATES (SOUTH AFRICA)
- PRIMEIRO DE AGOSTO (ANGOLA)
- STADE MALIEN (MALI)
- TP MAZEMBE (DR CONGO)

# ASIA AND OCEANIA

### "ASIAN FOOTBALL IS IN THE PROCESS OF MAKING A BIG STEP FORWARD."

FRENCH SUPERSTAR ZINEDINE ZIDANE

The A-League (Australia), J-League (Japan), and K-League (Republic of Korea) are just some of the logically named club championships of Asia and Oceania. Over the years, their up-and-coming teams have lured many notable players such as Kazuyoshi Miura and Dwight Yorke (Australia), Hristo Stoichkov, Patrick Mboma and Gary Lineker (Japan), and Alpay (Republic of Korea). The future looks bright for this rapidly developing soccer region.

## MELBOURNE VICTORY FC

TELSTRA DOME, MELBOURNE, AUSTRALIA

Australian football is on the way up, with Melbourne Victory leading the charge. Sydney FC won the first A-League in 2006, but captain Kevin Muscat helped take the title to Melbourne the next year and then added the Championship trophy after the top four played off in the Finals Series.

*Melbourne striker Archie Thompson is one of a growing number of A-league players to play for the Australian national team.*

## JEONBUK FC

JEONJU WORLD CUP STADIUM, JEONJU, REPUBLIC OF KOREA

Jeonbuk was the first South Korean team to win the AFC Champions League, in 2006. Despite domestic cup success, it still awaits its first K-League title, since the league has been largely monopolized by Seongnam Ilhwa Chunma.

Jeonbuk's players after winning the AFC Champions League 2006 trophy.

## WELLINGTON PHOENIX

WESTPAC STADIUM, WELLINGTON, NEW ZEALAND

Wellington Phoenix was formed in 2007 to replace New Zealand Knights in Australia's A-League.

*German-born New Zealand international Shane Smeltz plays for the Phoenix.*

## DEMPO SPORTS CLUB

JAWAHARLAL NEHRU FATORDA STADIUM, MARGAO, INDIA

Dempo won two of the last three titles of India's National Football League. The NFL finished in 2007 and was replaced by a new professional league called the I-League.

# FAMOUS CLUBS

Suwon Samsung Bluewings (South Korea)

Singapore Armed Forces FC (Singapore)

Júbilo Iwata (Japan)

Dalian Shide (China)

Adelaide United (Australia)

Central Coast Mariners (Australia)

# DALIAN SHIDE

**DALIAN PEOPLE'S STADIUM, DALIAN, CHINA**

Dalian Shide is the most successful team in China. It won seven out of 10 Jia league titles and has, so far, won the new Super League once.

Midfielder Zhu Ting scores for Dalian during its 2006 A3 Champions Cup match against Japan's JEF United Chiba.

# PAKISTAN ARMY FC

**ARMY STADIUM, RAWALPINDI, PAKISTAN**

Goalkeeper-captain Jaffar Khan and his Pakistan Army team marched to their fourth league title in 2006–2007, However, they remain five behind high-fliers Pakistan International Airlines.

Faheem Riaz (left) plays in midfield for Pakistan Army.

Midfielder Mitsuo Ogasawara (left) in action for the Kashima Antlers.

# KASHIMA ANTLERS

**KASHIMA STADIUM, KASHIMA, JAPAN**

Kashima Antlers clinched the J-League's most eye-catching transfer coup by signing Brazilian star Zico in 1993. The four-time league champion peaked in 2000 with a triple of the J-League, J- League Cup, and the Emperor's Cup.

# AL-ZAWRAA

**AL-ZAWRAA STADIUM, BAGHDAD, IRAQ**

Arguably Iraq's best player, Ahmed Radhi—1988 Asian Footballer of the Year—had three jubilant spells with the country's biggest club, Al-Zawraa. A single goal by Japan's Shimizu S-Pulse denied it the Asian Cup Winners' Cup in 2000.

# AL-HILAL

**KING FAHD INTERNATIONAL STADIUM, RIYADH, SAUDI ARABIA**

The Al-Hilal trophy cabinet has been crammed with 45 cups since 1957, thanks to talents such as Brazilian World Cup-winner Rivelino, who played for it from 1978 to1981.

Abdulsalam Abboud (left) of Al-Zawraa vies with Taweeq Abdul Razzaq of UAE club Al-Wahda.

# ESTEGHLAL FC

**AZADI STADIUM, TEHRAN, IRAN**

Rival Persepolis has won a few more league titles while sharing the same 90,000-capacity home, but Esteghlal can boast of being Asian champions in 1992 and runner-up eight years later.

*Al-Hilal striker Yasser al-Qahtani is also the captain of the Saudi Arabia national team.*

Melbourne Victory FC (Australia)

Newcastle Jets (Australia)

Perth Glory (Australia)

Queensland Roar (Australia)

Sydney FC (Australia)

Wellington Phoenix (New Zealand)

# WOMEN'S CLUBS

*"WE HAVE COME A LONG WAY IN DEVELOPING THE NATIONAL TEAMS—NOW THE TIME HAS COME TO WORK EVEN HARDER TO DEVELOP THE CLUBS."*

SUSANNE ERLANDSSON OF THE UEFA
WOMEN'S FOOTBALL COMMITTEE

As relatively recently as the end of the 20th century, women were banned from playing soccer in many countries, such as Brazil. However, in the 21st century things are slowly improving; the international game is gaining in popularity and domestic leagues are now flourishing, especially in Northern Europe and the US. Brazil's second place at the 2007 Women's World Cup has even prompted promises to set up a league there.

## L-LEAGUE
### JAPAN

Introduced in 1989, Japan's amateur L-League thrived thanks to big-money sponsorship and star players such as the US's Tiffeny Milbrett (Shiroki Serena) and Norway's Hege Riise (Nikko Securities Dream Ladies).

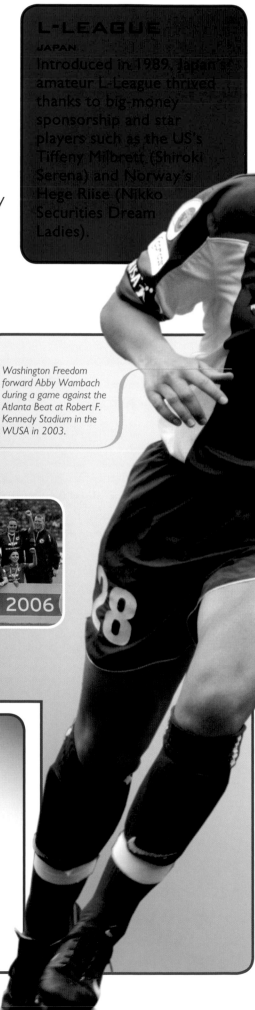

Washington Freedom forward Abby Wambach during a game against the Atlanta Beat at Robert F. Kennedy Stadium in the WUSA in 2003.

## FRAUEN-BUNDESLIGA
### GERMANY

Two clubs have dominated German women's soccer since the women's semipro league was founded in 1990—1. FFC Frankfurt and 1. FFC Turbine Potsdam. Domestic and European success, particularly for Frankfurt, has provided the foundation for Germany's many international triumphs.

Striker Birgit Prinz has collected six league titles, six German Cups, and six UEFA club championships since joining Frankfurt in 1998.

DFB-Pokalsieger 2006

1. FFC Turbine Potsdam celebrates winning the 2006 German Cup against Frankfurt.

## TOPPSERIEN
### NORWAY

Scandinavia has long been a stronghold for women's soccer and Norway first established a women's league in 1984. It began as three regional divisions that merged three years later to form a single league. The majority of titles have been shared between Trondheims-Ørn and Asker SK. In fact, during the 1998 season Asker SK won all of its 18 games!

## USA W-LEAGUE
USA

The US made history by setting up the world's first professional league for women in 2001, with 20 founding players including Kristine Lilly and Michelle Akers. However, the WUSA (Women's United Soccer Association) went bust after just three seasons, although hopes are high for a 2008 relaunch. For now, attention is back on the amateur W-League, running since 1995 and featuring international stars and up-and-coming college players.

Canada's Vancouver Whitecaps were W-League champions in 2004 and 2006, but the team now faces a tough challenge from ex-WUSA team Washington Freedom.

## SUPERLIGA FEMININA
SPAIN

The women's league clubs in Spain have maintained close links to their male counterparts since kicking off in 1983. As in La Liga's early years, the front-runner is Athletic Bilbao. However, in the women's game, Real Madrid remains absent from the top divison and Barcelona was relegated in 2006–2007.

Arsenal Ladies added the league title, league cup, and UEFA trophy to their FA Women's Cup in 2007 (above).

## PREMIER LEAGUE
ENGLAND

When Arsenal Ladies beat Sweden's Umeå IK to capture the UEFA Women's Cup in 2007 it was England's first victory in that competiton. It marked a clean sweep of trophies for the London club and also brought positive signs for the development of the women's game in England.

## DAMALLSVENSKAN
SWEDEN

Sweden seems to develop women's soccer better than anywhere else in the world. The Swedish league, known as the Damallsvenskan, dates back to 1973 and has attracted some of the best players from around the world. Stars such as the US's Kristine Lilly, China's Ma Xiaoxu, and Brazil's Marta combine with the finest homegrown talents such as Hanna Ljungberg. Top team Umeå IK has twice been UEFA Women's Cup champions. Despite club success, Sweden remains international soccer's runner-up, losing four major international finals.

Marta left Brazil for Sweden's Umeå IK in 2004 because Brazil did not have a serious women's league.

## RIVELINO
### BRAZIL

The midfielder's performances for Brazil between 1965 and 1978 earned him legendary status. Famed for his graceful play and thunderous left foot, Rivelino is unofficially credited with scoring the fastest ever goal—directly from the kickoff.

## JAIRZINHO
### BRAZIL

This powerful winger scored in every game of the 1970 World Cup tournament, the only player so far ever to achieve this feat. Immensely talented, Jairzinho made his professional debut at 15 and his international debut in 1964, at the age of 19.

## BRIAN LAUDRUP
### DENMARK

Highly skilled, with devastating pace, attacking midfielder Brian Laudrup was a key member of the Danish team that won the 1992 European Championship. He also helped Glasgow Rangers win nine consecutive league titles, before retiring in 2000.

## BIXENTE LIZARAZU
### FRANCE

Able to mark tightly, anchor the defense, and pass the ball expertly, Lizarazu was widely regarded as one of the finest left backs of all time. He was a key member of the France side that won the 1998 World Cup and 2000 European Championship.

## JORGE VALDANO
### ARGENTINA

The striker played for his country between 1975 and 1986, and also achieved fame as a player and coach with Real Madrid. Valdano's soccer knowledge and opinions of the game have earned him the nickname "The Philosopher of Football'."

# HALL OF FAME

"THE MOST CLEVER DO MATH, THE NEXT-BEST WRITE BOOKS. DANCERS ARE THE MOST CLEVER WITH THEIR FEET, NEXT ARE FOOTBALLERS." JOHAN CRUYFF

In this book we have set out to select the greatest players and best teams in world soccer. Sadly, it is impossible to include absolutely everyone and many true soccer legends have not managed to squeeze onto our pages. However, there are some heroes—old and new—that we simply had to find space for. This is our Hall of Fame.

## SÓCRATES
### BRAZIL

Skillful, inspirational and a fine reader of the game, Sócrates captained his country in the 1982 and 1986 World Cups. His trademark move was the blind heel pass, which involved passing the ball with his heel while looking in the opposite direction.

## JOHAN NEESKENS
### HOLLAND

A technically gifted midfielder, Neeskens provided the base for the great Johan Cruyff to work his magic in the great Dutch "Total Football" side of the 1970s. He played club football for Ajax and Barcelona and was known for his powerful penalty kicks.

## FERNANDO HIERRO
### SPAIN

A tough defender with superior passing ability, Hierro was a stalwart for Spain for more than a decade. He scored an impressive 29 goals for his country in 89 appearances and also helped Real Madrid to five league titles between 1989 and 2002.

## OLIVER KAHN
### GERMANY

Now retired from international soccer, this goalkeeper is nicknamed "King Kahn." He was regarded as the world's number one after the 2002 World Cup Finals when he become the first goalkeeper in history to win the Golden Ball for best player.

## OMAR SÍVORI
### ARGENTINA/ITALY

A wonderfully gifted, audacious forward who loved to dribble the ball and delighted in nutmegging defenders, his speed and invention make him one of the finest players ever. Sívori played for both Argentina and Italy between 1956 and 1962.

## LEV YASHIN
### USSR
Voted the best goalkeeper of the 20th century, Yashin was known for his athleticism and reflex saves. He played for the USSR between 1949 and 1967 and spent his entire club career at Dinamo Moscow. He is believed to have saved 150 penalties.

## IAN RUSH
### WALES
A deadly striker who combined lethal finishing with superb anticipation, "Rushie" formed half of what many regard as Britain's greatest-ever strike partnership alongside Liverpool teammate Kenny Dalglish. Rush is Liverpool's all-time highest scorer.

## ROY KEANE
### REPUBLIC OF IRELAND
Central midfielder Keane was seen as one of the best players of the modern era. A competitive and aggressive ball winner whose late runs into the box often led to goals, he achieved most success with Man Utd. and has recently moved into club management.

## SIR BOBBY CHARLTON
### ENGLAND
Graceful, athletic, quick, with a thunderbolt shot and fierce sense of fair play, Bobby Charlton's exploits with Manchester United and England during the 1950s and 1960s make him one of the greatest players of all time. He is still England's top scorer.

## JIMMY GREAVES
### ENGLAND
In the 1960s, nobody was better at scoring goals than striker Jimmy Greaves. He scored on every debut and netted 44 times in 57 England games—including six hat tricks. He also played for Chelsea, AC Milan, West Ham, and Tottenham Hotspur.

## MICHELLE AKERS
### USA
Dubbed "the Pele of women's football" and voted FIFA's Woman Player of the Century in 2002, Akers was part of the first-ever USA women's team in 1985. She was top scorer in the first women's World Cup in 1991, scoring twice in the final win over Norway.

## DENIS LAW
### SCOTLAND
The only Scotsman ever to be European Footballer of the Year, (in 1964), this fiercely competitive striker was a supreme goalscorer, incisive passer, and intelligent reader of the game. A legend at Manchester United, he also played for Manchester City.

## FRANCO BARESI
### ITALY
Able to play as a central defender or sweeper, Baresi was famous for his tough tackling. He captained Italy at the 1994 World Cup Finals. He was also a rock in the AC Milan defense for 20 years and AC Milan's no. 6 shirt has been retired in his honor.

## GEORGE BEST
### NORTHERN IRELAND
Possibly Britain's greatest ever player, Best was dazzlingly skillful. Fast, two-footed, an expert dribbler, and scorer of sublime goals. Best, unfortunately, never graced a World Cup Finals. As the saying goes "Maradona good, Pelé better, George Best."

## SIR STANLEY MATTHEWS
### ENGLAND
A classic winger, Matthews played for an astonishing 33 years—until he was 50! He was the first-ever European Footballer of the Year and the first player to be knighted. Matthews was a true gentleman of the game and never received a single booking.

## MARCEL DESAILLY
### FRANCE
One of the top center-backs in the world between 1993 and 2004, Desailly won every major club and international honor in the game with AC Milan, Chelsea and France. Chelsea fans voted him their greatest ever center-back, alongside John Terry.

## ERIC CANTONA
### FRANCE
One of the most influential players of the 1980s and 1990s, Cantona had everything. Dubbed "The King" by Man Utd. fans, he could score goals or create them, displayed superb ball control and breathtaking vision—a true entertainer.

### ROBERTO AYALA
#### ARGENTINA
This much-capped central defender is good in the air, a tenacious tackler, and an excellent passer of the ball. Ayala inherited the nickname of El Ratón (Mouse) from Argentine 1974 World Cup player Rubén Ayala, though they are not related.

### KRISTINE LILLY
#### USA
The USA's legendary captain has played more than 330 games for the national side—a world record for men or women. Nicknamed "Iron Woman," Lilly is a tireless worker who can score and create goals. She is the first woman to play in five World Cup Finals.

### TAB RAMOS
#### USA
One of the most technically gifted players to wear the USA shirt, midfielder Ramos won 81 caps between 1981 and 2000. Born in Uruguay, he was also one of the first US players to find success abroad, playing in both Spain and Mexico.

### ALFREDO DI STÉFANO
#### ARGENTINA/SPAIN
Considered by many the greatest player ever, di Stéfano's fitness and versatility saw him play in most outfield positions. Best known as a deadly center-forward, he inspired Real Madrid to five successive European Cups between 1956 and 1960.

### ROMÁRIO
#### BRAZIL
Still scoring at over 40 years old, this gifted center-forward claims a career total of more than 1,000 goals. His technique and sharpness in the box have fired PSV and Barcelona to success, as well as Brazil. Romário won the Golden Ball at the 94 World Cup Finals.

### EUSÉBIO
#### PORTUGAL
Portuguese but of Mozambican origin, striker Eusébio was the first African soccer superstar. Playing in the 1960s, Eusébio was fast, powerful, capable of superb ball-control, and had a deadly right foot. He is still all-time top scorer for his club Benfica.

### ALESSANDRO NESTA
#### ITALY
A powerful, confident central defender, widely acknowledged as one of the world's best, Nesta has won almost every major honor in the game, including the 2006 World Cup. Still a regular for AC Milan, he has retired from international soccer.

### MAHMOUD EL-KHATIB
#### EGYPT
A true legend of Egyptian soccer, striker El-Khatib was an accomplished goal scorer between 1972 and 1988. Nicknamed "Bibo," El-Khatib holds the dubious honor of sustaining the most injuries in the history of the Egyptian game.

### HRISTO STOICHKOV
#### BULGARIA
Probably his country's greatest player, this left-sided attacker could accelerate at speed, dribble superbly and unleash powerful shots from unpredictable situations. He inspired Bulgaria to fourth at the 1994 World Cup, and Barcelona to four league titles.

### DINO ZOFF
#### ITALY
One of the finest goalkeepers ever, Zoff holds the record for not conceding an international goal—1,142 minutes between 1972 and 1974. He captained Italy, most famously at the 1982 World Cup, and was a key member of the great Juventus team of the 1970s.

### "JAY-JAY" OKOCHA
#### NIGERIA
A skillful midfielder reknowned for his dazzling stepovers, Okocha helped establish his country as a world force in the 1990s and played for club sides across Europe. His fans at Bolton Wanderers used to say, he's "so good they named him twice."

### "DOCTOR" KHUMALO
#### SOUTH AFRICA
The man who made his country and his club side, Kaizer Chiefs, tick in the 1980 and 1990s, Khumalo's passing and movement were so good that he could run the game from his midfield position. He was also an accomplished ball juggler!

## TONY VIDMAR
### AUSTRALIA
One of the most successful Australians in club soccer, this left-sided defender achieved most success with Glasgow Rangers between 1997 and 2002. Versatile enough to play across the back line, he could also push up the left wing to support attacks.

## RUUD KROL
### NETHERLANDS
A legend of the 1970s "Total Football" sides of Ajax and the Netherlands, Krol was a technically gifted defender who could play across the back line, as a sweeper or defensive midfielder. He captained his country after Johan Cruyff retired.

## KARL-HEINZ RUMMENIGGE
### GERMANY
A prolific goal scorer for his country and club Bayern Munich, Rummenigge was Germany's soccer superstar after Franz Beckenbauer retired. Twice European Footballer of the Year (in 1980 and 1981), he retired from the game in 1989.

## JUAN ROMÁN RIQUELME
### ARGENTINA
With great ball control, pinpoint passing, and incisive vision, attacking midfielder Riquelme is considered by some to be the world's best current player. Watching him run with the ball is a joy, and he scores spectacular goals, often from free kicks.

## FRANCISCO GENTO
### SPAIN
Gento's ability to run with the ball and eye for goal were central to the success of the Real Madrid side of the 1950s and 1960s. He is still the only man to win six European Cups and was also part of Spain's 1964 European Championship winning side.

## FRITZ WALTER
### GERMANY
Named by the German soccer associations as the country's most outstanding player, this forward captained Germany to its first World Cup success in 1954. His ability to read the game and to control the ball kept him two steps ahead of opponents.

## LI MING
### CHINA
Hard-working midfielder Li Ming's reputation for striking the right balance between attack and defense made him a key part of the Dalian Shide team that won six Chinese league titles in the 1990s. He is also China's most-capped player.

## PAULINO ALCÁNTARA
### PHILIPPINES
Born in the Philippines to a Spanish father, striker Alcántara scored a remarkable 357 goals in 357 games for Barcelona between 1912 and 1927. The first Asian player ever to play for a European club, Alcántara is still Barcelona's top scorer.

## SALIF KEÏTA
### MALI
A hugely talented striker, Keïta was also a soccer pioneer. He was the first African Footballer of the Year (in 1970) and one of the first African players to play in Europe. In 2005, Keïta was elected president of the Malian Federation of Football (FEMAFOOT).

## KARIM ABDUL RAZAK
### GHANA
Midfielder Razak was blessed with superb ball control and ability to read the game. He was African Footballer of the Year in 1978 and was a key part of the Ghana team that won the African Cup of Nations in the same year. Razak is now a top coach in Ghana.

## MASAMI IHARA
### JAPAN
An accomplished sweeper and central defender, Ihara was a fixture in the national team throughout the 1990s. What he lacked in pace he made up for in awareness. His phenomenal record of 123 caps may never be equalled.

## MOHAMMED AL DEAYEA
### SAUDI ARABIA
A goalkeeper who played for his country in four World Cup Finals, Al-Deayea holds 181 caps, a record for a male player. His penalty saves in the 1996 Asian Cup final helped Saudi Arabia to victory. Al-Deayea has now retired from international soccer.

# INTERNATIONAL STATS

## FIFA WORLD CUP

A competition for national teams of member nations of FIFA, the international ruling body of soccer.

| | |
|---|---|
| 2006 | Italy |
| 2002 | Brazil |
| 1998 | France |
| 1994 | Brazil |
| 1990 | West Germany |
| 1986 | Argentina |
| 1982 | Italy |
| 1978 | Argentina |
| 1974 | West Germany |
| 1970 | Brazil |
| 1966 | England |
| 1962 | Brazil |
| 1958 | Brazil |
| 1954 | West Germany |
| 1950 | Uruguay |
| 1938 | Italy |
| 1934 | Italy |
| 1930 | Uruguay |

## FIFA WOMEN'S WORLD CUP

| | |
|---|---|
| 2007 | Germany |
| 2003 | Germany |
| 1999 | USA |
| 1995 | Norway |
| 1991 | USA |

## UEFA EUROPEAN CHAMPIONSHIP

A competition for national teams of nations governed by UEFA, the ruling body of European soccer.

| | |
|---|---|
| 2004 | Greece |
| 2000 | France |
| 1996 | Germany |
| 1992 | Denmark |
| 1988 | Netherlands |
| 1984 | France |
| 1980 | West Germany |
| 1976 | Czechoslovakia* |
| 1972 | West Germany |
| 1968 | Italy |
| 1964 | Spain |
| 1960 | USSR |

## UEFA WOMEN'S CHAMPIONSHIPS

| | |
|---|---|
| 2005 | Germany |
| 2001 | Germany |
| 1997 | Germany |
| 1995 | Germany |
| 1993 | Norway |
| 1991 | Germany |

* See p.45 for the current name of Czechoslovakia.

## CONMEBOL COPA AMÉRICA

A competition for national teams of nations governed by CONMEBOL, the ruling body of South American soccer.

| | |
|---|---|
| 2007 | Brazil |
| 2004 | Brazil |
| 2001 | Colombia |
| 1999 | Brazil |
| 1997 | Brazil |
| 1995 | Uruguay |
| 1993 | Argentina |
| 1991 | Argentina |
| 1989 | Brazil |
| 1987 | Uruguay |
| 1983 | Uruguay |
| 1979 | Paraguay |
| 1975 | Peru |
| 1967 | Uruguay |
| 1963 | Bolivia |
| 1959 | Uruguay (December) |
| 1959 | Argentina (April) |
| 1957 | Argentina |
| 1956 | Uruguay |
| 1955 | Argentina |
| 1953 | Paraguay |
| 1949 | Brazil |
| 1947 | Argentina |
| 1946 | Argentina |
| 1945 | Argentina |
| 1942 | Uruguay |
| 1941 | Argentina |
| 1939 | Peru |
| 1937 | Argentina |
| 1935 | Uruguay |
| 1929 | Argentina |
| 1927 | Argentina |
| 1926 | Uruguay |
| 1925 | Argentina |
| 1924 | Uruguay |
| 1923 | Uruguay |
| 1922 | Brazil |
| 1921 | Argentina |
| 1920 | Uruguay |
| 1919 | Brazil |
| 1917 | Uruguay |
| 1916 | Uruguay |

## CONCACAF GOLD CUP*

A competition for national teams of countries governed by CONCACAF, the ruling body of soccer in North America, Central America and the Caribbean.

| | |
|---|---|
| 2007 | USA |
| 2005 | USA |
| 2003 | Mexico |
| 2002 | USA |
| 2000 | Canada |
| 1998 | Mexico |
| 1996 | Mexico |
| 1993 | Mexico |
| 1991 | USA |
| 1989 | Costa Rica |
| 1985 | Canada |
| 1981 | Honduras |
| 1977 | Mexico |
| 1973 | Haiti |
| 1971 | Mexico |
| 1969 | Costa Rica |
| 1967 | Guatemala |
| 1965 | Mexico |
| 1963 | Costa Rica |

*1963–1989 competition known as CONCACAF Championship; 1991– present competition known as CONCACAF Gold Cup.

## CAF AFRICAN CUP OF NATIONS

A competition for national teams of African countries, sanctioned by CAF.

| | |
|---|---|
| 2006 | Egypt |
| 2004 | Tunisia |
| 2002 | Cameroon |
| 2000 | Cameroon |
| 1998 | Egypt |
| 1996 | South Africa |
| 1994 | Nigeria |
| 1992 | Côte d'Ivoire |
| 1990 | Algeria |
| 1988 | Cameroon |
| 1986 | Egypt |
| 1984 | Cameroon |
| 1982 | Ghana |
| 1980 | Nigeria |
| 1978 | Ghana |
| 1976 | Morocco |
| 1974 | Zaire |
| 1972 | Congo |
| 1970 | Sudan |
| 1968 | Congo Kinshasa (now DR Congo) |
| 1965 | Ghana |
| 1963 | Ghana |
| 1962 | Ethiopia |
| 1959 | Egypt |
| 1957 | Egypt |

## AFC ASIAN CUP

A competition for national teams of Asian countries, organized by AFC.

| | |
|---|---|
| 2007 | Iraq |
| 2004 | Japan |
| 2000 | Japan |
| 1996 | United Arab Emirates |
| 1992 | Japan |
| 1988 | Saudi Arabia |
| 1984 | Saudi Arabia |
| 1980 | Kuwait |
| 1976 | Iran |
| 1972 | Iran |
| 1968 | Iran |
| 1964 | Israel |
| 1960 | Republic of Korea |
| 1956 | Republic of Korea |

## OFC NATIONS CUP (OCEANIA)

A competition for national teams of member countries of OFC.

| | |
|---|---|
| 2004 | Australia |
| 2002 | New Zealand |
| 2000 | Australia |
| 1998 | New Zealand |
| 1996 | Australia |
| 1980 | Australia |
| 1973 | New Zealand |

## FIFA CONFEDERATIONS CUP

A competition for winners of the the AFC Asian Cup, the CAF African Cup of Nations, the CONCACAF Gold Cup, the CONMEBOL Copa America, the OFC Nations Cup, the UEFA European Championships, and the World Cup champions and host country.

| | |
|---|---|
| 2005 | Brazil |
| 2003 | France |
| 2001 | France |
| 1999 | Mexico |
| 1996 | Brazil |
| 1994 | Denmark |
| 1992 | Argentina |

## OLYMPIC GAMES – MEN'S SOCCER

A soccer competition that is part of an international event made up of multiple sporting competitions.

| | |
|---|---|
| 2004 | Argentina |
| 2000 | Cameroon |
| 1996 | Nigeria |
| 1992 | Spain |
| 1988 | USSR |
| 1984 | France |
| 1980 | Czechoslovakia* |
| 1976 | East Germany** |
| 1972 | Poland |
| 1968 | Hungary |
| 1964 | Hungary |
| 1960 | Yugoslavia*** |
| 1956 | USSR**** |
| 1952 | Hungary |
| 1948 | Sweden |
| 1936 | Italy |
| 1928 | Uruguay |
| 1924 | Uruguay |
| 1920 | Belgium |
| 1912 | Great Britain |
| 1908 | Great Britain |
| 1904 | Canada |
| 1900 | Great Britain |

*, ***, **** See p.45 for the current names of Czechoslovakia, Yugoslavia and the USSR.
** See p.38 and 39 for the current name of East Germany.

## OLYMPIC GAMES – WOMEN'S SOCCER

| | |
|---|---|
| 2004 | USA |
| 2000 | Norway |
| 1996 | USA |

## FIFA WORLD FOOTBALLER OF THE YEAR*

| | |
|---|---|
| 2006 | Fabio Cannavaro (Juventus, Real Madrid and Italy) |
| 2005 | Ronaldinho (Barcelona and Brazil) |
| 2004 | Ronaldinho (Barcelona and Brazil) |
| 2003 | Zinedine Zidane (Real Madrid and France) |
| 2002 | Ronaldo (Internazionale, Real Madrid and Brazil) |
| 2001 | Luis Figo (Real Madrid and Portugal) |
| 2000 | Zinedine Zidane (Juventus and France) |
| 1999 | Rivaldo (Barcelona and Brazil) |
| 1998 | Zinedine Zidane (Juventus and France) |
| 1997 | Ronaldo (Barcelona, Internazionale and Brazil) |
| 1996 | Ronaldo (PSV Eindhoven, Barcelona and Brazil) |
| 1995 | George Weah (AC Milan and Liberia) |
| 1994 | Romário (Barcelona and Brazil) |
| 1993 | Roberto Baggio (Juventus and Italy) |
| 1992 | Marco van Basten (AC Milan and Netherlands) |
| 1991 | Lothar Matthäus (Internazionale and Germany) |

* As voted by coaches and captains of international teams.

## EUROPEAN FOOTBALLER OF THE YEAR*

| | |
|---|---|
| 2007 | Kaká (AC Milan and Brazil) |
| 2006 | Fabio Cannavaro (Real Madrid and Italy) |
| 2005 | Ronaldinho (Barcelona and Brazil) |
| 2004 | Andriy Shevchenko (AC Milan and Ukraine) |
| 2003 | Pavel Nedved (Juventus and Czech Republic) |
| 2002 | Ronaldo (Internazionale, Real Madrid and Brazil) |
| 2001 | Michael Owen (Liverpool and England) |
| 2000 | Luís Figo (Real Madrid and Portugal) |
| 1999 | Rivaldo (Barcelona and Brazil) |
| 1998 | Zinedine Zidane (Juventus and France) |
| 1997 | Ronaldo (Barcelona, Internazionale and Brazil) |
| 1996 | Matthias Sammer (Borussia Dortmund and Germany) |
| 1995 | George Weah (Paris Saint-Germain, AC Milan and Liberia) |
| 1994 | Hristo Stoichkov (Barcelona and Bulgaria) |
| 1993 | Roberto Baggio (Juventus and Italy) |
| 1992 | Marco van Basten (AC Milan and Netherlands) |
| 1991 | Jean-Pierre Papin (Marseille and France) |
| 1990 | Lothar Matthäus (Internazionale and West Germany) |
| 1989 | Marco van Basten (AC Milan and Netherlands) |

## OLYMPIC GAMES

Olympic soccer, at least for men, has never quite enjoyed the prestige of other international tournaments, such as the World Cup. In 1992 FIFA ruled that Olympic players must be under 23 (with three exceptions allowed per squad). This has changed the nature of the tournament and allowed teams such as Cameroon and Nigeria to shine at the Olympics.

In the 2004 Olympic final, Argentina beat Paraguay 1–0. Argentina's Javier Mascherano (right) and Paraguay's Osvaldo Díaz (left) battle for the ball.

| | |
|---|---|
| 1988 | Marco van Basten (AC Milan and Netherlands) |
| 1987 | Ruud Gullit (PSV Eindhoven, Ajax and Netherlands) |
| 1986 | Igor Belanov (Dynamo Kiev and USSR) |
| 1985 | Michel Platini (Juventus and France) |
| 1984 | Michel Platini (Juventus and France) |
| 1983 | Michel Platini (Juventus and France) |
| 1982 | Paolo Rossi (Juventus and Italy) |
| 1981 | Karl-Heinz Rummenigge (Bayern Munich and West Germany) |
| 1980 | Karl-Heinz Rummenigge (Bayern Munich and West Germany) |
| 1979 | Kevin Keegan (Hamburg and England) |
| 1978 | Kevin Keegan (Hamburg and England) |
| 1977 | Allan Simonsen (Borussia Mönchengladbach and Denmark) |
| 1976 | Franz Beckenbauer (Bayern Munich and West Germany) |
| 1975 | Oleg Blokhin (Dynamo Kiev and USSR) |
| 1974 | Johan Cruyff (Barcelona and Netherlands) |
| 1973 | Johan Cruyff (Ajax, Barcelona and Netherlands) |
| 1972 | Franz Beckenbauer (Bayern Munich and West Germany) |
| 1971 | Johan Cruyff (Ajax and Netherlands) |
| 1970 | Gerd Müller (Bayern Munich and West Germany) |
| 1969 | Gianni Rivera (AC Milan and Italy) |
| 1968 | George Best (Manchester United and Northern Ireland) |
| 1967 | Flórián Albert (Ferencvaros and Hungary) |
| 1966 | Bobby Charlton (Manchester United and England) |
| 1965 | Eusébio (Benfica and Portugal) |
| 1964 | Denis Law (Manchester United and Scotland) |
| 1963 | Lev Yashin (Dynamo Moscow and USSR) |
| 1962 | Josef Masopust (Dukla Prague and Czechoslovakia) |
| 1961 | Omar Sívori (Juventus and Italy) |
| 1960 | Luis Suárez (Barcelona and Spain) |
| 1959 | Alfredo di Stéfano (Real Madrid and Spain) |
| 1958 | Raymond Kopa (Real Madrid and France) |
| 1957 | Alfredo di Stéfano (Real Madrid and Spain) |
| 1956 | Stanley Matthews (Blackpool and England) |

* As voted by France Soccer magazine.

## SOUTH AMERICAN FOOTBALLER OF THE YEAR*

**2006** Matías Fernández (Colo-Colo and Chile)

**2005** Carlos Tevéz (Corinthians and Argentina)

**2004** Carlos Tevéz (Boca Juniors and Argentina)

**2003** Carlos Tevéz (Boca Juniors and Argentina)

**2002** José Cardozo (Toluca and Paraguay)

**2001** Juan Román Riquelme (Boca Juniors and Argentina)

**2000** Romário (Vasco da Gama and Brazil)

**1999** Javier Saviola (River Plate and Argentina)

**1998** Martín Palermo (Boca Juniors and Argentina)

**1997** Marcelo Salas (River Plate and Chile)

**1996** José Luis Chilavert (Vélez Sársfield and Paraguay)

**1995** Enzo Francescoli (River Plate and Uruguay)

**1994** Cafú (São Paulo and Brazil)

**1993** Carlos Valderrama (Atlético Junior and Colombia)

**1992** Raí (São Paulo and Brazil)

**1991** Oscar Ruggeri (Vélez Sársfield and Argentina)

**1990** Raúl Vicente Amarilla (Olimpia and Paraguay)

**1989** Bebeto (Vasco da Gama and Brazil)

**1988** Rubén Paz (Racing Club and Uruguay)

**1987** Carlos Valderrama (Deportivo Cali and Colombia)

**1986** Antonio Alzamendi (River Plate and Uruguay)

**1985** Romerito (Fluminense and Paraguay)

**1984** Enzo Francescoli (River Plate and Uruguay)

**1983** Sócrates (Corinthians and Brazil)

**1982** Zico (Flamengo and Brazil)

**1981** Zico (Flamengo and Brazil)

**1980** Diego Maradona (Argentinos Juniors and Argentina)

**1979** Diego Maradona (Argentinos Juniors and Argentina)

**1978** Mario Kempes (Valencia and Argentina)

**1977** Zico (Flamengo and Brazil)

**1976** Elías Figueroa (Internacional and Chile)

**1975** Elías Figueroa (Internacional and Chile)

**1974** Elías Figueroa (Internacional and Chile)

**1973** Pelé (Santos and Brazil)

**1972** Teófilo Cubillas (Alianza Lima and Peru)

**1971** Tostão (Cruzeiro and Brazil)

* As voted by El Mundo magazine 1971–1986 and El Pais 1987–present.

## AFRICAN FOOTBALLER OF THE YEAR*

**2006** Didier Drogba (Chelsea and Côte d'Ivoire)

**2005** Samuel Eto'o (Barcelona and Cameroon)

**2004** Samuel Eto'o (Real Mallorca, Barcelona and Cameroon)

**2003** Samuel Eto'o (Real Mallorca and Cameroon)

**2002** El Hadji Diouf (Lens, Liverpool and Senegal)

**2001** El Hadji Diouf (Lens and Senegal)

**2000** Patrick Mboma (Parma and Cameroon)

**1999** Nwankwo Kanu (Arsenal and Nigeria)

**1998** Mustapha Hadji (Deportivo La Coruña and Morocco)

**1997** Viktor Ikpeba (Monaco and Nigeria)

**1996** Nwankwo Kanu (Ajax, Internazionale and Nigeria)

**1995** George Weah (Milan and Liberia)

**1994** Emmanuel Amuneke (Zamalek, Sporting Lisbon and Nigeria)

**1993** Rashidi Yekini (Vitória Setubal and Nigeria)

**1992** Abédi 'Pelé' Ayew (Lille and Ghana)

**1991** Abédi 'Pelé' Ayew (Marseille and Ghana)

**1990** Roger Milla (Cameroon)

**1989** George Weah (Monaco and Liberia)

**1988** Kalusha Bwalya (Cercle Brugge and Zambia)

**1987** Rabah Madjer (Porto and Algeria)

**1986** Badou Zaki (Real Mallorca and Morocco)

**1985** Mohamed Timoumi (FAR Rabat and Morocco)

**1984** Théophile Abega (Toulouse and Cameroon)

**1983** Mahmoud El-Khatib (Al-Ahly and Egypt)

**1982** Thomas Nkono (Espanyol and Cameroon)

**1981** Lakhdar Belloumi (GCR Mascara and Algeria)

**1980** Jean Manga-Onguene (Canon Yaoundé and Cameroon)

**1979** Thomas Nkono (Canon Yaoundé and Cameroon)

**1978** Abdul Razak (Asante Kotoko and Ghana)

**1977** Tarak Dhiab (Espérance and Tunisia)

**1976** Roger Milla (Canon Yaoundé and Cameroon)

**1975** Ahmed Faras (SC Chabab Mohammedia and Morocco)

**1974** Paul Moukila (CARA Brazzaville and People's Republic of Congo)

**1973** Tshimen Bwanga (TP Mazembe and Zaire)

**1972** Cherif Souleymane (Hafia Conakry and Guinea)

**1971** Ibrahim Sunday (Asante Kotoko and Ghana)

**1970** Salif Keita (Saint-Étienne/Mali)

*as voted by France Soccer magazine 1970–1992 and CAF 1992–present.

## ASIAN FOOTBALLER OF THE YEAR*

**2007** Yasser Al-Qahtani (Al-Hilal and Saudi Arabia)

**2006** Khalfan Ibrahim (Al-Sadd and Qatar)

**2005** Hamad Al-Montashari (Al-Ittihad and Saudi Arabia)

**2004** Ali Karimi (Al-Ahli and Iran)

**2003** Mehdi Mahdavikia (Hamburg and Iran)

**2002** Shinji Ono (Feyenoord and Japan)

**2001** Fan Zhiyi (Dundee and China)

**2000** Nawaf Al Temyat (Al-Hilal and Saudi Arabia)

**1999** Ali Daei (Hertha Berlin and Iran)

**1998** Hidetoshi Nakata (Perugia and Japan)

**1997** Hidetoshi Nakata (Bellmare Hiratsuka and Japan)

**1996** Khodadad Azizi (Bahman and Iran)

**1995** Masami Ihara (Yokohama Marinos and Japan)

**1994** Saeed Al-Owairan (Al-Shabab and Saudi Arabia)

**1993** Kazuyoshi Miura (Verdy Kawasaki and Japan)

**1992** Not awarded

**1991** Kim Joo-Sung (Daewoo Royals and Republic of Korea)

**1990** Kim Joo-Sung (Daewoo Royals and Republic of Korea)

**1989** Kim Joo-Sung (Daewoo Royals and Republic of Korea)

**1988** Ahmed Radhi (Al-Rasheed and Iraq)

* Awarded by AFC.

## OCEANIA FOOTBALLER OF THE YEAR*

**2004** Tim Cahill (Millwall, Everton and Australia)

**2003** Harry Kewell (Leeds United, Liverpool and Australia)

**2002** Brett Emerton (Feyenoord and Australia)

**2001** Harry Kewell (Leeds United and Australia)

**2000** Mark Viduka (Celtic, Leeds United and Australia)

**1999** Harry Kewell (Leeds United and Australia)

**1998** Christian Karembeu (Sampdoria and New Caledonia)

**1997** Mark Bosnich (Aston Villa and Australia)

**1996** Paul Okon (Club Brugge, Lazio and Australia)

**1995** Christian Karembeu (Nantes, Atlantique and New Caledonia)

**1994** Aurelio Vidmar (KSV Waregem, Standard Liége and Australia)

**1993** Robbie Slater (Anderlecht and Australia)

**1992** Wynton Rufer (Werder Bremen and New Zealand)

**1991** Robbie Slater (Anderlecht and Australia)

**1990** Wynton Rufer (Werder Bremen and New Zealand)

**1989** Wynton Rufer (Grasshopper Zurich, Werder Bremen and New Zealand)

**1988** Frank Farina (Marconi Fairfield, Club Brugge and Australia)

* As voted by a forum of journalists.

## UEFA CHAMPIONS LEAGUE/EUROPEAN CUP

A competition for the most successful soccer clubs in Europe, organized by UEFA.

| | |
|---|---|
| 2007 | AC Milan (Italy) |
| 2006 | Barcelona (Spain) |
| 2005 | Liverpool (England) |
| 2004 | Porto (Portugal) |
| 2003 | AC Milan (Italy) |
| 2002 | Real Madrid (Spain) |
| 2001 | Bayern Munich (Germany) |
| 2000 | Real Madrid (Spain) |
| 1999 | Manchester United (England) |
| 1998 | Real Madrid (Spain) |
| 1997 | Borussia Dortmund (Germany) |
| 1996 | Juventus (Italy) |
| 1995 | Ajax (Netherlands) |
| 1994 | AC Milan (Italy) |
| 1993 | Marseille (France) |
| 1992 | Barcelona (Spain) |
| 1991 | Red Star Belgrade (Yugoslavia*) |
| 1990 | AC Milan (Italy) |
| 1989 | AC Milan (Italy) |
| 1988 | PSV Eindhoven (Netherlands) |
| 1987 | Porto (Portugal) |
| 1986 | Steaua Bucharest (Romania) |
| 1985 | Juventus (Italy) |
| 1984 | Liverpool (England) |
| 1983 | Hamburg (West Germany) |
| 1982 | Aston Villa (England) |
| 1981 | Liverpool (England) |
| 1980 | Nottingham Forest (England) |
| 1979 | Nottingham Forest (England) |
| 1978 | Liverpool (England) |
| 1977 | Liverpool (England) |
| 1976 | Bayern Munich (West Germany) |
| 1975 | Bayern Munich (West Germany) |
| 1974 | Bayern Munich (West Germany) |
| 1973 | Ajax (Netherlands) |
| 1972 | Ajax (Netherlands) |
| 1971 | Ajax (Netherlands) |
| 1970 | Feyenoord (Netherlands) |
| 1969 | AC Milan (Italy) |
| 1968 | Manchester United (England) |
| 1967 | Celtic (Scotland) |
| 1966 | Real Madrid (Spain) |
| 1965 | Internazionale (Italy) |
| 1964 | Internazionale (Italy) |
| 1963 | AC Milan (Italy) |
| 1962 | Benfica (Portugal) |
| 1961 | Benfica (Portugal) |
| 1960 | Real Madrid (Spain) |
| 1959 | Real Madrid (Spain) |
| 1958 | Real Madrid (Spain) |
| 1957 | Real Madrid (Spain) |
| 1956 | Real Madrid (Spain) |

* See p.45 for current name of Yugoslavia.

## UEFA CUP*

A competition for European soccer clubs, organized by UEFA.

| | |
|---|---|
| 2006–2007 | Sevilla (Spain) |
| 2005–2006 | Sevilla (Spain) |
| 2004–2005 | CSKA Moscow (Russia) |
| 2003–2004 | Valencia (Spain) |
| 2002–2003 | Porto (Portugal) |
| 2001–2002 | Feyenoord (Netherlands) |
| 2000–2001 | Liverpool (England) |
| 1999–2000 | Galetasaray (Turkey) |
| 1998–1999 | Parma (Italy) |
| 1997–1998 | Internazionale (Italy) |
| 1996–1997 | Schalke (Germany) |
| 1995–1996 | Bayern Munich (Germany) |
| 1994–1995 | Parma (Italy) |
| 1993–1994 | Internazionale (Italy) |
| 1992–1993 | Juventus (Italy) |
| 1991–1992 | Ajax (Netherlands) |
| 1990–1991 | Internazionale (Italy) |
| 1989–1990 | Juventus (Italy) |
| 1988–1989 | Napoli (Italy) |
| 1987–1988 | Bayer Leverkusen (West Germany) |
| 1986–1987 | IFC Gothenburg (Sweden) |
| 1985–1986 | Real Madrid (Spain) |
| 1984–1985 | Real Madrid (Spain) |
| 1983–1984 | Tottenham Hotspur (England) |
| 1982–1983 | Anderlecht (Belgium) |
| 1981–1982 | IFK Gothenburg (Sweden) |
| 1980–1981 | Ipswich Town (England) |
| 1979–1980 | Eintracht Frankfurt (West Germany) |
| 1978–1979 | Borussia Mönchengladbach (West Germany) |
| 1977–1978 | PSV Eindhoven (Netherlands) |
| 1976–1977 | Juventus (Italy) |
| 1975–1976 | Liverpool (England) |
| 1974–1975 | Borussia Mönchengladbach (West Germany) |
| 1973–1974 | Feyenoord (Netherlands) |
| 1972–1973 | Liverpool (England) |
| 1971–1972 | Tottenham Hotspur (England) |
| 1970–1971 | Leeds United (England) |
| 1969–1970 | Arsenal (England) |
| 1968–1969 | Newcastle United (England) |
| 1967–1968 | Leeds United (England) |
| 1966–1967 | Dinamo Zagreb (Yugoslavia) |
| 1965–1966 | Barcelona (Spain) |
| 1964–1965 | Ferencvaros (Hungary) |
| 1963–1964 | Real Zaragoza (Spain) |
| 1962–1963 | Valencia (Spain) |
| 1961–1962 | Valencia (Spain) |
| 1960–1961 | Roma (Italy) |
| 1958–1960 | Barcelona (Spain) |
| 1955–1958 | Barcelona (Spain) |

* Before 1971 competition was known as the Inter-Cities Fairs Cup.

## EUROPEAN CUP WINNERS' CUP

A club competition for recent winners of European cup competitions, organized by UEFA.

| | |
|---|---|
| 1998–1999 | Lazio (Italy) |
| 1997–1998 | Chelsea (England) |
| 1996–1997 | Barcelona (Spain) |
| 1995–1996 | Paris Saint-Germain (France) |
| 1994–1995 | Real Zaragoza (Spain) |
| 1993–1994 | Arsenal (England) |
| 1992–1993 | Parma (Italy) |
| 1991–1992 | Werder Bremen (Germany) |
| 1990–1991 | Manchester United (England) |
| 1989–1990 | Sampdoria (Italy) |
| 1988–1989 | Barcelona (Spain) |
| 1987–1988 | Mechelen (Belgium) |
| 1986–1987 | Ajax (Netherlands) |
| 1985–1986 | Dinamo Kiev (USSR) |
| 1984–1985 | Everton (England) |
| 1983–1984 | Juventus (Italy) |
| 1982–1983 | Aberdeen (Scotland) |
| 1981–1982 | Barcelona (Spain) |
| 1980–1981 | Dinamo Tbilisi (USSR) |
| 1979–1980 | Valencia (Spain) |
| 1978–1979 | Barcelona (Spain) |
| 1977–1978 | Anderlecht (Belgium) |
| 1976–1977 | Hamburg (West Germany) |
| 1975–1976 | Anderlecht (Belgium) |
| 1974–1975 | Dinamo Kiev (USSR) |
| 1972–1973 | AC Milan (Italy) |
| 1973–1974 | 1. FC Magdeburg (East Germany) |
| 1971–1972 | Rangers (Scotland) |
| 1970–1971 | Chelsea (England) |
| 1969–1970 | Manchester City (England) |
| 1968–1969 | Slovan Bratislava (Czechoslovakia) |
| 1967–1968 | AC Milan (Italy) |
| 1966–1967 | Bayern Munich (West Germany) |
| 1965–1966 | Borussia Dortmund (West Germany) |
| 1964–1965 | West Ham United (England) |
| 1963–1964 | Sporting Lisbon (Portugal) |
| 1962–1963 | Tottenham Hotspur (England) |
| 1961–1962 | Atlético Madrid (Spain) |
| 1960–1961 | Fiorentina (Italy) |

## EUROPEAN SUPER CUP

An annual soccer match played between the current champions of the UEFA Cup and the Champions League.

| | |
|---|---|
| 2007 | AC Milan (Italy) |
| 2006 | Sevilla (Spain) |
| 2005 | Liverpool (England) |
| 2004 | Valencia (Spain) |
| 2003 | AC Milan (Italy) |
| 2002 | Real Madrid (Spain) |
| 2001 | Liverpool (England) |
| 2000 | Galatasaray (Turkey) |
| 1999 | Lazio (Italy) |
| 1998 | Chelsea (England) |
| 1997 | Barcelona (Spain) |
| 1996 | Juventus (Italy) |
| 1995 | Ajax (Netherlands) |
| 1994 | AC Milan (Italy) |
| 1993 | Parma (Italy) |
| 1992 | Barcelona (Spain) |
| 1991 | Manchester United (England) |
| 1990 | AC Milan (Italy) |
| 1989 | AC Milan (Italy) |
| 1988 | Mechelen (Belgium) |
| 1987 | Porto (Portugal) |
| 1986 | Steaua Bucharest (Romania) |
| 1985 | Not played |
| 1984 | Juventus (Italy) |
| 1983 | Aberdeen (Scotland) |
| 1982 | Aston Villa (England) |
| 1981 | Not played |
| 1980 | Valencia (Spain) |
| 1979 | Nottingham Forest (England) |
| 1978 | Anderlecht (Belgium) |
| 1977 | Liverpool (England) |
| 1976 | Anderlecht (Belgium) |
| 1975 | Dinamo Kiev (USSR) |
| 1974 | Not played |
| 1973 | Ajax (Netherlands) |
| 1972 | Ajax (Netherlands) |

Qatar's Khalfan Ibrahim was the 2006 Asian Footballer of the Year. The striker is famous for his tricks with the ball and is often compared to Ronaldinho.

# INTERNATIONAL STATS

## CONMEBOL COPA LIBERTADORES

A competition for the most successful soccer clubs in South America, organized by CONMEBOL.

| | |
|---|---|
| 2007 | Boca Juniors (Argentina) |
| 2006 | Internacional (Brazil) |
| 2005 | São Paulo (Brazil) |
| 2004 | Once Caldas (Colombia) |
| 2003 | Boca Juniors (Argentina) |
| 2002 | Olimpia (Paraguay) |
| 2001 | Boca Juniors (Argentina) |
| 2000 | Boca Juniors (Argentina) |
| 1999 | Palmeiras (Brazil) |
| 1998 | Vasco da Gama (Brazil) |
| 1997 | Cruzeiro (Brazil) |
| 1996 | River Plate (Argentina) |
| 1995 | Grêmio (Brazil) |
| 1994 | Vélez Sársfield (Argentina) |
| 1993 | São Paulo (Brazil) |
| 1992 | São Paulo (Brazil) |
| 1991 | Colo-Colo (Chile) |
| 1990 | Olimpia (Paraguay) |
| 1989 | Atlético Nacional (Colombia) |
| 1988 | Nacional (Uruguay) |
| 1987 | Peñarol (Uruguay) |
| 1986 | River Plate (Argentina) |
| 1985 | Argentinos Juniors (Argentina) |
| 1984 | Independiente (Argentina) |
| 1983 | Grêmio (Brazil) |
| 1982 | Peñarol (Uruguay) |
| 1981 | Flamengo (Brazil) |
| 1980 | Nacional (Uruguay) |
| 1979 | Olimpia (Paraguay) |
| 1978 | Boca Juniors (Argentina) |
| 1977 | Boca Juniors (Argentina) |
| 1976 | Cruzeiro (Brazil) |
| 1975 | Independiente (Argentina) |
| 1974 | Independiente (Argentina) |
| 1973 | Independiente (Argentina) |
| 1972 | Independiente (Argentina) |
| 1971 | Nacional (Uruguay) |
| 1970 | Estudiantes (Argentina) |
| 1969 | Estudiantes (Argentina) |
| 1968 | Estudiantes (Argentina) |
| 1967 | Racing Club (Argentina) |
| 1966 | Peñarol (Uruguay) |
| 1965 | Independiente (Argentina) |
| 1964 | Independiente (Argentina) |
| 1963 | Santos (Brazil) |
| 1962 | Santos (Brazil) |
| 1961 | Peñarol (Uruguay) |
| 1960 | Peñarol (Uruguay) |

## FIFA CLUB WORLD CUP

A competition between the winners of the 6 continental federations: UEFA, CONMEBOL, CONCACAF, CAF, AFC and OFC.

| | |
|---|---|
| 2006 | Internacional (Brazil) |
| 2005 | São Paulo (Brazil) |
| 2001–2004 | Not played until merged with Intercontinental Cup in 2005 |
| 2001 | Corinthians (Brazil) |

## INTERCONTINENTAL CUP*

A competition between the winners of the UEFA Champions League and the Copa Libertadores.

| | |
|---|---|
| 2004 | Porto (Portugal) |
| 2003 | Boca Juniors (Argentina) |
| 2002 | Real Madrid (Spain) |
| 2001 | Bayern Munich (Germany) |
| 2000 | Boca Juniors (Argentina) |
| 1999 | Manchester United (England) |
| 1998 | Real Madrid (Spain) |
| 1997 | Borussia Dortmund (Germany) |
| 1996 | Juventus (Italy) |
| 1995 | Ajax (Netherlands) |
| 1994 | Vélez Sársfield (Argentina) |
| 1993 | São Paulo (Brazil) |
| 1992 | São Paulo (Brazil) |
| 1991 | Red Star Belgrade (Yugoslavia**) |
| 1990 | AC Milan (Italy) |
| 1989 | AC Milan (Italy) |
| 1988 | Nacional (Uruguay) |
| 1987 | Porto (Portugal) |
| 1986 | River Plate (Argentina) |
| 1985 | Juventus (Italy) |
| 1984 | Independiente (Argentina) |
| 1983 | Grêmio (Brazil) |
| 1982 | Peñarol (Uruguay) |
| 1981 | Flamengo (Brazil) |
| 1980 | Nacional (Uruguay) |
| 1979 | Olimpia (Paraguay) |
| 1978 | Not played |
| 1977 | Boca Juniors (Argentina) |
| 1976 | Bayern Munich (West Germany) |
| 1975 | Not played |
| 1974 | Atlético Madrid (Spain) |
| 1973 | Independiente (Argentina) |
| 1972 | Ajax (Netherlands) |
| 1971 | Nacional (Uruguay) |
| 1970 | Feyenoord (Netherlands) |
| 1969 | AC Milan (Italy) |
| 1968 | Estudiantes (Argentina) |
| 1967 | Racing Club (Argentina) |
| 1966 | Peñarol (Uruguay) |
| 1965 | Internazionale (Italy) |
| 1964 | Internazionale (Italy) |
| 1963 | Santos (Brazil) |
| 1962 | Santos (Brazil) |
| 1961 | Peñarol (Uruguay) |
| 1960 | Real Madrid (Spain) |

* Known as the World Club Championship until 2000. From 2005, competition replaced by FIFA Club World Cup.

** See p.45 for the current name of Yugoslavia.

## CONCACAF CHAMPIONS' CUP

A competition for the most successful soccer clubs in North America, Central America and the Caribbean, organized by CONCACAF.

| | |
|---|---|
| 2007 | Pachuca (Mexico) |
| 2006 | Club América (Mexico) |
| 2005 | Deportivo Saprissa (Costa Rica) |
| 2004 | Alajuelense (Costa Rica) |
| 2003 | Toluca (Mexico) |
| 2002 | Pachuca (Mexico) |
| 2001 | Not played |
| 2000 | Los Angeles Galaxy (USA) |
| 1999 | Necaxa (Mexico) |
| 1998 | DC United (USA) |
| 1997 | Cruz Azul (Mexico) |
| 1996 | Cruz Azul (Mexico) |
| 1995 | Deportivo Saprissa (Costa Rica) |
| 1994 | CS Cartaginés (Costa Rica) |
| 1993 | Deportivo Saprissa (Costa Rica) |
| 1992 | Club América (Mexico) |
| 1991 | Puebla (Mexico) |
| 1990 | Club America (Mexico) |
| 1989 | UNAM Pumas (Mexico) |
| 1988 | Olimpia (Honduras) |
| 1987 | Club América (Mexico) |
| 1986 | Alajuelense (Costa Rica) |
| 1985 | Defence Force (Trinidad and Tobago) |
| 1984 | Violette AC (Haiti) awarded the trophy after Guadalajara (Mexico) and New York Freedoms (USA) were disqualified |
| 1983 | Atlante (Mexico) |
| 1982 | UNAM Pumas (Mexico) |
| 1981 | Transvaal (Surinam) |
| 1980 | UNAM Pumas (Mexico) |
| 1979 | FAS (El Salvador) |
| 1978 | Universidad de Guadalajara (Mexico) awarded the trophy |
| 1977 | Club America (Mexico) |
| 1976 | Aguila (El Salvador) |
| 1975 | Atlético Español (Mexico) |
| 1974 | CSD Municipal (Guatemala) won 4–2 on aggregate |
| 1973 | Transvaal (Surinam) awarded the trophy after Northern and Central region teams withdrew |
| 1972 | Olimpia (Honduras) |
| 1971 | Cruz Azul (Mexico) |
| 1970 | Cruz Azul (Mexico) awarded the trophy after Transvaal (Surinam) and Deportivo Saprissa (Costa Rica) withdrew |
| 1969 | Cruz Azul (Mexico) |
| 1968 | Toluca (Mexico) awarded a walkover win after Aurora (Guatemala) and Transvaal (Surinam) were suspended |
| 1967 | Alianza (El Salvador) |
| 1964–1966 | Not played |
| 1963 | Racing Club (Haiti) awarded the cup after Guadalajara withdrew |
| 1962 | Guadalajara (Mexico) |

## CAF AFRICAN CHAMPIONS LEAGUE*

A competition for the most successful soccer clubs in Africa, organized by CAF.

| | |
|---|---|
| 2007 | Étoile du Sahel (Tunisia) |
| 2006 | Al-Ahly (Egypt) |
| 2005 | Al-Ahly (Egypt) |
| 2004 | Enyimba (Nigeria) |
| 2003 | Enyimba (Nigeria) |
| 2002 | Zamalek (Egypt) |
| 2001 | Al-Ahly (Egypt) |
| 2000 | Hearts of Oak (Ghana) |
| 1999 | Raja Casablanca (Morocco) |
| 1998 | ASEC Abidjan (Côte d'Ivoire) |
| 1997 | Raja Casablanca (Morocco) |
| 1996 | Zamalek (Egypt) |
| 1995 | Orlando Pirates (South Africa) |
| 1994 | Espérance (Tunisia) |
| 1993 | Zamalek (Egypt) |
| 1992 | Wydad Casablanca (Morocco) |
| 1991 | Club Africain (Algeria) |
| 1990 | JS Kabylie (Algeria) |
| 1989 | Raja Casablanca (Morocco) |
| 1988 | EP Sétif (Algeria) |
| 1987 | Al-Ahly (Egypt) |
| 1986 | Zamalek (Egypt) |
| 1985 | FAR Rabat (Morocco) |
| 1984 | Zamalek (Egypt) |
| 1983 | Asante Kotoko (Ghana) |
| 1982 | Al-Ahly (Egypt) |
| 1981 | JE Tizi-Ouzou (Algeria) |
| 1980 | Canon Yaoundé (Cameroon) |
| 1979 | Union Douala (Cameroon) |
| 1978 | Canon Yaoundé (Cameroon) |
| 1977 | Hafia Conakry (Ghana) |
| 1976 | MC Algiers (Algeria) |
| 1975 | Hafia Conakry (Ghana) |
| 1974 | CARA Brazzaville (Congo) |
| 1973 | As Vita Club (Zaire) |
| 1972 | Hafia Conakry (Ghana) |
| 1971 | Canon Yaoundé (Cameroon) |
| 1970 | Asante Kotoko (Ghana) |
| 1969 | Ismaily (Egypt) |
| 1968 | TP Englebert (Zaire) |
| 1967 | Trophy awarded to TP Englebert (Zaire) after Asante Kotoko (Ghana) refused to take part in a play-off |
| 1966 | Stade Abidjan (Côte d'Ivoire) |
| 1965 | Not played |
| 1964 | Oryz Douala (Cameroon) |

* Known as the African Cup of Champions until 1997, and since then as the CAF Champions League.

## CAF AFRICAN CONFEDERATION CUP*

A competition for African Soccer clubs, organized by CAF.

| | |
|---|---|
| 2006 | Étoile du Sahel (Tunisia) |
| 2005 | FAR Rabat (Morocco) |
| 2004 | Hearts of Oak (Ghana) |

* Competition was formed when the CAF Cup and the CAF African Cup winners Cup merged.

## CAF CUP

A competition for African clubs, organized by CAF.

| | |
|---|---|
| 2003 | Raja Casablanca (Morocco) |
| 2002 | JS Kabylie (Algeria) |
| 2001 | JS Kabylie (Algeria) |
| 2000 | JS Kabylie (Algeria) |
| 1999 | Étoile du Sahel (Tunisia) |
| 1998 | CS Sfaxien (Tunisia) |
| 1997 | Espérance (Tunisia) |
| 1996 | Kawkab Marrakech (Morocco) |
| 1995 | Étoile du Sahel (Tunisia) |
| 1994 | Bendel Insurance (Nigeria) |
| 1993 | Stella Abidjan (Côte d'Ivoire) |
| 1992 | Shooting Stars (Nigeria) |

## CAF AFRICAN CUP WINNERS' CUP

A competition for African clubs who were winners of national competitions, organized by CAF.

| | |
|---|---|
| 2003 | Étoile du Sahel (Tunisia) |
| 2002 | Wydad Casablanca (Morocco) |
| 2001 | Kaizer Chiefs (South Africa) |
| 2000 | Zamalek (Egypt) |
| 1999 | Africa Sports (Côte d'Ivoire) |
| 1998 | Espérance (Tunisia) |
| 1997 | Étoile du Sahel (Tunisia) |
| 1996 | Al-Mokawloon al-Arab (Egypt) |
| 1995 | JS Kabylie (Algeria) |
| 1994 | DC Motemba Pemba (Zaire) |
| 1993 | Al-Ahly (Egypt) |
| 1992 | Africa Sports (Côte d'Ivoire) |
| 1991 | Power Dynamos (Zambia) |
| 1990 | BBC Lions (Nigeria) |
| 1989 | Al-Merrick (Sudan) |
| 1988 | CA Bizertin (Algeria) |
| 1987 | Gor Mahia (Kenya) |
| 1986 | Al-Ahly (Egypt) |
| 1985 | Al-Ahly (Egypt) |
| 1984 | Al-Ahly (Egypt) |
| 1983 | Al-Mokawloon al-Arab (Egypt) |
| 1982 | Al-Mokawloon al-Arab (Egypt) |
| 1981 | Union Douala (Cameroon) |
| 1980 | TP Mazembe (Zaire) |
| 1979 | Canon Yaoundé (Cameroon) |
| 1978 | Horoya AC (Guinea) |
| 1977 | Enugu Rangers (Nigeria) |
| 1976 | Shooting Stars (Nigeria) |
| 1975 | Tonnerre Yaoundé (Cameroon) |

## CAF AFRICAN SUPER CUP

A competition match between the current champions of the CAF Confederation Cup and the CAF Champions League.

| | |
|---|---|
| 2007 | Al-Ahly (Egypt) |
| 2006 | Al-Ahly (Egypt) |
| 2005 | Enyimba (Nigeria) |
| 2004 | Enyimba (Nigeria) |
| 2003 | Zamalek (Egypt) |
| 2002 | Al-Ahly (Egypt) |
| 2001 | Hearts of Oak (Ghana) |
| 2000 | Raja Casablanca (Morocco) |

| | |
|---|---|
| 1999 | ASEC Abidjan (Côte d'Ivoire) |
| 1998 | Étoile du Sahel (Tunisia) |
| 1997 | Zamalek (Egypt) |
| 1996 | Orlando Pirates (South Africa) |
| 1995 | Espérance (Tunisia) |
| 1994 | Zamalek (Egypt) |
| 1993 | Africa Sports (Côte d'Ivoire) |

## AFC ASIAN CHAMPIONS LEAGUE*

A competition between champions and cup winners of the top 14 Asian leagues.

| | |
|---|---|
| 2006–2007 | Urawa Red Diamonds (Japan) |
| 2005–2006 | Jeonbuk Hyundai Motors (Republic of Korea) |
| 2004–2005 | Al-Ittihad (Saudi Arabia) |
| 2003–2004 | Al-Ittihad (Saudi Arabia) |
| 2002–2003 | Al Ain (United Arab Emirates) |

* Competition formed when the Asian Cup Winners Cup and the Asian Champions Cup merged.

## AFC ASIAN CUP WINNERS' CUP

A competition for Asian domestic cup winners, organized by AFC.

| | |
|---|---|
| 2001–2002 | Al-Hilal (Saudi Arabia) |
| 2000–2001 | Al-Shabab (Saudi Arabia) |
| 1999–2000 | Shimizu S-Pulse (Japan) |
| 1998–1999 | Al-Ittihad (Saudi Arabia) |
| 1997–1998 | Al-Nasr (Saudi Arabia) |
| 1996–1997 | Al-Hilal (Saudi Arabia) |
| 1995–1996 | Bellmare Hiratsuka (Japan) |
| 1994–1995 | Yokohama Flügels (Japan) |
| 1993–1994 | Al-Qadisiya (Saudi Arabia) |
| 1992–1993 | Yokohama Marinos (formerly Nissan) |
| 1991–1992 | Nissan (Japan) |
| 1990–1991 | Persepolis (Iran) |

## AFC ASIAN CHAMPIONS CUP*

A competition for champions of Asian leagues.

| | |
|---|---|
| 2001–2002 | Suwon Samsung Bluewings (Republic of Korea) |
| 2000–2001 | Suwon Samsung Bluewings (Republic of Korea) |
| 1999–2000 | Al-Hilal (Saudi Arabia) |
| 1998–1999 | Júbilo Iwata (Japan) |
| 1997–1998 | Pohang Steelers (South Korea) |
| 1996–1997 | Pohang Steelers (Republic of Korea) |
| 1995–1996 | Ilhwa Chunma (South Korea) |
| 1994–1995 | Thai Farmers Bank (Thailand) |

| | |
|---|---|
| 1993–1994 | Thai Farmers Bank (Thailand) |
| 1991–1992 | Al-Hilal (Saudi Arabia) |
| 1990–1991 | Esteghlal (Iran) |
| 1989–1990 | Liaoning (China) |
| 1988–1989 | Al-Sadd (Qatar) |
| 1987–1988 | Yomiuri (Japan) awarded the trophy after Al-Hilal (Saudi Arabia) withdrew |
| 1986–1987 | Furukawa Electric (Japan) |
| 1985–1986 | Daewoo Royals (South Korea) |
| 1972–1984 | Not played |
| 1970–1971 | Maccabi Tel Aviv (Israel) awarded the trophy after Al Shorta (Iraq) withdrew |
| 1969–1970 | Taj (Iran) |
| 1968–1969 | Maccabi Tel Aviv (Israel) |
| 1966–1967 | Hapoel Tel Aviv (Israel) |

* 1967–1971 known as the Asian Club Championship; 1985–2002 known as the Asian Champions Cup. Not played 1967–1968 and 1972–1984.

## AFC ASIAN SUPER CUP

A competition between the winners of the Asian Champions Cup and the Asian Cup Winners Cup. Came to an end after the Asian Champions League was formed.

| | |
|---|---|
| 2002 | Suwon Samsung Bluewings (Republic of Korea) |
| 2001 | Suwon Samsung Bluewings (Republic of Korea) |
| 2000 | Al-Hilal (Saudi Arabia) |
| 1999 | Júbilo Iwata (Japan) |
| 1998 | Al-Nasr (Saudi Arabia) |
| 1997 | Al-Hilal (Saudi Arabia) |
| 1996 | Ilhwa Chunma (Republic of Korea) |
| 1995 | Yokohama Flugels (Japan) |

## ARAB CHAMPIONS LEAGUE*

A competition for clubs in the Arab world.

| | |
|---|---|
| 2007 | ES Sétif (Algeria) |
| 2006 | Raja Casablanca (Morocco) |
| 2005 | Al-Ittihad (Saudi Arabia) |
| 2004 | CS Sfaxien (Tunisia) |
| 2003 | Zamalek (Egypt) |
| 2002 | Al-Ahli (Saudi Arabia) |
| 2001 | Al-Sadd (Qatar) |
| 2000 | CS Sfaxien (Tunisia) |
| 1999 | Al-Shabab (Saudi Arabia) |
| 1998 | WA Tlemcen (Algeria) |
| 1997 | Club Africain (Algeria) |
| 1996 | Al-Ahly (Egypt) |
| 1995 | Al-Hilal (Saudi Arabia) |
| 1994 | Al-Hilal (Saudi Arabia) |
| 1993 | Espérance (Tunisia) |
| 1992 | Al-Shabab (Saudi Arabia) |
| 1991 | Not played |
| 1990 | Not played |
| 1989 | Wydad Casablanca (Morocco) |
| 1988 | Al-Ittifaq (Saudi Arabia) |

| | |
|---|---|
| 1987 | Al-Rasheed (Iraq) |
| 1986 | Al-Rasheed (Iraq) |
| 1985 | Al-Rasheed (Iraq) |
| 1984 | Al-Ittifaq (Saudi Arabia) |
| 1983 | Not played |
| 1982 | Al-Shorta (Iraq) |

* Known as the Arab Club Champions Cup until 2001, when it merged with the Arab Cup Winners Cup. New tournament known as the Prince Faysal bin Fahad Tournament for Arab Clubs until 2003.

## ARAB CUP WINNERS CUP*

A competition between winners of national club competitions in Arab nations.

| | |
|---|---|
| 2001–2002 | Stade Tunisien (Tunisia) |
| 2000–2001 | Al-Hilal (Saudi Arabia) |
| 1999–2000 | Al Ittihad (Qatar) |
| 1998–1999 | MC Oran (Algeria) |
| 1997–1998 | MC Oran (Algeria) |
| 1996–1997 | OC Khouribga (Morocco) |
| 1995–1996 | Club Africain (Tunisia) |
| 1994–1995 | Al-Ahly (Egypt) |
| 1993–1994 | Olympique Casablanca (Morocco) |
| 1992–1993 | Olympique Casablanca (Morocco) |
| 1991–1992 | Olympique Casablanca (Morocco) |
| 1989–1990 | Stade Tunisien (Tunisia) |

* 1990–1991 not played.

## OCEANIA CHAMPIONS LEAGUE*

A competition for Oceanian soccer clubs, organized by OFC.

| | |
|---|---|
| 2007 | Waitakere United (New Zealand) |
| 2006 | Auckland City (New Zealand) |
| 2004–2005 | Sydney (Australia) |
| 2001–2004 | Not played |
| 2000–2001 | Wollongong Wolves (Australia) |
| 1999 | South Melbourne (Australia) |
| 1987 | Adelaide City (Australia) |

* Known as Oceania Club Championship until 2007.

## UEFA WOMENS CUP

| | |
|---|---|
| 2006–2007 | Arsenal (England) |
| 2005–2006 | 1. FFC Frankfurt (Germany) |
| 2004–2005 | Turbine Potsdam (Germany) |
| 2003–2004 | Umeå IK (Sweden) |
| 2002–2003 | Umeå IK (Sweden) |
| 2001–2002 | 1. FFC Frankfurt (Germany) |

# DOMESTIC STATS

## ENGLAND: PREMIER LEAGUE*

| | |
|---|---|
| 2006–2007 | Manchester United |
| 2005–2006 | Chelsea |
| 2004–2005 | Chelsea |
| 2003–2004 | Arsenal |
| 2002–2003 | Manchester United |
| 2001–2002 | Arsenal |
| 2000–2001 | Manchester United |
| 1999–2000 | Manchester United |
| 1998–1999 | Manchester United |
| 1997–1998 | Arsenal |
| 1996–1997 | Manchester United |
| 1995–1996 | Manchester United |
| 1994–1995 | Blackburn Rovers |
| 1993–1994 | Manchester United |
| 1992–1993 | Manchester United |
| 1991–1992 | Leeds United |
| 1990–1991 | Arsenal |
| 1989–1990 | Liverpool |
| 1988–1989 | Arsenal |
| 1987–1988 | Liverpool |
| 1986–1987 | Everton |
| 1985–1986 | Liverpool |
| 1984–1985 | Everton |
| 1983–1984 | Liverpool |
| 1982–1983 | Liverpool |
| 1981–1982 | Liverpool |
| 1980–1981 | Aston Villa |
| 1979–1980 | Liverpool |
| 1978–1979 | Liverpool |
| 1977–1978 | Nottingham Forest |
| 1976–1977 | Liverpool |
| 1975–1976 | Liverpool |
| 1974–1975 | Derby County |
| 1973–1974 | Leeds United |
| 1972–1973 | Liverpool |
| 1971–1972 | Derby County |
| 1970–1971 | Arsenal |
| 1969–1970 | Everton |
| 1968–1969 | Leeds United |
| 1967–1968 | Manchester City |
| 1966–1967 | Manchester United |
| 1965–1966 | Liverpool |
| 1964–1965 | Manchester United |
| 1963–1964 | Liverpool |
| 1962–1963 | Everton |
| 1961–1962 | Ipswich Town |
| 1960–1961 | Tottenham Hotspur |
| 1959–1960 | Burnley |
| 1958–1959 | Wolverhampton Wanderers |
| 1957–1958 | Wolverhampton Wanderers |
| 1956–1957 | Manchester United |
| 1955–1956 | Manchester United |
| 1954–1955 | Chelsea |
| 1953–1954 | Wolverhampton Wanderers |
| 1952–1953 | Arsenal |
| 1951–1952 | Manchester United |
| 1950–1951 | Tottenham Hotspur |
| 1949–1950 | Portsmouth |
| 1948–1949 | Portsmouth |
| 1947–1948 | Arsenal |
| 1946–1947 | Liverpool |
| 1938–1939 | Everton |
| 1937–1938 | Arsenal |
| 1936–1937 | Manchester City |
| 1935–1936 | Sunderland |
| 1934–1935 | Arsenal |
| 1933–1934 | Arsenal |
| 1932–1933 | Arsenal |
| 1931–1932 | Everton |
| 1930–1931 | Arsenal |
| 1929–1930 | Sheffield Wednesday |
| 1928–1929 | Sheffield Wednesday |
| 1927–1928 | Everton |
| 1926–1927 | Newcastle United |
| 1925–1926 | Huddersfield Town |
| 1924–1925 | Huddersfield Town |
| 1923–1924 | Huddersfield Town |
| 1922–1923 | Liverpool |
| 1921–1922 | Liverpool |
| 1920–1921 | Burnley |
| 1919–1920 | West Bromwich Albion |
| 1914–1915 | Everton |
| 1913–1914 | Blackburn Rovers |
| 1912–1913 | Sunderland |
| 1911–1912 | Blackburn Rovers |
| 1910–1911 | Manchester United |
| 1909–1910 | Aston Villa |
| 1908–1909 | Newcastle United |
| 1907–1908 | Manchester United |
| 1906–1907 | Newcastle United |
| 1905–1906 | Liverpool |
| 1904–1905 | Newcastle United |
| 1903–1904 | Sheffield Wednesday |
| 1902–1903 | Sheffield Wednesday |
| 1901–1902 | Sunderland |
| 1900–1901 | Liverpool |
| 1899–1900 | Aston Villa |
| 1898–1899 | Aston Villa |
| 1897–1898 | Sheffield United |
| 1896–1897 | Aston Villa |
| 1895–1896 | Aston Villa |
| 1894–1895 | Sunderland |
| 1893–1894 | Aston Villa |
| 1892–1893 | Sunderland |
| 1891–1892 | Sunderland |
| 1890–1891 | Everton |
| 1889–1890 | Preston North End |
| 1888–1889 | Preston North End |

* Known as First Division 1888–1992. Not played 1916–1919 due to the First World War and 1940–1946 due to the Second World War.

## ENGLAND: FA CUP*

| | |
|---|---|
| 2006–2007 | Chelsea |
| 2005–2006 | Liverpool |
| 2004–2005 | Arsenal |
| 2003–2004 | Manchester United |
| 2002–2003 | Arsenal |
| 2001–2002 | Arsenal |
| 2000–2001 | Liverpool |
| 1999–2000 | Chelsea |
| 1998–1999 | Manchester United |
| 1997–1998 | Arsenal |
| 1996–1997 | Chelsea |
| 1995–1996 | Manchester United |
| 1994–1995 | Everton |
| 1993–1994 | Manchester United |
| 1992–1993 | Arsenal |
| 1991–1992 | Liverpool |
| 1990–1991 | Tottenham Hotspur |
| 1989–1990 | Manchester United |
| 1988–1989 | Liverpool |
| 1987–1988 | Wimbledon |
| 1986–1987 | Coventry City |
| 1985–1986 | Liverpool |
| 1984–1985 | Manchester United |
| 1983–1984 | Everton |
| 1982–1983 | Manchester United |
| 1981–1982 | Tottenham Hotspur |
| 1980–1981 | Tottenham Hotspur |
| 1979–1980 | West Ham United |
| 1978–1979 | Arsenal |
| 1977–1978 | Ipswich Town |
| 1976–1977 | Manchester United |
| 1975–1976 | Southampton |
| 1974–1975 | West Ham United |
| 1973–1974 | Liverpool |
| 1972–1973 | Sunderland |
| 1971–1972 | Leeds United |
| 1970–1971 | Arsenal |
| 1969–1970 | Chelsea |
| 1969–1960 | Wanderers |
| 1968–1969 | Manchester City |
| 1967–1968 | West Bromwich Albion |
| 1966–1967 | Tottenham Hotspur |
| 1965–1966 | Everton |
| 1964–1965 | Liverpool |
| 1963–1964 | West Ham United |
| 1962–1963 | Manchester United |
| 1961–1962 | Tottenham Hotspur |
| 1960–1961 | Tottenham Hotspur |
| 1958–1959 | Nottingham Forest |
| 1957–1958 | Bolton Wanderers |
| 1956–1957 | Aston Villa |
| 1955–1956 | Manchester City |
| 1954–1955 | Newcastle United |
| 1953–1954 | West Bromwich Albion |
| 1952–1953 | Blackpool |
| 1951–1952 | Newcastle United |
| 1950–1951 | Newcastle United |
| 1949–1950 | Arsenal |
| 1948–1949 | Wolverhampton Wanderers |
| 1947–1948 | Manchester City |
| 1946–1947 | Charlton Athletic |
| 1945–1946 | Derby County |
| 1938–1939 | Portsmouth |
| 1937–1938 | Preston North End |
| 1936–1937 | Sunderland |
| 1935–1936 | Arsenal |
| 1934–1935 | Sheffield Wednesday |
| 1933–1934 | Manchester City |
| 1932–1933 | Everton |
| 1931–1932 | Newcastle United |
| 1930–1931 | West Bromwich Albion |
| 1929–1930 | Arsenal |
| 1928–1929 | Bolton Wanderers |
| 1927–1928 | Blackburn Rovers |
| 1926–1927 | Cardiff City |
| 1925–1926 | Bolton Wanderers |
| 1924–1925 | Sheffield United |
| 1923–1924 | Newcastle United |
| 1922–1923 | Bolton Wanderers |
| 1921–1922 | Huddersfield Town |
| 1920–1921 | Tottenham Hotspur |
| 1919–1920 | Aston Villa |
| 1914–1915 | Sheffield United |
| 1913–1914 | Burnley |
| 1912–1913 | Aston Villa |
| 1911–1912 | Barnsley |
| 1910–1911 | Bradford City |
| 1909–1910 | Newcastle United |
| 1908–1909 | Manchester United |
| 1907–1908 | Wolverhampton Wanderers |
| 1906–1907 | Sheffield Wednesday |
| 1905–1906 | Everton |
| 1904–1905 | Aston Villa |
| 1903–1904 | Manchester City |
| 1902–1903 | Bury |
| 1901–1902 | Sheffield United |
| 1900–1901 | Tottenham Hotspur |
| 1899–1900 | Bury |
| 1898–1899 | Sheffield United |
| 1897–1898 | Nottingham Forest |
| 1896–1897 | Aston Villa |
| 1895–1896 | Sheffield Wednesday |
| 1894–1895 | Aston Villa |
| 1893–1894 | Notts County |
| 1892–1893 | Wolverhampton Wanderers |
| 1891–1892 | West Bromwich Albion |
| 1890–1891 | Blackburn Rovers |
| 1889–1890 | Blackburn Rovers |
| 1888–1889 | Preston North End |
| 1887–1888 | West Bromwich Albion |
| 1886–1887 | Aston Villa |
| 1885–1886 | Blackburn Rovers |
| 1884–1885 | Blackburn Rovers |
| 1883–1884 | Blackburn Rovers |
| 1882–1883 | Blackburn Olympic |
| 1881–1882 | Old Etonians |
| 1880–1881 | Old Carthusians |
| 1879–1880 | Clapham Rovers |
| 1878–1879 | Old Etonians |
| 1877–1878 | Wanderers |
| 1876–1877 | Wanderers |
| 1875–1876 | Wanderers |
| 1874–1875 | Royal Engineers |
| 1873–1874 | Oxford University |
| 1872–1873 | Wanderers |
| 1871–1872 | Wanderers |

* Not played 1915–1919 due to the First World War and 1939–1945 due to the Second World War.

## ENGLAND: LEAGUE CUP

| | |
|---|---|
| 2006–2007 | Chelsea |
| 2005–2006 | Manchester United |
| 2004–2005 | Chelsea |
| 2003–2004 | Middlesbrough |
| 2002–2003 | Liverpool |
| 2001–2002 | Blackburn Rovers |
| 2000–2001 | Liverpool |
| 1999–2000 | Leicester City |
| 1998–1999 | Tottenham Hotspur |
| 1997–1998 | Chelsea |
| 1996–1997 | Leicester City |
| 1995–1996 | Aston Villa |
| 1994–1995 | Liverpool |
| 1993–1994 | Aston Villa |
| 1992–1993 | Arsenal |
| 1991–1992 | Manchester United |
| 1990–1991 | Sheffield Wednesday |
| 1989–1990 | Nottingham Forest |
| 1988–1989 | Nottingham Forest |
| 1987–1988 | Luton Town |
| 1986–1987 | Arsenal |
| 1985–1986 | Oxford United |
| 1984–1985 | Norwich City |
| 1983–1984 | Liverpool |
| 1982–1983 | Liverpool |
| 1981–1982 | Liverpool |
| 1980–1981 | Liverpool |
| 1979–1980 | Wolverhampton Wanderers |
| 1978–1979 | Nottingham Forest |
| 1977–1978 | Nottingham Forest |
| 1976–1977 | Aston Villa |
| 1975–1976 | Manchester City |
| 1974–1975 | Aston Villa |
| 1973–1974 | Wolverhampton Wanderers |
| 1972–1973 | Tottenham Hotspur |
| 1971–1972 | Stoke City |
| 1970–1971 | Tottenham Hotspur |
| 1969–1970 | Manchester City |
| 1968–1969 | Swindon Town |
| 1967–1968 | Leeds United |
| 1966–1967 | Queens Park Rangers |
| 1965–1966 | West Bromwich Albion |
| 1964–1965 | Chelsea |
| 1963–1964 | Leicester City |
| 1962–1963 | Birmingham City |
| 1961–1962 | Norwich City |
| 1960–1961 | Aston Villa |

## ENGLAND: LEAGUE TOP SCORERS*

| | |
|---|---|
| 2006–2007 | Didier Drogba (Chelsea) 20 |
| 2005–2006 | Thierry Henry (Arsenal ) 27 |
| 2004–2005 | Thierry Henry (Arsenal) 25 |
| 2003–2004 | Thierry Henry (Arsenal) 30 |
| 2002–2003 | Ruud van Nistelrooy (Manchester United) 25 |
| 2001–2002 | Thierry Henry (Arsenal) 24 |
| 2000–2001 | Jimmy Floyd Hasselbaink (Chelsea) 23 |
| 1999–2000 | Kevin Philips (Sunderland) 30 |
| 1998–1999 | Jimmy Floyd Hasselbaink (Leeds United) 18 |
| | Michael Owen (Liverpool) 18 |
| | Dwight Yorke (Manchester United) 18 |
| 1997–1998 | Chris Sutton (Blackburn Rovers) 18 |
| | Dion Dublin (Coventry City) 18 |
| | Michael Owen (Liverpool) 18 |
| 1996–1997 | Alan Shearer (Newcastle United) 25 |
| 1995–1996 | Alan Shearer (Blackburn Rovers) 31 |
| 1994–1995 | Alan Shearer (Blackburn Rovers) 34 |
| 1993–1994 | Andy Cole (Newcastle United) 34 |
| 1992–1993 | Teddy Sheringham (Tottenham Hotspur) 22 |
| 1991–1992 | Ian Wright (Crystal Palace and Arsenal) 29 |
| 1990–1991 | Alan Smith (Arsenal) 22 |
| 1989–1990 | Gary Lineker (Tottenham Hotspur) 24 |
| 1988–1989 | Alan Smith (Arsenal) 23 |
| 1987–1988 | John Aldridge (Liverpool) 26 |
| 1986–1987 | Clive Allen (Tottenham Hotspur) 33 |
| 1985–1986 | Gary Lineker (Everton) 30 |
| 1984–1985 | Kerry Dixon (Chelsea) 24 |
| | Gary Lineker (Leicester City) 24 |
| 1983–1984 | Ian Rush (Liverpool) 32 |
| 1982–1983 | Luther Blissett (Watford) 27 |
| 1981–1982 | Kevin Keegan (Southampton) 26 |
| 1980–1981 | Peter Withe (Aston Villa) 20 |
| | Steve Archibald (Tottenham Hotspur) 20 |
| 1979–1980 | Phil Boyer (Southampton) 23 |
| 1978–1979 | Frank Worthington (Bolton Wanderers) 24 |
| 1977–1978 | Bob Latchford (Everton) 30 |
| 1976–1977 | Malcolm Macdonald (Arsenal) 25 |
| | Andy Gray (Aston Villa) 25 |
| 1975–1976 | Ted MacDougall (Norwich City) 23 |
| 1974–1975 | Malcolm Macdonald (Newcastle United) 21 |
| 1973–1974 | Mick Channon (Southampton) 21 |
| 1972–1973 | Bryan "Pop" Robson (West Ham United) 28 |
| 1971–1972 | Francis Lee (Manchester City) 33 |
| 1970–1971 | Tony Brown (West Bromwich Albion) 28 |
| 1969–1970 | Jeff Astle (West Bromwich Albion) 25 |
| 1968–1969 | Jimmy Greaves |
| | (Tottenham Hotspur) 27 |
| 1967–1968 | George Best (Manchester United) 28 |
| | Ron Davies (Southampton) 28 |
| 1966–1967 | Ron Davies (Southampton) 37 |
| 1965–1966 | Willie Irvine (Burnley) 29 |
| 1964–1965 | Andy McEvoy (Blackburn Rovers) 29 |
| | Jimmy Greaves (Tottenham Hotspur) 29 |
| 1963–1964 | Jimmy Greaves (Tottenham Hotspur) 35 |
| 1962–1963 | Jimmy Greaves (Tottenham Hotspur) 37 |
| 1961–1962 | Ray Crawford (Ipswich Town) 33 |
| | Derek Kevan (West Bromwich Albion) 33 |
| 1960–1961 | Jimmy Greaves (Chelsea) 41 |
| 1959–1960 | Dennis Viollet (Manchester United) 32 |
| 1958–1959 | Jimmy Greaves (Chelsea) 33 |
| 1957–1958 | Bobby Smith (Tottenham Hotspur) 36 |
| 1956–1957 | John Charles (Leeds United) 38 |
| 1955–1956 | Nat Lofthouse (Bolton Wanderers) 33 |
| 1954–1955 | Ronnie Allen (West Bromwich Albion) 27 |
| 1953–1954 | Jimmy Glazzard (Huddersfield Town) 29 |
| 1952–1953 | Charlie Wayman (Preston North End) 24 |
| 1951–1952 | George Robledo (Newcastle United) 33 |
| 1950–1951 | Stan Mortensen (Blackpool) 30 |
| 1949–1950 | Dickie Davis (Sunderland) 25 |
| 1948–1949 | Willie Moir (Bolton Wanderers) 25 |
| 1947–1948 | Ronnie Rooke (Arsenal) 33 |
| 1946–1947 | Dennis Westcott (Wolverhampton Wanderers) 37 |
| 1938–1939 | Tommy Lawton (Everton) 35 |
| 1937–1938 | Tommy Lawton (Everton) 28 |
| 1936–1937 | Freddie Steel (Stoke City) 33 |
| 1935–1936 | Pat Glover (Grimsby Town) 31 |
| | Raich Carter (Sunderland) 31 |
| | Bobby Gurney (Sunderland) 31 |
| 1934–1935 | Ted Drake (Arsenal) 42 |
| 1933–1934 | Jack Bowers (Derby County) 34 |
| 1932–1933 | Jack Bowers (Derby County) 35 |
| 1931–1932 | Dixie Dean (Everton) 44 |
| 1930–1931 | Tom "Pongo" Waring (Aston Villa) 49 |
| 1929–1930 | Vic Watson (West Ham United) 41 |
| 1928–1929 | Dave Halliday (Sunderland) 43 |
| 1927–1928 | Dixie Dean (Everton) 60 |
| 1926–1927 | Jimmy Trotter (Sheffield Wednesday) 37 |
| 1925–1926 | Ted Harper (Blackburn Rovers) 43 |
| 1924–1925 | Frank Roberts (Manchester City) 31 |
| 1923–1924 | Wilf Chadwick (Everton) 28 |
| 1922–1923 | Charlie Buchan (Sunderland) 30 |
| 1921–1922 | Andy Wilson (Middlesbrough) 31 |
| 1920–1921 | Joe Smith (Bolton Wanderers) 38 |
| 1919–1920 | Fred Morris (West Bromwich Albion) 37 |
| 1914–1915 | Bobby Parker (Everton) 35 |
| 1913–1914 | George Elliot (Middlesbrough) 32 |
| 1912–1913 | David McLean (Sheffield Wednesday) 30 |
| 1911–1912 | Harry Hampton (Aston Villa) 25 |
| | George Holley (Sunderland) 25 |
| | David McLean (Sheffield Wednesday) 25 |
| 1910–1911 | Albert Shepherd (Newcastle United) 25 |
| 1909–1910 | Jack Parkinson (Liverpool) 30 |
| 1908–1909 | Bert Freeman (Everton) 38 |
| 1907–1908 | Enoch West (Nottingham Forest) 27 |
| 1906–1907 | Alf Young (Everton) 30 |
| 1905–1906 | Albert Shepherd (Bolton Wanderers) 26 |
| 1904–1905 | Arthur Brown (Sheffield United) 22 |
| 1903–1904 | Steve Bloomer (Derby County) 20 |
| 1902–1903 | Sam Raybould (Liverpool) 31 |
| 1901–1902 | Jimmy Settle (Everton) 18 |
| 1900–1901 | Steve Bloomer (Derby County) 23 |
| 1899–1900 | Billy Garraty (Aston Villa) 27 |
| 1898–1899 | Steve Bloomer (Derby County) 23 |
| 1897–1898 | Fred Wheldon (Aston Villa) 21 |
| 1896–1897 | Steve Bloomer (Derby County) 22 |
| 1895–1896 | Johnny Campbell (Aston Villa) 20 |
| | Steve Bloomer (Derby County) 20 |
| 1894–1895 | Johnny Campbell (Sunderland) 22 |
| 1893–1894 | Jack Southworth (Everton) 27 |

| | |
|---|---|
| 1892–1893 | Johnny Campbell (Sunderland) 31 |
| 1891–1892 | Johnny Campbell (Sunderland 32) |
| 1890–1891 | Jack Southworth (Blackburn Rovers) 26 |
| 1889–1890 | Jimmy Ross (Preston North End) 24 |
| 1888–1889 | John Goodall (Preston North End) 21 |

* Not played 1916–1919 due to the First World War and 1940–1946 due to the Second World War.

## SCOTLAND: LEAGUE CHAMPIONS* **

| | |
|---|---|
| 2006–2007 | Celtic |
| 2005–2006 | Celtic |
| 2004–2005 | Rangers |
| 2003–2004 | Celtic |
| 2002–2003 | Rangers |
| 2001–2002 | Celtic |
| 2000–2001 | Celtic |
| 1999–2000 | Rangers |
| 1998–1999 | Rangers |
| 1997–1998 | Celtic |
| 1996–1997 | Rangers |
| 1995–1996 | Rangers |
| 1994–1995 | Rangers |
| 1993–1994 | Rangers |
| 1992–1993 | Rangers |
| 1991–1992 | Rangers |
| 1990–1991 | Rangers |
| 1989–1990 | Rangers |
| 1988–1989 | Rangers |
| 1987–1988 | Celtic |
| 1986–1987 | Rangers |
| 1985–1986 | Celtic |
| 1984–1985 | Aberdeen |
| 1983–1984 | Aberdeen |
| 1982–1983 | Dundee United |
| 1981–1982 | Celtic |
| 1980–1981 | Celtic |
| 1979–1980 | Aberdeen |
| 1978–1979 | Celtic |
| 1977–1978 | Rangers |
| 1976–1977 | Celtic |
| 1975–1976 | Rangers |
| 1974–1975 | Rangers |
| 1973–1974 | Celtic |
| 1972–1973 | Celtic |
| 1971–1972 | Celtic |
| 1970–1971 | Celtic |
| 1969–1970 | Celtic |
| 1968–1969 | Celtic |
| 1967–1968 | Celtic |
| 1966–1967 | Celtic |
| 1965–1966 | Celtic |
| 1964–1965 | Kilmarnock |
| 1963–1964 | Rangers |
| 1962–1963 | Rangers |
| 1961–1962 | Dundee |
| 1960–1961 | Rangers |
| 1959–1960 | Heart of Midlothian |
| 1958–1959 | Rangers |
| 1957–1958 | Heart of Midlothian |
| 1956–1957 | Rangers |
| 1955–1956 | Rangers |

| | |
|---|---|
| 1954–1955 | Aberdeen |
| 1953–1954 | Celtic |
| 1952–1953 | Rangers |
| 1951–1952 | Hibernian |
| 1950–1951 | Hibernian |
| 1949–1950 | Rangers |
| 1948–1949 | Rangers |
| 1947–1948 | Hibernian |
| 1946–1947 | Rangers |
| 1938–1939 | Rangers |
| 1937–1938 | Celtic |
| 1936–1937 | Rangers |
| 1935–1936 | Celtic |
| 1934–1935 | Rangers |
| 1933–1934 | Rangers |
| 1932–1933 | Rangers |
| 1931–1932 | Motherwell |
| 1930–1931 | Rangers |
| 1929–1930 | Rangers |
| 1928–1929 | Rangers |
| 1927–1928 | Rangers |
| 1926–1927 | Rangers |
| 1925–1926 | Celtic |
| 1924–1925 | Rangers |
| 1923–1924 | Rangers |
| 1922–1923 | Rangers |
| 1921–1922 | Celtic |
| 1920–1921 | Rangers |
| 1919–1920 | Rangers |
| 1918–1919 | Celtic |
| 1917–1918 | Rangers |
| 1916–1917 | Celtic |
| 1915–1916 | Celtic |
| 1914–1915 | Celtic |
| 1913–1914 | Celtic |
| 1912–1913 | Rangers |
| 1911–1912 | Rangers |
| 1910–1911 | Rangers |
| 1909–1910 | Celtic |
| 1908–1909 | Celtic |
| 1907–1908 | Celtic |
| 1906–1907 | Celtic |
| 1905–1906 | Celtic |
| 1904–1905 | Celtic |
| 1903–1904 | Third Lanark |
| 1902–1903 | Hibernian |
| 1901–1902 | Rangers |
| 1900–1901 | Rangers |
| 1899–1900 | Rangers |
| 1898–1899 | Rangers |
| 1897–1898 | Celtic |
| 1896–1897 | Heart of Midlothian |
| 1895–1896 | Celtic |
| 1894–1895 | Heart of Midlothian |
| 1893–1894 | Celtic |
| 1892–1893 | Celtic |
| 1891–1892 | Dumbarton |
| 1890–1891 | Dumbarton/Rangers (shared title) |

* Top league known as the First Division until 1975.
** Not played 1940–1946 due to the Second World War.

## SCOTLAND: FA CUP*

| | |
|---|---|
| 2006–2007 | Celtic |
| 2005–2006 | Heart of Midlothian |

| | |
|---|---|
| 2004–2005 | Celtic |
| 2003–2004 | Celtic |
| 2002–2003 | Rangers |
| 2001–2002 | Rangers |
| 2000–2001 | Celtic |
| 1999–2000 | Rangers |
| 1998–1999 | Rangers |
| 1997–1998 | Heart of Midlothian |
| 1996–1997 | Kilmarnock |
| 1995–1996 | Rangers |
| 1994–1995 | Celtic |
| 1993–1994 | Dundee United |
| 1992–1993 | Rangers |
| 1991–1992 | Rangers |
| 1990–1991 | Motherwell |
| 1989–1990 | Aberdeen |
| 1988–1989 | Celtic |
| 1987–1988 | Celtic |
| 1986–1987 | St Mirren |
| 1985–1986 | Aberdeen |
| 1984–1985 | Celtic |
| 1983–1984 | Aberdeen |
| 1982–1983 | Aberdeen |
| 1981–1982 | Aberdeen |
| 1980–1981 | Rangers |
| 1979–1980 | Celtic |
| 1978–1979 | Rangers |
| 1977–1978 | Rangers |
| 1976–1977 | Celtic |
| 1975–1976 | Rangers |
| 1974–1975 | Celtic |
| 1973–1974 | Celtic |
| 1972–1973 | Rangers |
| 1971–1972 | Celtic |
| 1970–1971 | Celtic |
| 1969–1970 | Aberdeen |
| 1968–1969 | Celtic |
| 1967–1968 | Dunfermline Athletic |
| 1966–1967 | Celtic |
| 1965–1966 | Rangers |
| 1964–1965 | Celtic |
| 1963–1964 | Rangers |
| 1962–1963 | Rangers |
| 1961–1962 | Rangers |
| 1960–1961 | Dunfermline Athletic |
| 1959–1960 | Rangers |
| 1958–1959 | St Mirren |
| 1957–1958 | Clyde |
| 1956–1957 | Falkirk |
| 1955–1956 | Heart of Midlothian |
| 1954–1955 | Clyde |
| 1953–1954 | Celtic |
| 1952–1953 | Rangers |
| 1951–1952 | Motherwell |
| 1950–1951 | Celtic |
| 1949–1950 | Rangers |
| 1948–1949 | Rangers |
| 1947–1948 | Rangers |
| 1946–1947 | Aberdeen |
| 1938–1939 | Clyde |
| 1937–1938 | East Fife |
| 1936–1937 | Celtic |
| 1935–1936 | Rangers |
| 1934–1935 | Rangers |
| 1933–1934 | Rangers |
| 1932–1933 | Celtic |
| 1931–1932 | Rangers |

| | |
|---|---|
| 1930–1931 | Celtic |
| 1929–1930 | Rangers |
| 1928–1929 | Kilmarnock |
| 1927–1928 | Rangers |
| 1926–1927 | Celtic |
| 1925–1926 | St Mirren |
| 1924–1925 | St Mirren |
| 1923–1924 | Airdrieonians |
| 1922–1923 | Celtic |
| 1921–1922 | Morton |
| 1920–1921 | Partick Thistle |
| 1919–1920 | Kilmarnock |
| 1913–1914 | Celtic |
| 1912–1913 | Falkirk |
| 1911–1912 | Celtic |
| 1910–1911 | Celtic |
| 1909–1910 | Dundee |
| 1908–1909 | Trophy withheld after a riot during Celtic vs Rangers |
| 1907–1908 | Celtic |
| 1906–1907 | Celtic |
| 1905–1906 | Heart of Midlothian |
| 1904–1905 | Third Lanark |
| 1903–1904 | Celtic |
| 1902–1903 | Rangers |
| 1901–1902 | Hibernian |
| 1900–1901 | Heart of Midlothian |
| 1899–1900 | Celtic |
| 1898–1899 | Celtic |
| 1897–1898 | Rangers |
| 1896–1897 | Rangers |
| 1895–1896 | Heart of Midlothian |
| 1894–1895 | St Bernard's |
| 1893–1894 | Rangers |
| 1892–1893 | Queen's Park |
| 1891–1892 | Celtic |
| 1890–1891 | Heart of Midlothian |
| 1889–1890 | Queen's Park |
| 1888–1889 | Third Lanark |
| 1887–1888 | Renton |
| 1886–1887 | Hibernian |
| 1885–1886 | Queen's Park |
| 1884–1885 | Renton |
| 1883–1884 | Queen's Park |
| 1882–1883 | Dumbarton |
| 1881–1882 | Queen's Park |
| 1880–1881 | Queen's Park |
| 1879–1880 | Queen's Park |
| 1878–1879 | Vale of Leven |
| 1877–1878 | Vale of Leven |
| 1876–1877 | Vale of Leven |
| 1875–1876 | Queen's Park |
| 1874–1875 | Queen's Park |
| 1873–1874 | Queen's Park |

* Not played 1914–1919 due to the First World War and 1939–1946 due to the Second World War.

## SCOTTISH LEAGUE CUP*

| | |
|---|---|
| 2006–2007 | Hibernian |
| 2005–2006 | Celtic |
| 2004–2005 | Rangers |
| 2003–2004 | Livingston |
| 2002–2003 | Rangers |
| 2001–2002 | Rangers |
| 2000–2001 | Celtic |

| 1999–2000 | Celtic |
|---|---|
| 1998–1999 | Rangers |
| 1997–1998 | Celtic |
| 1996–1997 | Rangers |
| 1995–1996 | Aberdeen |
| 1994–1995 | Raith Rovers |
| 1993–1994 | Rangers |
| 1992–1993 | Rangers |
| 1991–1992 | Hibernian |
| 1990–1991 | Rangers |
| 1989–1990 | Aberdeen |
| 1988–1989 | Rangers |
| 1987–1988 | Rangers |
| 1986–1987 | Rangers |
| 1985–1986 | Aberdeen |
| 1984–1985 | Rangers |
| 1983–1984 | Rangers |
| 1982–1983 | Celtic |
| 1981–1982 | Rangers |
| 1980–1981 | Dundee United |
| 1979–1980 | Dundee United |
| 1978–1979 | Rangers |
| 1977–1978 | Rangers |
| 1976–1977 | Aberdeen |
| 1975–1976 | Rangers |
| 1974–1975 | Celtic |
| 1973–1974 | Dundee |
| 1972–1973 | Hibernian |
| 1971–1972 | Partick Thistle |
| 1970–1971 | Rangers |
| 1969–1970 | Celtic |
| 1968–1969 | Celtic |
| 1967–1968 | Celtic |
| 1966–1967 | Celtic |
| 1965–1966 | Celtic |
| 1964–1965 | Rangers |
| 1963–1964 | Rangers |
| 1962–1963 | Heart of Midlothian |
| 1961–1962 | Rangers |
| 1960–1961 | Rangers |
| 1959–1960 | Heart of Midlothian |
| 1958–1959 | Heart of Midlothian |
| 1957–1958 | Celtic |
| 1956–1957 | Celtic |
| 1955–1956 | Aberdeen |
| 1954–1955 | Heart of Midlothian |
| 1953–1954 | East Fife |
| 1952–1953 | Dundee |
| 1951–1952 | Dundee |
| 1950–1951 | Motherwell |
| 1949–1950 | East Fife |
| 1948–1949 | Rangers |
| 1947–1948 | East Fife |
| 1946–1947 | Rangers |

## SCOTLAND: LEAGUE TOP SCORERS

| 2006–2007 | Kris Boyd (Rangers) 19 |
|---|---|
| 2005–2006 | Kris Boyd (Rangers) 32 |
| 2004–2005 | John Hartson (Celtic) 25 |
| 2003–2004 | Henrik Larsson (Celtic) 30 |
| 2002–2003 | Henrik Larsson (Celtic) 28 |
| 2001–2002 | Henrik Larsson (Celtic) 29 |
| 2000–2001 | Henrik Larsson (Celtic) 35 |
| 1999–2000 | Mark Viduka (Celtic) 25 |
| 1998–1999 | Henrik Larsson (Celtic) 29 |
| 1997–1998 | Marco Negri (Rangers) 32 |
| 1996–1997 | Jorge Cadete (Celtic) 25 |
| 1995–1996 | Pierre van Hooijdonk (Celtic) 26 |

| 1994–1995 | Tommy Coyne (Motherwell) 16 |
|---|---|
| 1993–1994 | Mark Hateley (Rangers) 22 |
| 1992–1993 | Ally McCoist (Rangers) 34 |
| 1991–1992 | Ally McCoist (Rangers) 34 |
| 1990–1991 | Tommy Coyne (Celtic) 18 |
| 1989–1990 | John Robertson (Heart of Midlothian) 17 |
| 1988–1989 | Mark McGhee (Celtic) 16 Charlie Nicholas (Aberdeen 16) |
| 1987–1988 | Tommy Coyne (Dundee) 33 |
| 1986–1987 | Brian McClair (Celtic) 35 |
| 1985–1986 | Ally McCoist (Rangers) 24 |
| 1984–1985 | Frank McDougall (Aberdeen) 22 |
| 1983–1984 | Brian McClair (Celtic) 23 |
| 1982–1983 | Charlie Nicholas (Celtic) 29 |
| 1981–1982 | George McCluskey (Celtic) 21 |
| 1980–1981 | Frank McGarvey (Celtic) 23 |
| 1979–1980 | Douglas Somner (St Mirren) 25 |
| 1978–1979 | Andy Ritchie (Morton) 22 |
| 1977–1978 | Derek Johnstone (Rangers) 25 |
| 1976–1977 | Willie Pettigrew (Motherwell) 21 |
| 1975–1976 | Kenny Dalglish (Celtic) 24 |
| 1974–1975 | Andy Gray (Motherwell) 20 Willie Pettigrew (Motherwell) 20 |
| 1973–1974 | John "Dixie" Deans (Celtic) 26 |
| 1972–1973 | Alan Gordon (Hibernian) 27 |
| 1971–1972 | Joe Harper (Aberdeen) 33 |
| 1970–1971 | Harry Hood (Celtic) 22 |
| 1969–1970 | Colin Stein (Rangers) 24 |
| 1968–1969 | Kenny Cameron (Dundee United) 26 |
| 1967–1968 | Bobby Lennox (Celtic) 32 |
| 1966–1967 | Stevie Chalmers (Celtic) 21 |
| 1965–1966 | Joe McBride (Celtic) 31 Alex Ferguson (Dunfermline) 31 |
| 1964–1965 | Jim Forrest (Rangers) 30 |
| 1963–1964 | Alan Gilzean (Dundee) 32 |
| 1962–1963 | Jimmy Millar (Rangers) 27 |
| 1961–1962 | Alan Gilzean (Dundee) 24 |
| 1960–1961 | Alex Harley (Third Lanark) 42 |
| 1959–1960 | Joe Baker (Hibernian) 42 |
| 1958–1959 | Joe Baker (Hibernian) 25 |
| 1957–1958 | Jimmy Wardhaugh (Heart of Midlothian) 28 Jimmy Murray (Heart of Midlothian) 28 |
| 1956–1957 | Hugh Baird (Airdrieonians) 33 |
| 1955–1956 | Jimmy Wardhaugh (Heart of Midlothian) 28 |
| 1954–1955 | Willie Bauld (Heart of Midlothian) 21 |
| 1953–1954 | Jimmy Wardhaugh (Heart of Midlothian) 27 |
| 1952–1953 | Lawrie Reilly (Hibernian) 30 Charles Fleming (East Fife) 30 |
| 1951–1952 | Lawrie Reilly (Hibernian) 27 |
| 1950–1951 | Lawrie Reilly (Hibernian) 22 |

| 1949–1950 | Willie Bauld (Hearts) 30 |
|---|---|
| 1948–1949 | Alexander Stott (Dundee) 30 |
| 1947–1948 | Archie Aikman (Falkirk) 20 |
| 1946–1947 | Bobby Mitchell (Third Lanark) 22 |
| 1938–1939 | Alex Venters (Rangers) 35 |
| 1937–1938 | Andy Black (Heart of Midlothian) 40 |
| 1936–1937 | David Wilson (Hamilton Academical) 34 |
| 1935–1936 | Jimmy McGrory (Celtic) 50 |
| 1934–1935 | Dave McCulloch (Heart of Midlothian) 38 |
| 1933–1934 | Jimmy Smith (Rangers) 41 |
| 1932–1933 | Willie McFadden (Motherwell) 45 |
| 1931–1932 | Willie McFadden (Motherwell) 52 |
| 1930–1931 | Barney Battles (Heart of Midlothian) 44 |
| 1929–1930 | Benny Yorston (Aberdeen) 38 |
| 1928–1929 | Evelyn Morrison (Falkirk) 43 |
| 1927–1928 | Jimmy McGrory (Celtic) 47 |
| 1926–1927 | Jimmy McGrory (Celtic) 49 |
| 1925–1926 | Willie Devlin (Cowdenbeath) 40 |
| 1924–1925 | Willie Devlin (Cowdenbeath) 33 |
| 1923–1924 | David Halliday (Dundee) 38 |
| 1922–1923 | John White (Heart of Midlothian) 30 |
| 1921–1922 | Duncan Walker (St Mirren) 45 |
| 1920–1921 | Hugh Ferguson (Motherwell) 43 |
| 1919–1920 | Hugh Ferguson (Motherwell) 33 |
| 1918–1919 | David McLean (Rangers) 29 |
| 1917–1918 | Hugh Ferguson (Motherwell) 35 |
| 1916–1917 | Bert Yarnall (Airdrieonians) 39 |
| 1915–1916 | James McColl (Celtic) 34 |
| 1914–1915 | Tom Gracie (Heart of Midlothian) 29 James Richardson (Ayr) 29 |
| 1913–1914 | James Reid (Airdrieonians) 27 |
| 1912–1913 | James Reid (Airdrieonians) 30 |
| 1911–1912 | Willie Reid (Rangers) 33 |
| 1910–1911 | Willie Reid (Rangers) 38 |
| 1909–1910 | Jimmy Quinn (Celtic) 24 John Simpson (Falkirk) 24 |
| 1908–1909 | John Hunter (Dundee) 29 |
| 1907–1908 | John Simpson (Falkirk) 32 |
| 1906–1907 | Jimmy Quinn (Celtic) 29 |
| 1905–1906 | Jimmy Quinn (Celtic) 20 |
| 1904–1905 | Robert C Hamilton (Rangers) 19 Jimmy Quinn (Celtic) 19 |
| 1903–1904 | Robert C Hamilton (Rangers) 28 |
| 1902–1903 | David Reid (Hibernian) 14 |
| 1901–1902 | William Maxwell (Third Lanark) 10 |
| 1900–1901 | Robert C Hamilton (Rangers) 20 |

| 1899–1900 | Robert C Hamilton (Rangers) 15 William Michael (Heart of Midlothian) 15 |
|---|---|
| 1898–1899 | Robert C Hamilton (Rangers) 25 |
| 1897–1898 | Robert C Hamilton (Rangers) 18 |
| 1896–1897 | William Taylor (Heart of Midlothian) 12 |
| 1895–1896 | Allan Martin (Celtic) 19 |
| 1894–1895 | James Miller (Clyde) 12 |
| 1893–1894 | Sandy McMahon (Celtic) 16 |
| 1892–1893 | Sandy McMahon (Celtic) 11 John Campbell (Celtic) 11 |
| 1891–1892 | John Bell (Dumbarton) 23 |
| 1890–1891 | John Bell (Dumbarton) 20 |

* Not played 1940–1946 due to the Second World War.

## LEAGUE OF WALES CHAMPIONS

| 2006–2007 | TNS |
|---|---|
| 2005–2006 | TNS |
| 2004–2005 | TNS |
| 2003–2004 | Rhyl |
| 2002–2003 | Barry Town |
| 2001–2002 | Barry Town |
| 2000–2001 | Barry Town |
| 1999–2000 | TNS |
| 1998–1999 | Barry Town |
| 1997–1998 | Barry Town |
| 1996–1997 | Barry Town |
| 1995–1996 | Barry Town |
| 1994–1995 | Bangor City |
| 1993–1994 | Bangor City |
| 1992–1993 | Cwmbran Town |

## WELSH CUP*

| 2006–2007 | Carmarthen Town |
|---|---|
| 2005–2006 | Rhyl |
| 2004–2005 | TNS |
| 2003–2004 | Rhyl |
| 2002–2003 | Barry Town |
| 2001–2002 | Barry Town |
| 2000–2001 | Barry Town |
| 1999–2000 | Bangor City |
| 1998–1999 | Inter Cardiff |
| 1997–1998 | Bangor City |
| 1996–1997 | Barry Town |
| 1995–1996 | Llansantffraid |
| 1994–1995 | Wrexham |
| 1993–1994 | Barry Town |
| 1992–1993 | Cardiff City |
| 1991–1992 | Cardiff City |
| 1990–1991 | Swansea City |
| 1989–1990 | Hereford United |
| 1988–1989 | Swansea City |
| 1987–1988 | Cardiff City |
| 1986–1987 | Merthyr Tydfil |
| 1985–1986 | Kidderminster Harriers |
| 1984–1985 | Shrewsbury Town |
| 1983–1984 | Shrewsbury Town |
| 1982–1983 | Swansea City |
| 1981–1982 | Swansea City |
| 1980–1981 | Swansea City |
| 1979–1980 | Newport County |
| 1978–1979 | Shrewsbury Town |
| 1977–1978 | Wrexham |
| 1976–1977 | Shrewsbury Town |

| | |
|---|---|
| 1975–1976 | Cardiff City |
| 1974–1975 | Wrexham |
| 1973–1974 | Cardiff City |
| 1972–1973 | Cardiff City |
| 1971–1972 | Wrexham |
| 1970–1971 | Cardiff City |
| 1969–1970 | Cardiff City |
| 1968–1969 | Cardiff City |
| 1967–1968 | Cardiff City |
| 1966–1967 | Cardiff City |
| 1965–1966 | Swansea Town |
| 1964–1965 | Cardiff City |
| 1963–1964 | Cardiff City |
| 1962–1963 | Borough United |
| 1961–1962 | Bangor City |
| 1960–1961 | Swansea Town |
| 1959–1960 | Wrexham |
| 1958–1959 | Cardiff City |
| 1957–1958 | Wrexham |
| 1956–1957 | Wrexham |
| 1955–1956 | Cardiff City |
| 1954–1955 | Barry Town |
| 1953–1954 | Flint Town United |
| 1952–1953 | Rhyl |
| 1951–1952 | Rhyl |
| 1950–1951 | Merthyr Tydfil |
| 1949–1950 | Swansea Town |
| 1948–1949 | Merthyr Tydfil |
| 1947–1948 | Lovells Athletic |
| 1946–1947 | Chester |
| 1939–1940 | Wellington |
| 1938–1939 | South Liverpool |
| 1937–1938 | Shrewsbury Town |
| 1936–1937 | Crewe Alexandra |
| 1935–1936 | Crewe Alexandra |
| 1934–1935 | Tranmere Rovers |
| 1933–1934 | Bristol City |
| 1932–1933 | Chester |
| 1931–1932 | Swansea Town |
| 1930–1931 | Wrexham |
| 1929–1930 | Cardiff City |
| 1928–1929 | Connah's Quay |
| 1927–1928 | Cardiff City |
| 1926–1927 | Cardiff City |
| 1925–1926 | Ebbw Vale |
| 1924–1925 | Wrexham |
| 1923–1924 | Wrexham |
| 1922–1923 | Cardiff City |
| 1921–1922 | Cardiff City |
| 1920–1921 | Wrexham |
| 1919–1920 | Cardiff City |
| 1914–1915 | Wrexham |
| 1913–1914 | Wrexham |
| 1912–1913 | Swansea Town |
| 1911–1912 | Cardiff City |
| 1910–1911 | Wrexham |
| 1909–1910 | Wrexham |
| 1908–1909 | Wrexham |
| 1907–1908 | Chester |
| 1906–1907 | Oswestry |
| 1905–1906 | Wellington |
| 1904–1905 | Wrexham |
| 1903–1904 | Druids |
| 1902–1903 | Wrexham |
| 1901–1902 | Wellington |
| 1900–1901 | Oswestry |
| 1899–1900 | Aberystwyth |

| | |
|---|---|
| 1898–1899 | Druids |
| 1897–1898 | Druids |
| 1896–1897 | Wrexham |
| 1895–1896 | Bangor Town |
| 1894–1895 | Newtown |
| 1893–1894 | Chirk |
| 1892–1893 | Wrexham |
| 1891–1892 | Chirk |
| 1890–1891 | Shrewsbury Town |
| 1889–1890 | Chirk |
| 1888–1889 | Bangor City |
| 1887–1888 | Chirk |
| 1886–1887 | Chirk |
| 1886–1886 | Druids |
| 1884–1885 | Druids |
| 1883–1884 | Oswestry |
| 1882–1883 | Wrexham |
| 1881–1882 | Druids |
| 1880–1881 | Druids |
| 1879–1880 | Druids |
| 1878–1879 | Newtown |
| 1877–1878 | Wrexham |

* Not played 1915–1919 due to the First World War and 1940–1946 due to the Second World War.

## WALES: LEAGUE TOP SCORERS

| | |
|---|---|
| 2006–2007 | Rhys Griffiths (Llanelli) 30 |
| 2005–2006 | Rhys Griffith (Llanelli) 28 |
| 2004–2005 | Marc Lloyd–Williams (TNS) 34 |
| 2003–2004 | Andy Moran (Rhyl) 27 |
| 2002–2003 | Graham Evans (Caersws) 24 |
| 2001–2002 | Marc Lloyd–Williams (Bangor City) 47 |
| 2000–2001 | Graham Evans (Caersws) 25 |
| 1999–2000 | Chris Summers (Cwmbran Town) 28 |
| 1998–1999 | Eifion Williams (Barry Town) 28 |
| 1997–1998 | Eifion Williams (Barry Town) 40 |
| 1996–1997 | Tony Bird (Barry Town) 42 |
| 1995–1996 | Ken McKenna (Conwy United) 38 |
| 1994–1995 | Frank Mottram (Bangor City) 30 |
| 1993–199 | David Taylor (Porthmadog) 43 |
| 1992–1993 | Steve Woods (Ebbw Vale) 29 |

## NORTHERN IRELAND: IRISH PREMIER LEAGUE* **

| | |
|---|---|
| 2006–2007 | Linfield |
| 2005–2006 | Linfield |
| 2004–2005 | Glentoran |
| 2003–2004 | Linfield |
| 2002–2003 | Glentoran |
| 2001–2002 | Portadown |
| 2000–2001 | Linfield |
| 1999–2000 | Linfield |
| 1998–1999 | Glentoran |
| 1997–1998 | Cliftonville |
| 1996–1997 | Crusaders |
| 1995–1996 | Portadown |

| | |
|---|---|
| 1994–1995 | Crusaders |
| 1993–1994 | Linfield |
| 1992–1993 | Linfield |
| 1991–1992 | Glentoran |
| 1990–1991 | Portadown |
| 1989–1990 | Portadown |
| 1988–1989 | Linfield |
| 1987–1988 | Glentoran |
| 1986–1987 | Linfield |
| 1985–1986 | Linfield |
| 1984–1985 | Linfield |
| 1983–1984 | Linfield |
| 1982–1983 | Linfield |
| 1981–1982 | Linfield |
| 1980–1981 | Glentoran |
| 1979–1980 | Linfield |
| 1978–1979 | Linfield |
| 1977–1978 | Linfield |
| 1976–1977 | Glentoran |
| 1975–1976 | Crusaders |
| 1974–1975 | Crusaders |
| 1973–1974 | Coleraine |
| 1972–1973 | Crusaders |
| 1971–1972 | Glentoran |
| 1970–1971 | Linfield |
| 1969–1970 | Glentoran |
| 1968–1969 | Linfield |
| 1967–1968 | Glentoran |
| 1966–1967 | Glentoran |
| 1965–1966 | Linfield |
| 1964–1965 | Derry City |
| 1963–1964 | Glentoran |
| 1962–1963 | Distillery |
| 1961–1962 | Linfield |
| 1960–1961 | Linfield |
| 1959–1960 | Glenavon |
| 1958–1959 | Linfield |
| 1957–1958 | Ards |
| 1956–1957 | Glenavon |
| 1955–1956 | Linfield |
| 1954–1955 | Linfield |
| 1953–1954 | Linfield |
| 1952–1953 | Glentoran |
| 1951–1952 | Glenavon |
| 1950–1951 | Glentoran |
| 1949–1950 | Linfield |
| 1948–1949 | Linfield |
| 1947–1948 | Belfast Celtic |
| 1939–1940 | Belfast Celtic |
| 1938–1939 | Belfast Celtic |
| 1937–1938 | Belfast Celtic |
| 1936–1937 | Belfast Celtic |
| 1935–1936 | Belfast Celtic |
| 1934–1935 | Linfield |
| 1933–1934 | Linfield |
| 1932–1933 | Belfast Celtic |
| 1931–1932 | Linfield |
| 1930–1931 | Glentoran |
| 1929–1930 | Linfield |
| 1928–1929 | Belfast Celtic |
| 1927–1928 | Belfast Celtic |
| 1926–1927 | Belfast Celtic |
| 1925–1926 | Belfast Celtic |
| 1924–1925 | Glentoran |
| 1923–1924 | Queen's Island |
| 1922–1923 | Linfield |
| 1921–1922 | Linfield |
| 1920–1921 | Glentoran |

| | |
|---|---|
| 1919–1920 | Belfast Celtic |
| 1914–1915 | Belfast Celtic |
| 1913–1914 | Linfield |
| 1912–1913 | Glentoran |
| 1911–1912 | Glentoran |
| 1910–1911 | Linfield |
| 1909–1910 | Cliftonville |
| 1908–1909 | Linfield |
| 1907–1908 | Linfield |
| 1906–1907 | Linfield |
| 1905–1906 | Cliftonville/Distillery (shared title) |
| 1904–1905 | Glentoran |
| 1903–1904 | Linfield |
| 1902–1903 | Distillery |
| 1901–1902 | Linfield |
| 1900–1901 | Distillery |
| 1899–1900 | Belfast Celtic |
| 1898–1899 | Distillery |
| 1897–1898 | Linfield |
| 1896–1897 | Glentoran |
| 1895–1896 | Distillery |
| 1894–1895 | Linfield |
| 1893–1894 | Glentoran |
| 1892–1893 | Linfield |
| 1891–1892 | Linfield |
| 1890–1891 | Linfield |

* Known as the Irish Football League until 2003.
** Not played 1915–1919 due to the First World War and 1941–1947 due to the Second World War.

## NORTHERN IRELAND: IRISH CUP

| | |
|---|---|
| 2006–2007 | Linfield |
| 2005–2006 | Linfield |
| 2004–2005 | Portadown |
| 2003–2004 | Glentoran |
| 2002–2003 | Coleraine |
| 2001–2002 | Linfield |
| 2000–2001 | Glentoran |
| 1999–2000 | Glentoran |
| 1998–1999 | Portadown awarded cup after Cliftonville's disqualification |
| 1997–1998 | Glentoran |
| 1996–1997 | Glenavon |
| 1995–1996 | Glentoran |
| 1994–1995 | Linfield |
| 1993–1994 | Linfield |
| 1992–1993 | Bangor |
| 1991–1992 | Glenavon |
| 1990–1991 | Portadown |
| 1989–1990 | Glentoran |
| 1988–1989 | Ballymena |
| 1987–1988 | Glentoran |
| 1986–1987 | Glentoran |
| 1985–1986 | Glentoran |
| 1984–1985 | Glentoran |
| 1983–1984 | Ballymena United |
| 1982–1983 | Glentoran |
| 1981–1982 | Linfield |
| 1980–1981 | Ballymena United |
| 1979–1980 | Linfield |
| 1978–1979 | Cliftonville |
| 1977–1978 | Linfield |
| 1976–1977 | Coleraine |
| 1975–1976 | Carrick Rangers |

| | |
|---|---|
| 1974–1975 | Coleraine |
| 1973–1974 | Ards |
| 1972–1973 | Glentoran |
| 1971–1972 | Coleraine |
| 1970–1971 | Distillery |
| 1969–1970 | Linfield |
| 1968–1969 | Ards |
| 1967–1968 | Crusaders |
| 1966–1967 | Crusaders |
| 1965–1966 | Glentoran |
| 1964–1965 | Coleraine |
| 1963–1964 | Derry City |
| 1962–1963 | Linfield |
| 1961–1962 | Linfield |
| 1960–1961 | Glenavon |
| 1959–1960 | Linfield |
| 1958–1959 | Glenavon |
| 1957–1958 | Ballymena United |
| 1956–1957 | Glenavon |
| 1955–1956 | Distillery |
| 1954–1955 | Dundela |
| 1953–1954 | Derry City |
| 1952–1953 | Linfield |
| 1951–1952 | Ards 1 |
| 1950–1951 | Glentoran |
| 1949–1950 | Linfield |
| 1948–1949 | Derry City |
| 1947–1948 | Linfield |
| 1946–1947 | Belfast Celtic |
| 1945–1946 | Linfield |
| 1944–1945 | Linfield |
| 1943–1944 | Belfast Celtic |
| 1942–1943 | Belfast Celtic |
| 1941–1942 | Linfield |
| 1940–1941 | Belfast Celtic |
| 1939–1940 | United |
| 1938–1939 | Linfield |
| 1937–1938 | Belfast Celtic |
| 1936–1937 | Belfast Celtic |
| 1935–1936 | Linfield |
| 1934–1935 | Glentoran |
| 1933–1934 | Linfield |
| 1932–1933 | Glentoran |
| 1931–1932 | Glentoran |
| 1930–1931 | Linfield |
| 1929–1930 | Linfield |
| 1928–1929 | Ballymena United |
| 1927–1928 | Willowfield |
| 1926–1927 | Ards |
| 1925–1926 | Belfast Celtic |
| 1924–1925 | Distillery |
| 1923–1924 | Queen's Island |
| 1922–1923 | Linfield |
| 1921–1922 | Linfield |
| 1920–1921 | Glentoran |
| 1919–1920 | Shelbourne awarded cup after Belfast Celtic and Glentoran were expelled from the competition |
| 1918–1919 | Linfield |
| 1917–1918 | Belfast Celtic |
| 1916–1917 | Glentoran |
| 1915–1916 | Linfield |
| 1914–1915 | Linfield |
| 1913–1914 | Glentoran |
| 1912–1913 | Linfield |
| 1911–1912 | Linfield awarded cup after withdrawal of others |
| 1910–1911 | Shelbourne |
| 1909–1910 | Distillery |

| | |
|---|---|
| 1908–1909 | Cliftonville |
| 1907–1908 | Bohemians |
| 1906–1907 | Cliftonville |
| 1905–1906 | Shelbourne |
| 1904–1905 | Distillery |
| 1903–1904 | Linfield |
| 1902–1903 | Distillery |
| 1901–1902 | Linfield |
| 1900–1901 | Cliftonville |
| 1899–1900 | Cliftonville |
| 1898–1899 | Linfield |
| 1897–1898 | Linfield |
| 1896–1897 | Cliftonville |
| 1895–1896 | Distillery |
| 1894–1895 | Linfield |
| 1893–1894 | Distillery |
| 1892–1893 | Linfield |
| 1891–1892 | Linfield |
| 1890–1891 | Linfield |
| 1889–1890 | Gordon Highlanders |
| 1888–1889 | Distillery |
| 1887–1888 | Cliftonville |
| 1886–1887 | Ulster |
| 1885–1886 | Distillery |
| 1884–1885 | Distillery |
| 1883–1884 | Distillery |
| 1882–1883 | Cliftonville |
| 1881–1882 | Queen's Island |
| 1880–1881 | Moyola Park |

## NORTHERN IRELAND: LEAGUE TOP SCORERS

| | |
|---|---|
| 2006–2007 | Gary Hamilton (Glentoran) 27 |
| 2005–2006 | Peter Thompson (Linfield) 25 |
| 2004–2005 | Chris Morgan (Glentoran) 19 |
| 2003–2004 | Glenn Ferguson (Linfield) 25 |
| 2002–2003 | Vinny Arkins (Portadown) 29 |
| 2001–2002 | Vinny Arkins (Portadown) 30 |
| 2000–2001 | Davy Larmour (Linfield) 17 |
| 1999–2000 | Vinny Arkins (Portadown) 29 |
| 1998–1999 | Vinny Arkins (Portadown) 19 |
| 1997–1998 | Vinny Arkins (Portadown) 22 |
| 1996–1997 | Garry Haylock (Portadown) 16 |
| 1995–1996 | Garry Haylock (Portadown) 19 |
| 1994–1995 | Glenn Ferguson (Glenavon) 27 |
| 1993–1994 | Darren Erskine (Ards) 22, Stephen McBride (Glenavon) 22 |
| 1992–1993 | Stevie Cowan (Portadown) 27 |
| 1991–1992 | Harry McCourt (Omagh Town) 18, Stephen McBride (Glenavon) 18 |
| 1990–1991 | Stephen McBride (Glenavon) 22 |
| 1989–1990 | Martin McGaughey (Linfield) 19 |
| 1988–1989 | Stephen Baxter (Linfield) 17 |

| | |
|---|---|
| 1987–1988 | Martin McGaughey (Linfield) 18 |
| 1986–1987 | Ray McCoy (Coleraine) 14, Gary McCartney (Glentoran) 14 |
| 1985–1986 | Trevor Anderson (Linfield) 14 |
| 1984–1985 | Martin McGaughey (Linfield) 34 |
| 1983–1984 | Martin McGaughey (Linfield) 15, Trevor Anderson (Linfield) 15 |
| 1982–1983 | Jim Campbell (Ards) 15 |
| 1981–1982 | Gary Blackledge (Glentoran) 18 |
| 1980–1981 | Des Dickson (Coleraine) 18, Paul Malone (Ballymena United) 18 |
| 1979–1980 | Jimmy Martin (Glentoran) 17 |
| 1978–1979 | Tommy Armstrong (Ards) 21 |
| 1977–1978 | Warren Feeney (Glentoran) 17 |
| 1976–1977 | Ronnie McAteer (Crusaders) 20 |
| 1975–1976 | Des Dickson (Coleraine) 23 |
| 1974–1975 | Martin Malone (Portadown) 19 |
| 1973–1974 | Des Dickson (Coleraine) 24 |
| 1972–1973 | Des Dickson (Coleraine) 23 |
| 1971–1972 | Peter Watson (Distillery) 15, Des Dickson (Coleraine) 15 |
| 1970–1971 | Bryan Hamilton (Linfield) 18 |
| 1969–1970 | Des Dickson (Coleraine) 21 |
| 1968–1969 | Danny Hale (Derry City) 21 |
| 1967–1968 | Sammy Pavis (Linfield) 30 |
| 1966–1967 | Sammy Pavis (Linfield) 25 |
| 1965–1966 | Sammy Pavis (Linfield) 28 |
| 1964–1965 | Kenny Halliday (Coleraine) 19, Dennis Guy (Glenavon) 19 |
| 1963–1964 | Trevor Thompson (Glentoran) 12 |
| 1962–1963 | Joe Meldrum (Distillery) 27 |
| 1961–1962 | Mick Lynch (Ards) 20 |
| 1960–1961 | Trevor Thompson (Glentoran) 22 |
| 1959–1960 | Jimmy Jones (Glenavon) 29 |
| 1958–1959 | Jackie Milburn (Linfield) 26 |
| 1957–1958 | Jackie Milburn (Linfield) 29 |
| 1956–1957 | Jimmy Jones (Glenavon) 33 |
| 1955–1956 | Jimmy Jones (Glenavon) 26 |
| 1954–1955 | Fay Coyle (Coleraine) 20 |
| 1953–1954 | Jimmy Jones (Glenavon) 32 |
| 1952–1953 | Sammy Hughes (Glentoran) 28 |
| 1951–1952 | Jimmy Jones (Glenavon) 27 |
| 1950–1951 | Sammy Hughes (Glentoran) 23, Walter Allen |

| | |
|---|---|
| | (Portadown) 23 |
| 1949–1950 | Sammy Hughes (Glentoran) 23 |
| 1948–1949 | Billy Simpson (Linfield) 19 |
| 1947–1948 | Jimmy Jones (Belfast Celtic) 28 |

## FRANCE LEAGUE 1 CHAMPIONS*

| | |
|---|---|
| 2006–2007 | Lyon |
| 2005–2006 | Lyon |
| 2004–2005 | Lyon |
| 2003–2004 | Lyon |
| 2002–2003 | Lyon |
| 2001–2002 | Lyon |
| 2000–2001 | Nantes |
| 1999–2000 | Monaco |
| 1998–1999 | Bordeaux |
| 1997–1998 | Lens |
| 1996–1997 | Monaco |
| 1995–1996 | Auxerre |
| 1994–1995 | Nantes |
| 1993–1994 | Paris Saint–Germain |
| 1992–1993 | No winner (Marseille stripped of title) |
| 1991–1992 | Marseille |
| 1990–1991 | Marseille |
| 1989–1990 | Marseille |
| 1988–1989 | Marseille |
| 1987–1988 | Monaco |
| 1986–1987 | Bordeaux |
| 1985–1986 | Paris Saint–Germain |
| 1984–1985 | Bordeaux |
| 1983–1984 | Bordeaux |
| 1982–1983 | Nantes |
| 1981–1982 | Monaco |
| 1980–1981 | Saint–Étienne |
| 1979–1980 | Nantes |
| 1978–1979 | Strasbourg |
| 1977–1978 | Monaco |
| 1976–1977 | Nantes |
| 1975–1976 | Saint–Étienne |
| 1974–1975 | Saint–Étienne |
| 1973–1974 | Saint–Étienne |
| 1972–1973 | Nantes |
| 1971–1972 | Marseille |
| 1970–1971 | Marseille |
| 1969–1970 | Saint–Étienne |
| 1968–1969 | Saint–Étienne |
| 1967–1968 | Saint–Étienne |
| 1966–1967 | Saint–Étienne |
| 1965–1966 | Nantes |
| 1964–1965 | Nantes |
| 1963–1964 | Saint–Étienne |
| 1962–1963 | Monaco |
| 1961–1962 | Stade Reims |
| 1960–1961 | Monaco |
| 1959–1960 | Stade Reims |
| 1958–1959 | Nice |
| 1957–1958 | Stade Reims |
| 1956–1957 | Saint–Étienne |
| 1955–1956 | Nice |
| 1954–1955 | Stade Reims |
| 1953–1954 | Lille |
| 1952–1953 | Stade Reims |
| 1951–1952 | Nice |
| 1950–1951 | Nice |
| 1949–1950 | Bordeaux |
| 1948–1949 | Stade Reims |
| 1947–1948 | Marseille |
| 1946–1947 | CO Roubaix–Tourcoing |

| | |
|---|---|
| 1945–1946 | Lille |
| 1938–1939 | Sète |
| 1937–1938 | Sochaux |
| 1936–1937 | Marseille |
| 1935–1936 | RCF Paris |
| 1934–1935 | Sochaux |
| 1933–1934 | Sète |
| 1932–1933 | Lille |

\* Not played 1939–1945 due to the Second World War.

## COUPE DE FRANCE (FRENCH CUP)

| | |
|---|---|
| 2007 | Sochaux |
| 2006 | Paris Saint–Germain |
| 2005 | Auxerre |
| 2004 | Paris Saint–Germain |
| 2003 | Auxerre |
| 2002 | Lorient |
| 2001 | RC Strasbourg |
| 2000 | Nantes |
| 1999 | Nantes |
| 1998 | Paris Saint–Germain |
| 1997 | Nice |
| 1996 | Auxerre |
| 1995 | Paris Saint–Germain |
| 1994 | Auxerre |
| 1993 | Paris Saint–Germain |
| 1992 | Not played due to Furiani Stadium disaster in Bastia |
| 1991 | Monaco |
| 1990 | Montpellier |
| 1989 | Marseille |
| 1988 | Metz |
| 1987 | Girondins |
| 1986 | Girondins |
| 1985 | Monaco |
| 1984 | Metz |
| 1983 | Paris Saint–Germain |
| 1982 | Paris Saint–Germain |
| 1981 | Bastia |
| 1980 | Monaco |
| 1979 | Nantes |
| 1978 | AS Nancy |
| 1977 | Saint–Étienne |
| 1976 | Marseille |
| 1975 | Saint–Étienne |
| 1974 | Saint–Étienne |
| 1973 | Lyon |
| 1972 | Marseille |
| 1971 | Rennes |
| 1970 | Saint–Étienne |
| 1969 | Marseille |
| 1968 | Saint–Étienne |
| 1967 | Lyon |
| 1966 | RC Strasbourg |
| 1965 | Rennes |
| 1964 | Lyon |
| 1963 | Monaco |
| 1962 | Saint–Étienne |
| 1961 | CS Sedan |
| 1960 | Monaco |
| 1959 | Le Havre |
| 1958 | Stade Reims |
| 1957 | Toulouse FC (1937) |
| 1956 | CS Sedan |
| 1955 | Lille |

| | |
|---|---|
| 1954 | Nice |
| 1953 | Lille |
| 1952 | Nice |
| 1951 | Strasbourg |
| 1950 | Stade Reims |
| 1949 | RCF Paris |
| 1948 | Lille |
| 1947 | Lille |
| 1946 | Lille |
| 1945 | RCF Paris |
| 1944 | ÉF Nancy–Lorraine |
| 1943 | Marseille |
| 1942 | Red Star |
| 1941 | Girondins |
| 1940 | RCF Paris |
| 1939 | RCF Paris |
| 1938 | Marseille |
| 1937 | Sochaux |
| 1936 | RCF Paris |
| 1935 | Marseille |
| 1934 | Sète |
| 1933 | Excelsior AC Roubaix |
| 1932 | Cannes |
| 1931 | Club Français |
| 1930 | Sète |
| 1929 | Montpellier |
| 1928 | Red Star |
| 1927 | Marseille |
| 1926 | Marseille |
| 1925 | CASG Paris |
| 1924 | Marseille |
| 1923 | Red Star |
| 1922 | Red Star |
| 1921 | Red Star |
| 1920 | CA Paris |
| 1919 | CASG Paris |
| 1918 | Olympique de Paris |

## FRANCE: LEAGUE TOP SCORERS*

| | |
|---|---|
| 2006–2007 | Pauleta (Paris Saint–Germain) 15 |
| 2005–2006 | Pauleta (Paris Saint–Germain) 21 |
| 2004–2005 | Alexander Frei (Rennes) 20 |
| 2003–2004 | Djibril Cissé (Auxerre) 26 |
| 2002–2003 | Shabani Nonda (Monaco) 26 |
| 2001–2002 | Djibril Cissé (Auxerre) 22 Pauleta (Bordeaux) 22 |
| 2000–2001 | Sonny Anderson (Lyon) 22 |
| 1999–2000 | Sonny Anderson (Lyon) 23 |
| 1998–1999 | Sylvain Wiltord (Bordeaux) 22 |
| 1997–1998 | Stéphane Guivarc'h (Auxerre) 21 |
| 1996–1997 | Stéphane Guivarc'h (Rennes) 22 |
| 1995–1996 | Sonny Anderson (Monaco) 21 |
| 1994–1995 | Patrice Loko (Nantes) 22 |
| 1993–1994 | Youri Djorkaeff (Monaco) 20 Roger Boli (Lens) 20 Nicolas Ouédec(Nantes) 20 |
| 1992–1993 | Alen Boksic (Marseille) 22 |
| 1991–1992 | Jean–Pierre Papin |

| | |
|---|---|
| | (Marseille) 27 |
| 1990–1991 | Jean–Pierre Papin (Marseille) 23 |
| 1989–1990 | Jean–Pierre Papin (Marseille) 30 |
| 1988–1989 | Jean–Pierre Papin (Marseille) 22 |
| 1987–1988 | Jean–Pierre Papin (Marseille) 19 |
| 1986–1987 | Bernard Zénier (Metz) 18 |
| 1985–1986 | Jules Bocandé (Metz) 23 |
| 1984–1985 | Vahid Halilhodzic (Nantes) 28 |
| 1983–1984 | Patrice Garande (Auxerre) 21 Delio Onnis (Sporting Toulon Var) 21 |
| 1982–1983 | Vahid Halilhodzic (Nantes) 27 |
| 1981–1982 | Delio Onnis (Tours) 29 |
| 1980–1981 | Delio Onnis (Tours) 24 |
| 1979–1980 | Delio Onnis (Monaco) 21 Erwin Kostedde (Stade Laval) 21 |
| 1978–1979 | Carlos Bianchi (Paris Saint–Germain) 27 |
| 1977–1978 | Carlos Bianchi (Paris Saint–Germain) 37 |
| 1976–1977 | Carlos Bianchi (Stade Reims) 28 |
| 1975–1976 | Carlos Bianchi (Stade Reims) 34 |
| 1974–1975 | Delio Onnis (Monaco) 30 |
| 1973–1974 | Carlos Bianchi (Stade Reims) 30 |
| 1972–1973 | Josip Skoblar (Marseille) 26 |
| 1971–1972 | Josip Skoblar (Marseille) 30 |
| 1970–1971 | Josip Skoblar (Marseille) 44 |
| 1969–1970 | Hervé Revelli (Saint–Étienne) 28 |
| 1968–1969 | André Guy (Lyon) 25 |
| 1967–1968 | Étienne Sansonetti (AC Ajaccio) 26 |
| 1966–1967 | Hervé Revelli (Saint–Étienne) 31 |
| 1965–1966 | Philippe Gondet (Nantes) 36 |
| 1964–1965 | Jacques Simon (Nantes) 24 |
| 1963–1964 | Ahmed Oudjani (Lens) 30 |
| 1962–1963 | Serge Masnaghetti (Valenciennes) 35 |
| 1961–1962 | Sékou Touré (Montpellier HSC) 25 |
| 1960–1961 | Roger Piantoni (Stade Reims) 28 |
| 1959–1960 | Just Fontaine (Stade Reims) 28 |
| 1958–1959 | Tadeusz Cisowski (RCF Paris) 30 |
| 1957–1958 | Just Fontaine (Stade Reims) 34 |
| 1956–1957 | Tadeusz Cisowski (RCF Paris) 33 |
| 1955–1956 | Tadeusz Cisowski (RCF Paris) 31 |
| 1954–1955 | René Bliard (Stade Reims) 30 |

| | |
|---|---|
| 1953–1954 | Édouard Kargulewicz (Bordeaux) 27 |
| 1952–1953 | Gunnar Andersson (Marseille) 35 |
| 1951–1952 | Gunnar Andersson (Marseille) 31 |
| 1950–1951 | Roger Piantoni (FC Nancy) 28 |
| 1949–1950 | Jean Grumellon (Rennes) 24 |
| 1948–1949 | Jean Baratte (Lille) 26 Jozef Humpal (Sochaux) 26 |
| 1947–1948 | Jean Baratte (Lille) 31 |
| 1946–1947 | Pierre Sinibaldi (Stade Reims) 33 |
| 1945–1946 | René Bihel (Lille) 28 |
| 1938–1939 | Roger Courtois (Sochaux) 27 Désiré Koranyi (Sète) 27 |
| 1937–1938 | Jean Nicolas (Rouen) 26 |
| 1936–1937 | Oskar Rohr (Strasbourg) 30 |
| 1935–1936 | Roger Courtois (Sochaux) 34 |
| 1934–1935 | André Abbeglen (Sochaux) 30 |
| 1933–1934 | István Lukacs (Sète) 28 |
| 1932–1933 | Robert Mercier (Club Français) 15 Walter Kaiser (Rennes) 15 |

\* Not played 1939–1945 due to the Second World War.

## ITALY: SERIE A CHAMPIONS*

| | |
|---|---|
| 2006–2007 | Internazionale |
| 2005–2006 | Internazionale (Juventus stripped of title) |
| 2004–2005 | Not awarded (Juventus stripped of title) |
| 2003–2004 | AC Milan |
| 2002–2003 | Juventus |
| 2001–2002 | Juventus |
| 2000–2001 | Roma |
| 1999–2000 | Lazio |
| 1998–1999 | AC Milan |
| 1997–1998 | Juventus |
| 1996–1997 | Juventus |
| 1995–1996 | AC Milan |
| 1994–1995 | Juventus |
| 1993–1994 | AC Milan |
| 1992–1993 | AC Milan |
| 1991–1992 | AC Milan |
| 1990–1991 | Sampdoria |
| 1989–1990 | Napoli |
| 1988–1989 | Internazionale |
| 1987–1988 | AC Milan |
| 1986–1987 | Napoli |
| 1985–1986 | Juventus |
| 1984–1985 | Hellas Verona |
| 1983–1984 | Juventus |
| 1982–1983 | Roma |
| 1981–1982 | Juventus |
| 1980–1981 | Juventus |
| 1979–1980 | Internazionale |
| 1978–1979 | AC Milan |
| 1977–1978 | Juventus |
| 1976–1977 | Juventus |

| | |
|---|---|
| 1975–1976 | Torino |
| 1974–1975 | Juventus |
| 1973–1974 | Lazio |
| 1972–1973 | Juventus |
| 1971–1972 | Juventus |
| 1970–1971 | Internazionale |
| 1969–1970 | Cagliari |
| 1968–1969 | Fiorentina |
| 1967–1968 | AC Milan |
| 1966–1967 | Juventus |
| 1965–1966 | Internazionale |
| 1964–1965 | Internazionale |
| 1963–1964 | Bologna |
| 1962–1963 | Internazionale |
| 1961–1962 | AC Milan |
| 1960–1961 | Juventus |
| 1959–1960 | Juventus |
| 1958–1959 | AC Milan |
| 1957–1958 | Juventus |
| 1956–1957 | AC Milan |
| 1955–1956 | Fiorentina |
| 1954–1955 | AC Milan |
| 1953–1954 | Internazionale |
| 1952–1953 | Internazionale |
| 1951–1952 | Juventus |
| 1950–1951 | AC Milan |
| 1949–1950 | Juventus |
| 1948–1949 | Torino |
| 1947–1948 | Torino |
| 1946–1947 | Torino |
| 1945–1946 | Torino |
| 1942–1943 | Torino |
| 1941–1942 | Roma |
| 1940–1941 | Bologna |
| 1939–1940 | Ambrosiana–Inter |
| 1938–1939 | Bologna |
| 1937–1938 | Ambrosiana–Inter |
| 1936–1937 | Bologna |
| 1935–1936 | Bologna |
| 1934–1935 | Juventus |
| 1933–1934 | Juventus |
| 1932–1933 | Juventus |
| 1931–1932 | Juventus |
| 1930–1931 | Juventus |
| 1929–1930 | Ambrosiana–Inter |
| 1928–1929 | Bologna |
| 1927–1928 | Torino |
| 1926–1927 | Not awarded (Torino stripped of title) |
| 1925–1926 | Juventus |
| 1924–1925 | Bologna |
| 1923–1924 | Genoa |
| 1922–1923 | Genoa |
| 1921–1922 | Pro Vercelli (awarded by the CCI federation) US Novese (awarded by the FIGC federation) |
| 1920–1921 | Pro Vercelli |
| 1919–1920 | Internazionale |
| 1914–1915 | Genoa |
| 1913–1914 | AS Casale |
| 1912–1913 | Pro Vercelli |
| 1911–1912 | Pro Vercelli |
| 1910–1911 | Pro Vercelli |
| 1909–1910 | Internazionale |
| 1909 | Pro Vercelli |
| 1908 | Pro Vercelli |
| 1907 | AC Milan |
| 1906 | AC Milan |
| 1905 | Juventus |

| | |
|---|---|
| 1904 | Genoa |
| 1903 | Genoa |
| 1902 | Genoa |
| 1901 | AC Milan |
| 1900 | Genoa |
| 1899 | Genoa |
| 1898 | Genoa |

* Not played 1915–1919 due to the First World War and 1943–1945 due to the Second World War.

## COPPA ITALIA (ITALIAN CUP)

| | |
|---|---|
| 2006–2007 | Roma |
| 2005–2006 | Internazionale |
| 2004–2005 | Internazionale |
| 2003–2004 | Lazio |
| 2002–2003 | AC Milan |
| 2001–2002 | Parma |
| 2000–2001 | Fiorentina |
| 1999–2000 | Lazio |
| 1998–1999 | Parma |
| 1997–1998 | Lazio |
| 1996–1997 | Vicenza |
| 1995–1996 | Fiorentina |
| 1994–1995 | Juventus |
| 1993–1994 | Sampdoria |
| 1992–1993 | Torino |
| 1991–1992 | Parma |
| 1990–1991 | Roma |
| 1989–1990 | Juventus |
| 1988–1989 | Sampdoria |
| 1987–1988 | Sampdoria |
| 1986–1987 | Napoli |
| 1985–1986 | Roma |
| 1984–1985 | Sampdoria |
| 1983–1984 | Roma |
| 1982–1983 | Juventus |
| 1981–1982 | Internazionale |
| 1980–1981 | Roma |
| 1979–1980 | Roma |
| 1978–1979 | Juventus |
| 1977–1978 | Internazionale |
| 1976–1977 | AC Milan |
| 1975–1976 | Napoli |
| 1974–1975 | Fiorentina |
| 1973–1974 | Bologna |
| 1972–1973 | AC Milan |
| 1971–1972 | AC Milan |
| 1970–1971 | Torino |
| 1969–1970 | Bologna |
| 1968–1969 | Roma |
| 1967–1968 | Torino |
| 1966–1967 | AC Milan |
| 1965–1966 | Fiorentina |
| 1964–1965 | Juventus |
| 1963–1964 | Roma |
| 1962–1963 | Atalanta |
| 1961–1962 | Napoli |
| 1960–1961 | Fiorentina |
| 1959–1960 | Juventus |
| 1958–1959 | Juventus |
| 1957–1958 | Lazio |
| 1942–1943 | Torino |
| 1941–1942 | Juventus |
| 1940–1941 | Venezia |
| 1939–1940 | Fiorentina |
| 1938–1939 | Internazionale |
| 1937–1938 | Juventus |
| 1936–1937 | Genoa |
| 1935–1936 | Torino |

## ITALY: LEAGUE TOP SCORERS*

| | |
|---|---|
| 2006–2007 | Francesco Totti (Roma) 26 |
| 2005–2006 | Luca Toni (Fiorentina) 31 |
| 2004–2005 | Cristiano Lucarelli (Livorno) 24 Alberto Gilardino (Parma) 24 |
| 2003–2004 | Andriy Shevchenko (AC Milan) 24 |
| 2002–2003 | Christian Vieri (Internazionale) 24 |
| 2001–2002 | David Trézéguet (Juventus) 24 Dario Hubner (Piacenza) 24 |
| 2000–2001 | Hernán Crespo (Lazio) 26 |
| 1999–2000 | Andriy Shevchenko (AC Milan) 24 |
| 1998–1999 | Márcio Amoroso (Udinese) 22 |
| 1997–1998 | Oliver Bierhoff (Udinese) 27 |
| 1996–1997 | Filippo Inzaghi (Atalanta) 24 |
| 1995–1996 | Giuseppe Signori (Lazio) 24 Igor Protti (Bari) 24 |
| 1994–1995 | Gabriel Batistuta (Fiorentina) 26 |
| 1993–1994 | Giuseppe Signori (Lazio) 23 |
| 1992–1993 | Giuseppe Signori (Lazio) 26 |
| 1991–1992 | Marco van Basten (AC Milan) 25 |
| 1990–1991 | Gianluca Vialli (Sampdoria) 17 |
| 1989–1990 | Marco van Basten (AC Milan) 19 |
| 1988–1989 | Aldo Serena (Internazionale) 22 |
| 1987–1988 | Diego Maradona (Napoli) 15 |
| 1986–1987 | Pietro Paolo Virdis (AC Milan) 17 |
| 1985–1986 | Roberto Pruzzo (Roma) 19 |
| 1984–1985 | Michel Platini (Juventus) 18 |
| 1983–1984 | Michel Platini (Juventus) 20 |
| 1982–1983 | Michel Platini (Juventus) 16 |
| 1981–1982 | Roberto Pruzzo (Roma) 15 |
| 1980–1981 | Roberto Pruzzo (Roma) 18 |
| 1979–1980 | Roberto Bettega (Juventus) 16 |
| 1978–1979 | Bruno Giordano (Lazio) 19 |
| 1977–1978 | Paolo Rossi (Vicenza) 24 |
| 1976–1977 | Francesco Graziani (Torino) 21 |
| 1975–1976 | Paolino Pulici (Torino) 21 |
| 1974–1975 | Paolino Pulici (Torino) 18 |
| 1973–1974 | Giorgio Chinaglia (Lazio) 24 |
| 1972–1973 | Paolino Pulici (Torino) 17 Gianni Rivera (AC Milan) 17 Giuseppe Savoldi (Bologna) 17 |
| 1971–1972 | Roberto Boninsegna (Internazionale) 22 |
| 1970–1971 | Roberto Boninsegna (Internazionale) 24 |
| 1969–1970 | Gigi Riva (Cagliari) 21 |
| 1968–1969 | Gigi Riva (Cagliari) 20 |
| 1967–1968 | Pierino Prati (AC Milan) 15 |
| 1966–1967 | Gigi Riva (Cagliari) 18 |
| 1965–1966 | Luis Vinicio (Vicenza) 25 |
| 1964–1965 | Sandro Mazzola (Internazionale) 17 Alberto Orlando (Fiorentina) 17 |
| 1963–1964 | Harald Nielsen (Bologna) 21 |
| 1962–1963 | Pedro Manfredini (Roma) 19 Harald Nielsen (Bologna) 19 |
| 1961–1962 | José Altafini (AC Milan) 22 Aurelio Milani (Fiorentina) 22 |
| 1960–1961 | Sergio Brighenti (Sampdoria) 27 |
| 1959–1960 | Omar Sivori (Juventus) 27 |
| 1958–1959 | Antonio Valentin Angelillo (Internazionale) 33 |
| 1957–1958 | John Charles (Juventus) 28 |
| 1956–1957 | Dino Da Costa (Roma) 22 |
| 1955–1956 | Gino Pivatelli (Bologna) 29 |
| 1954–1955 | Gunnar Nordahl (AC Milan) 27 |
| 1953–1954 | Gunnar Nordahl (AC Milan) 23 |
| 1952–1953 | Gunnar Nordahl (AC Milan) 26 |
| 1951–1952 | John Hansen (Juventus) 30 |
| 1950–1951 | Gunnar Nordahl (AC Milan) 34 |
| 1949–1950 | Gunnar Nordahl (AC Milan) 35 |
| 1948–1949 | Stefano Nyers (Internazionale) 26 |
| 1947–1948 | Giampiero Boniperti (Juventus) 27 |
| 1946–1947 | Valentino Mazzola (Torino) 29 |
| 1945–1946 | Eusebio Castigliano (Torino) 13 |
| 1942–1943 | Silvio Piola (Lazio) 21 |
| 1941–1942 | Aldo Boffi (AC Milan) 22 |
| 1940–1941 | Ettore Puricelli (Bologna) 22 |
| 1939–1940 | Aldo Boffi (AC Milan) 24 |
| 1938–1939 | Aldo Boffi (AC Milan) 19 Ettore Puricelli (Bologna) 19 |
| 1937–1938 | Giuseppe Meazza (Internazionale) 20 |
| 1936–1937 | Silvio Piola (Lazio) 21 |
| 1935–1936 | Giuseppe Meazza (Internazionale) 25 |
| 1934–1935 | Enrico Guaita (Roma) 28 |
| 1933–1934 | Felice Borel (Juventus) 31 |
| 1932–1933 | Felice Borel (Juventus) 29 |
| 1931–1932 | Pedro Petrone (Fiorentina) 25 Angelo Schiavio (Bologna) 25 |
| 1930–1931 | Rodolfo Volk (Roma) 29 |
| 1929–1930 | Giuseppe Meazza (Internazionale) 31 |

* Not played 1943–1945 due to the 2nd World War.

## GERMANY: BUNDELIGA CHAMPIONS

| | |
|---|---|
| 2006–2007 | VfB Stuttgart |
| 2005–2006 | Bayern Munich |
| 2004–2005 | Bayern Munich |
| 2003–2004 | Werder Bremen |
| 2002–2003 | Bayern Munich |
| 2001–2002 | Borussia Dortmund |
| 2000–2001 | Bayern Munich |

| | |
|---|---|
| 1923–1935 | Not played |
| 1922 | Vado |

**1999–2000** Bayern Munich
**1998–1999** Bayern Munich
**1997–1998** Kaiserslautern
**1996–1997** Bayern Munich
**1995–1996** Borussia Dortmund
**1994–1995** Borussia Dortmund
**1993–1994** Bayern Munich
**1992–1993** Werder Bremen
**1991–1992** VfB Stuttgart
**1990–1991** Kaiserslautern
**1989–1990** Bayern Munich
**1988–1989** Bayern Munich
**1987–1988** Werder Bremen
**1986–1987** Bayern Munich
**1985–1986** Bayern Munich
**1984–1985** Bayern Munich
**1983–1984** VfB Stuttgart
**1982–1983** Hamburg
**1981–1982** Hamburg
**1980–1981** Bayern Munich
**1979–1980** Bayern Munich
**1978–1979** Hamburg
**1977–1978** Köln
**1976–1977** Borussia Mönchengladbach
**1975–1976** Borussia Mönchengladbach
**1974–1975** Borussia Mönchengladbach
**1973–1974** Bayern Munich
**1972–1973** Bayern Munich
**1971–1972** Bayern Munich
**1970–1971** Borussia Mönchengladbach
**1969–1970** Borussia Mönchengladbach
**1968–1969** Bayern Munich
**1967–1968** Nürnberg
**1966–1967** Eintracht Braunschweig
**1965–1966** 1860 Munich
**1964–1965** Werder Bremen
**1963–1964** Köln

## GERMANY: DFB–POKAL (GERMAN CUP)

**2007** Nürnberg
**2006** Bayern Munich
**2005** Bayern Munich
**2004** Werder Bremen
**2003** Bayern Munich
**2002** Schalke
**2001** Schalke
**2000** Bayern Munich
**1999** Werder Bremen
**1998** Bayern Munich
**1997** VfB Stuttgart
**1996** Kaiserslautern
**1995** Borussia Mönchengladbach
**1994** Werder Bremen
**1993** Bayer Leverkusen
**1992** Hannover 96
**1991** Werder Bremen
**1990** Kaiserslautern
**1989** Borussia Dortmund
**1988** Eintracht Frankfurt
**1987** Hamburg
**1986** Bayern Munich

**1985** Bayer Uerdingen
**1984** Bayern Munich
**1983** Köln
**1982** Bayern Munich
**1981** Eintracht Frankfurt
**1980** Fortuna Düsseldorf
**1979** Fortuna Düsseldorf
**1978** Köln
**1977** Köln
**1976** Hamburg
**1975** Eintracht Frankfurt
**1974** Frankfurt
**1973** Borussia Mönchengladbach
**1972** Schalke
**1971** Bayern Munich
**1970** Kickers Offenbach
**1969** Bayern Munich
**1968** Köln
**1967** Bayern Munich
**1966** Bayern Munich
**1965** Borussia Dortmund
**1964** 1860 Munich
**1963** Hamburg
**1962** Nürnberg
**1961** Werder Bremen
**1960** Borussia Mönchengladbach
**1959** Schwarz–Weiss Essen
**1958** Stuttgart
**1957** Bayern Munich
**1956** Karlsruher
**1955** Karlsruher
**1954** VfB Stuttgart
**1953** Rot–Weiss Essen
**1944–1952** Not played
**1943** First Vienna
**1942** 1860 Munich
**1941** Dresdner SC
**1940** Dresdner SC
**1939** Nürnberg
**1938** Rapid Vienna
**1937** Schalke
**1936** VfB Leipzig
**1935** Nürnberg

## GERMANY: TOP SCORERS

**2006–2007** Theofanis Gekas (VfL Bochum) 20
**2005–2006** Miroslav Klose (Werder Bremen) 25
**2004–2005** Marek Mintál (Nürnberg) 24
**2003–2004** Ailton (Werder Bremen) 28
**2002–2003** Thomas Christiansen (VfL Bochum) 21
Giovane Elber (Bayern Munich) 21
**2001–2002** Márcio Amoroso (Borussia Dortmund) 18
Martin Max (1860 Munich) 18
**2000–2001** Sergej Barbarez (Hamburg) 22
Ebbe Sand (Schalke) 22
**1999–2000** Martin Max (1860 Munich) 19
**1998–1999** Michael Preetz (Hertha Berlin) 23
**1997–1998** Ulf Kirsten

(Bayer Leverkusen) 22
**1996–1997** Ulf Kirsten (Bayer Leverkusen) 22
**1995–1996** Fredi Bobic (VfB Stuttgart) 17
**1994–1995** Mario Basler (Werder Bremen) 20
Heiko Herrlich (Borussia Mönchengladbach) 20
**1993–1994** Stefan Kuntz (Kaiserslautern) 18
Tony Yeboah (Eintracht Frankfurt) 18
**1992–1993** Ulf Kirsten (Bayer Leverkusen) 20
Tony Yeboah (Eintracht Frankfurt) 20
**1991–1992** Fritz Walter (VfB Stuttgart) 22
**1990–1991** Roland Wohlfarth (Bayern Munich) 21
**1989–1990** Jørn Andersen (Eintracht Frankfurt) 18
**1988–1989** Thomas Allofs (Köln) 17
Roland Wohlfarth (Bayern Munich) 17
**1987–1988** Jürgen Klinsmann (VfB Stuttgart) 19
**1986–1987** Uwe Rahn (Borussia Mönchengladbach) 24
**1985–1986** Stefan Kuntz (VfL Bochum) 22
**1984–1985** Klaus Allofs (Köln) 26
**1983–1984** Karl–Heinz Rummenigge (Bayern Munich) 26
**1982–1983** Rudolf Völler (Werder Bremen) 23
**1981–1982** Horst Hrubesch (Hamburg) 27
**1980–1981** Karl–Heinz Rummenigge (Bayern Munich) 29
**1979–1980** Karl–Heinz Rummenigge (Bayern Munich) 26
**1978–1979** Klaus Allofs (Fortuna Düsseldorf) 22
**1977–1978** Dieter Müller (Köln) 24
Gerd Müller (Bayern Munich) 24
**1976–1977** Dieter Müller (Köln) 34
**1975–1976** Klaus Fischer (Schalke) 29
**1974–1975** Jupp Heynckes (Borussia Mönchengladbach) 27
**1973–1974** Gerd Müller (Bayern Munich) 30
Jupp Heynckes (Borussia Mönchengladbach) 30
**1972–1973** Gerd Müller (Bayern Munich) 36
**1971–1972** Gerd Müller (Bayern Munich) 40
**1970–1971** Lothar Kobluhn (Rot–Weiß Oberhausen) 24
**1969–1970** Gerd Müller (Bayern Munich) 38
**1968–1969** Gerd Müller (Bayern Munich) 30
**1967–1968** Johannes Löhr (Köln) 27

**1966–1967** Lothar Emmerich (Borussia Dortmund) 28
Gerd Müller (Bayern Munich) 28
**1965–1966** Lothar Emmerich (Borussia Dortmund) 31
**1964–1965** Rudolf Brunnenmeier (1860 Munich) 24
**1963–1964** Uwe Seeler (Hamburg) 30

## NETHERLANDS: EREDIVISIE CHAMPIONS

**2006–2007** PSV Eindhoven
**2005–2006** PSV Eindhoven
**2004–2005** PSV Eindhoven
**2003–2004** Ajax
**2002–2003** PSV Eindhoven
**2001–2002** Ajax
**2000–2001** PSV Eindhoven
**1999–2000** PSV Eindhoven
**1998–1999** Feyenoord
**1997–1998** Ajax
**1996–1997** PSV Eindhoven
**1995–1996** Ajax
**1994–1995** Ajax
**1993–1994** Ajax
**1992–1993** Feyenoord
**1991–1992** PSV Eindhoven
**1990–1991** PSV Eindhoven
**1989–1990** Ajax
**1988–1989** PSV Eindhoven
**1987–1988** PSV Eindhoven
**1986–1987** PSV Eindhoven
**1985–1986** PSV Eindhoven
**1984–1985** Ajax
**1983–1984** Feyenoord
**1982–1983** Ajax
**1981–1982** Ajax
**1980–1981** AZ Alkmaar
**1979–1980** Ajax
**1978–1979** Ajax
**1977–1978** PSV Eindhoven
**1976–1977** Ajax
**1975–1976** PSV Eindhoven
**1974–1975** PSV Eindhoven
**1973–1974** Feyenoord
**1972–1973** Ajax
**1971–1972** Ajax
**1970–1971** Feyenoord
**1969–1970** Ajax
**1968–1969** Feyenoord
**1967–1968** Ajax
**1966–1967** Ajax
**1965–1966** Ajax
**1964–1965** Feyenoord
**1963–1964** DWS
**1962–1963** PSV Eindhoven
**1961–1962** Feyenoord
**1960–1961** Feyenoord
**1959–1960** Ajax
**1958–1959** Sparta Rotterdam
**1957–1958** DOS
**1956–1957** Ajax
**1955–1956** Rapid JC
**1954–1955** Willem II
**1953–1954** FC Eindhoven
**1952–1953** RCH

| | |
|---|---|
| 1951–1952 | Willem II |
| 1950–1951 | PSV Eindhoven |
| 1949–1950 | Limburgia |
| 1948–1949 | SVV |
| 1947–1948 | BVV |
| 1946–1947 | Ajax |
| 1945–1946 | HFC Haarlem |
| 1943–1944 | Volewijckers |
| 1942–1943 | ADO Den Haag |
| 1941–1942 | ADO Den Haag |
| 1940–1941 | Heracles |
| 1939–1940 | Feyenoord |
| 1938–1939 | Ajax |
| 1937–1938 | Feyenoord |
| 1936–1937 | Ajax |
| 1935–1936 | Feyenoord |
| 1934–1935 | PSV Eindhoven |
| 1933–1934 | Ajax |
| 1932–1933 | Go Ahead |
| 1931–1932 | Ajax |
| 1930–1931 | Ajax |
| 1929–1930 | Go Ahead |
| 1928–1929 | PSV Eindhoven |
| 1927–1928 | Feyenoord |
| 1926–1927 | Heracles |
| 1925–1926 | Sportclub Enschede |
| 1924–1925 | HBS |
| 1923–1924 | Feyenoord |
| 1922–1923 | RCH |
| 1921–1922 | Go Ahead |
| 1920–1921 | NAC Breda |
| 1919–1920 | Be Quick |
| 1918–1919 | Ajax |
| 1917–1918 | Ajax |
| 1916–1917 | Go Ahead |
| 1915–1916 | Willem II |
| 1914–1915 | Sparta Rotterdam |
| 1913–1914 | Kon HVV |
| 1912–1913 | Sparta Rotterdam |
| 1911–1912 | Sparta Rotterdam |
| 1910–1911 | Sparta Rotterdam |
| 1909–1910 | Kon HVV |
| 1908–1909 | Sparta Rotterdam |
| 1907–1908 | Quick |
| 1906–1907 | Kon HVV |
| 1905–1906 | Kon HBS |
| 1904–1905 | Kon HVV |
| 1903–1904 | HBS |
| 1902–1903 | Kon HVV |
| 1901–1902 | Kon HVV |
| 1900–1901 | Kon HVV |
| 1899–1900 | Kon HVV |
| 1898–1899 | RAP |
| 1897–1898 | RAP |

## KNVB CUP (DUTCH CUP)

| | |
|---|---|
| 2006–2007 | Ajax |
| 2005–2006 | Ajax |
| 2004–2005 | PSV Eindhoven |
| 2003–2004 | Utrecht |
| 2002–2003 | Utrecht |
| 2001–2002 | Ajax |
| 2000–2001 | FC Twente |
| 1999–2000 | Roda JC |
| 1998–1999 | Ajax |
| 1997–1998 | Ajax |
| 1996–1997 | Roda JC |
| 1995–1996 | PSV Eindhoven |
| 1994–1995 | Feyenoord |
| 1993–1994 | Feyenoord |

| | |
|---|---|
| 1992–1993 | Ajax |
| 1991–1992 | Feyenoord |
| 1990–1991 | Feyenoord |
| 1989–1990 | PSV Eindhoven |
| 1988–1989 | PSV Eindhoven |
| 1987–1988 | PSV Eindhoven |
| 1986–1987 | Ajax |
| 1985–1986 | Ajax |
| 1984–1985 | Utrecht |
| 1983–1984 | Feyenoord |
| 1982–1983 | Ajax |
| 1981–1982 | AZ Alkmaar |
| 1980–1981 | AZ Alkmaar |
| 1979–1980 | Feyenoord |
| 1978–1979 | Ajax |
| 1977–1978 | AZ Alkmaar |
| 1976–1977 | FC Twente |
| 1975–1976 | PSV Eindhoven |
| 1974–1975 | FC Den Haag |
| 1973–1974 | PSV Eindhoven |
| 1972–1973 | NAC Breda |
| 1971–1972 | Ajax |
| 1970–1971 | Ajax |
| 1969–1970 | Ajax |
| 1968–1969 | Feyenoord |
| 1967–1968 | ADO Den Haag |
| 1966–1967 | Ajax |
| 1965–1966 | Sparta Rotterdam |
| 1964–1965 | Feyenoord |
| 1963–1964 | Fortuna Sittard |
| 1962–1963 | Willem II |
| 1961–1962 | Sparta Rotterdam |
| 1960–1961 | Ajax |
| 1959–19660 | Not played |
| 1958–1959 | VVV |
| 1957–1958 | Sparta Rotterdam |
| 1956–1957 | Fortuna Sittard |
| 1950–1956 | Not played |
| 1949–1950 | PSV Eindhoven |
| 1948–1949 | Quick |
| 1947–1948 | Wageningen |
| 1944–1947 | Not played |
| 1943–1944 | Willem II |
| 1942–1943 | Ajax |
| 1939–1942 | Not played |
| 1938–1939 | Wageningen |
| 1937–1938 | VSV |
| 1936–1937 | FC Eindhoven |
| 1935–1936 | Roermond |
| 1934–1935 | Feyenoord |
| 1933–1934 | Groningen |
| 1932–1933 | Not played |
| 1931–1932 | DFC |
| 1930–1931 | Not played |
| 1929–1930 | Feyenoord |
| 1928–1929 | Not played |
| 1927–1928 | RCH |
| 1926–1927 | VUC |
| 1925–1926 | LONGA |
| 1924–1925 | ZFC |
| 1923–1924 | Not played |
| 1922–1923 | Not played |
| 1921–1922 | Not played |
| 1920–1921 | Schoten |
| 1919–1920 | CVV |
| 1918–1919 | Not played |
| 1917–1918 | RCH |
| 1916–1917 | Ajax |
| 1915–1916 | Quick |
| 1914–1915 | HFC |

| | |
|---|---|
| 1913–1914 | DFC |
| 1912–1913 | HFC |
| 1911–1912 | Haarlem |
| 1910–1911 | Quick |
| 1909–1910 | Quick |
| 1908–1909 | Quick |
| 1907–1908 | HBS |
| 1906–1907 | VOC |
| 1905–1906 | Concordia |
| 1904–1905 | VOC |
| 1903–1904 | HFC |
| 1902–1903 | HVV |
| 1901–1902 | Haarlem |
| 1900–1901 | HBS |
| 1899–1900 | Velocitas Breda |
| 1898–1899 | RAP |

## NETHERLANDS: LEAGUE TOP SCORERS

| | |
|---|---|
| 2006–2007 | Afonso Alves (SSC Heerenveen) 34 |
| 2005–2006 | Klaas-Jan Huntelaar (SC Heerenveen and Ajax) 33 |
| 2004–2005 | Dirk Kuyt (Feyenoord) 29 |
| 2003–2004 | Mateja Kežman (PSV Eindhoven) 31 |
| 2002–2003 | Mateja Kežman (PSV Eindhoven) 35 |
| 2001–2002 | Pierre van Hooijdonk (Feyenoord) 24 |
| 2000–2001 | Mateza Kežman (PSV Eindhoven) 24 |
| 1999–2000 | Ruud van Nistelrooy (PSV Eindhoven) 29 |
| 1998–1999 | Ruud van Nistelrooy (PSV Eindhoven) 29 |
| 1997–1998 | Nikos Machlas (Vitesse) 34 |
| 1996–1997 | Luc Nilis (PSV Eindhoven) 21 |
| 1995–1996 | Luc Nilis (PSV Eindhoven) 21 |
| 1994–1995 | Ronaldo (PSV Eindhoven) 30 |
| 1993–1994 | Jari Litmanen (Ajax) 26 |
| 1992–1993 | Dennis Bergkamp (Ajax) 26 |
| 1991–1992 | Dennis Bergkamp (Ajax) 22 |
| 1990–1991 | Romário (PSV Eindhoven) 25 Dennis Bergkamp (Ajax) 25 |
| 1989–1990 | Romário (PSV Eindhoven) 23 |
| 1988–1989 | Romário (PSV Eindhoven) 19 |
| 1987–1988 | Wim Kieft (PSV Eindhoven) 29 |
| 1986–1987 | Marco van Basten (Ajax) 31 |
| 1985–1986 | Marco van Basten (Ajax) 37 |
| 1984–1985 | Marco van Basten (Ajax) 22 |
| 1983–1984 | Marco van Basten (Ajax) 28 |
| 1982–1983 | Peter Houtman (Feyenoord) 30 |
| 1981–1982 | Wim Kieft (Ajax) 32 |
| 1980–1981 | Ruud Geels (Sparta Rotterdam) 22 |
| 1979–1980 | Kees Kist (AZ Almaar) 27 |
| 1978–1979 | Kees Kist (AZ Alkmaar) 34 |
| 1977–1978 | Ruud Geels (Ajax) 30 |
| 1976–1977 | Ruud Geels (Ajax) 34 |
| 1975–1976 | Ruud Geels (Ajax) 29 |
| 1974–1975 | Ruud Geels (Ajax) 30 |
| 1973–1974 | Willy van der Kuijlen (PSV Eindhoven) 27 |
| 1972–1973 | Cas Janssens (NEC) 18 Willy Brokamp (MVV Maastricht) 18 |
| 1971–1972 | Johan Cruyff (Ajax) 25 |

| | |
|---|---|
| 1970–1971 | Ove Kindvall (Feyenoord) 24 |
| 1969–1970 | Willy van der Kuijlen (PSV Eindhoven) 26 |
| 1968–1969 | Dick van Dijk (FC Twente) 30 Ove Kindvall (Feyenoord) 30 |
| 1967–1968 | Ove Kindvall (Feyenoord) 28 |
| 1966–1967 | Johan Cruyff (Ajax) 33 |
| 1965–1966 | Willy van Kuijlen (PSV Eindhoven) 23 Piet Kruiver (Feyenoord) 23 |
| 1964–1965 | Frans Geurtsen (DWS) 23 |
| 1963–1964 | Frans Geurtsen (DWS) 28 |
| 1962–1963 | Pierre Kerkhofs (PSV Eindhoven) 22 |
| 1961–1962 | Dick Tol (Volendam) 27 |
| 1960–1961 | Henk Groot (Ajax) 41 |
| 1959–1960 | Henk Groot (Ajax) 38 |
| 1958–1959 | Leon Canjels (NAC Breda) 34 |
| 1957–1958 | Leo Canjels (NAC Breda) 32 |
| 1956–1957 | Coen Dillon (PSV Eindhoven) 43 |

## SPAIN: LA LIGA CHAMPIONS

| | |
|---|---|
| 2006–2007 | Real Madrid |
| 2005–2006 | Barcelona |
| 2004–2005 | Barcelona |
| 2003–2004 | Valencia |
| 2002–2003 | Real Madrid |
| 2001–2002 | Valencia |
| 2000–2001 | Real Madrid |
| 1999–2000 | Deportivo La Coruña |
| 1998–1999 | Barcelona |
| 1997–1998 | Barcelona |
| 1996–1997 | Real Madrid |
| 1995–1996 | Atlético Madrid |
| 1994–1995 | Real Madrid |
| 1993–1994 | Barcelona |
| 1992–1993 | Barcelona |
| 1991–1992 | Barcelona |
| 1990–1991 | Barcelona |
| 1989–1990 | Real Madrid |
| 1988–1989 | Real Madrid |
| 1987–1988 | Real Madrid |
| 1986–1987 | Real Madrid |
| 1985–1986 | Real Madrid |
| 1984–1985 | Barcelona |
| 1983–1984 | Athletic Bilbao |
| 1982–1983 | Athletic Bilbao |
| 1981–1982 | Real Sociedad |
| 1980–1981 | Real Sociedad |
| 1979–1980 | Real Madrid |
| 1978–1979 | Real Madrid |
| 1977–1978 | Real Madrid |
| 1976–1977 | Atlético Madrid |
| 1975–1976 | Real Madrid |
| 1974–1975 | Real Madrid |
| 1973–1974 | Barcelona |
| 1972–1973 | Atlético Madrid |
| 1971–1972 | Real Madrid |
| 1970–1971 | Valencia |
| 1969–1970 | Atlético Madrid |
| 1968–1969 | Real Madrid |
| 1967–1968 | Real Madrid |
| 1966–1967 | Real Madrid |
| 1965–1966 | Atlético Madrid |
| 1964–1965 | Real Madrid |
| 1963–1964 | Real Madrid |

| Season | Champion |
|---|---|
| 1962–1963 | Real Madrid |
| 1961–1962 | Real Madrid |
| 1960–1961 | Real Madrid |
| 1959–1960 | Barcelona |
| 1958–1959 | Barcelona |
| 1957–1958 | Real Madrid |
| 1956–1957 | Real Madrid |
| 1955–1956 | Athletic Bilbao |
| 1954–1955 | Real Madrid |
| 1953–1954 | Real Madrid |
| 1952–1953 | Barcelona |
| 1951–1952 | Barcelona |
| 1950–1951 | Atlético Madrid |
| 1949–1950 | Atlético Madrid |
| 1948–1949 | Barcelona |
| 1947–1948 | Barcelona |
| 1946–1947 | Valencia |
| 1945–1946 | Sevilla |
| 1944–1945 | Barcelona |
| 1943–1944 | Valencia |
| 1942–1943 | Athletic Bilbao |
| 1941–1942 | Valencia |
| 1940–1941 | Atlético Madrid |
| 1939–1940 | Atlético Madrid |
| 1936–1939 | Not played due to the Spanish Civil War |
| 1935–1936 | Athletic Bilbao |
| 1934–1935 | Real Betis |
| 1933–1934 | Athletic Bilbao |
| 1932–1933 | Real Madrid |
| 1931–1932 | Real Madrid |
| 1930–1931 | Athletic Bilbao |
| 1929–1930 | Athletic Bilbao |
| 1928–1929 | Barcelona |

## SPAIN: COPA DEL REY (SPANISH CUP)

|  |  |
|---|---|
| 2007 | Sevilla |
| 2006 | Espanyol |
| 2005 | Real Betis |
| 2004 | Real Zaragoza |
| 2003 | Mallorca |
| 2002 | Deportivo La Coruña |
| 2001 | Real Zaragoza |
| 2000 | Espanyol |
| 1999 | Valencia |
| 1998 | Barcelona |
| 1997 | Barcelona |
| 1996 | Atlético Madrid |
| 1995 | Deportivo La Coruña |
| 1994 | Real Zaragoza |
| 1993 | Real Madrid |
| 1992 | Atlético Madrid |
| 1991 | Atlético Madrid |
| 1990 | Barcelona |
| 1989 | Real Madrid |
| 1988 | Barcelona |
| 1987 | Real Sociedad |
| 1986 | Real Zaragoza |
| 1985 | Atlético Madrid |
| 1984 | Athletic Bilbao |
| 1983 | Barcelona |
| 1982 | Real Madrid |
| 1981 | Barcelona |
| 1980 | Real Madrid |
| 1979 | Valencia |
| 1978 | Barcelona |
| 1977 | Real Betis |
| 1976 | Atlético Madrid |
| 1975 | Real Madrid |
| 1974 | Real Madrid |
| 1973 | Athletic Bilbao |
| 1972 | Atlético Madrid |
| 1971 | Barcelona |
| 1970 | Real Madrid |
| 1969 | Athletic Bilbao |
| 1968 | Barcelona |
| 1967 | Valencia |
| 1966 | Real Zaragoza |
| 1965 | Atlético Madrid |
| 1964 | Real Zaragoza |
| 1963 | Barcelona |
| 1962 | Real Madrid |
| 1961 | Atlético Madrid |
| 1960 | Atlético Madrid |
| 1959 | Barcelona |
| 1958 | Athletic Bilbao |
| 1957 | Barcelona |
| 1956 | Athletic Bilbao |
| 1955 | Athletic Bilbao |
| 1954 | Valencia |
| 1953 | Barcelona |
| 1952 | Barcelona |
| 1951 | Barcelona |
| 1950 | Athletic Bilbao |
| 1949 | Valencia |
| 1948 | Sevilla |
| 1947 | Real Madrid |
| 1946 | Real Madrid |
| 1945 | Athletic Bilbao |
| 1944 | Athletic Bilbao |
| 1943 | Athletic Bilbao |
| 1942 | Barcelona |
| 1941 | Valencia |
| 1940 | Espanyol |
| 1939 | Sevilla |
| 1938 | Not played due to Spanish Civil War |
| 1937 | Not played due to Spanish Civil War |
| 1936 | Real Madrid |
| 1935 | Sevilla |
| 1934 | Real Madrid |
| 1933 | Athletic Bilbao |
| 1932 | Athletic Bilbao |
| 1931 | Athletic Bilbao |
| 1930 | Athletic Bilbao |
| 1929 | Espanyol |
| 1928 | Barcelona |
| 1927 | Real Unión |
| 1926 | Barcelona |
| 1925 | Barcelona |
| 1924 | Real Unión |
| 1923 | Athletic Bilbao |
| 1922 | Barcelona |
| 1921 | Athletic Bilbao |
| 1920 | Barcelona |
| 1919 | Arenas de Getxo |
| 1918 | Real Unión |
| 1917 | Real Madrid |
| 1916 | Athletic Bilbao |
| 1915 | Athletic Bilbao |
| 1914 | Athletic Bilbao |
| 1913 | Racing Irún |
| 1913 | Barcelona |
| 1912 | Barcelona |
| 1911 | Athletic Bilbao |
| 1910 | Barcelona |
| 1910 | Athletic Bilbao |
| 1909 | Ciclista (later Real Sociedad) |
| 1908 | Real Madrid |
| 1907 | Real Madrid |
| 1906 | Real Madrid |
| 1905 | Real Madrid |
| 1904 | Not played, Athletic Bilbao awarded the trophy |
| 1903 | Athletic Bilbao |
| 1902 | Club Vizcaya (later Athletic Bilbao) |

## SPAIN: LEAGUE TOP SCORERS

| Season | Player |
|---|---|
| 2006–2007 | Ruud van Nistelrooy (Real Madrid) 25 |
| 2005–2006 | Samuel Eto'o (Barcelona) 26 |
| 2004–2005 | Diego Forlán (Villareal) 25 |
| 2003–2004 | Ronaldo (Real Madrid) 24 |
| 2002–2003 | Roy Makaay (Deportivo La Coruña) 29 |
| 2001–2002 | Diego Tristán (Deportivo La Coruña) 21 |
| 2000–2001 | Raúl (Real Madrid) 24 |
| 1999–2000 | Salva Ballesta (Racing Santander) 27 |
| 1998–1999 | Raúl (Real Madrid) 23 |
| 1997–1998 | Christian Vieri (Atlético Madrid) 24 |
| 1996–1997 | Ronaldo (Barcelona) 34 |
| 1995–1996 | Juan Antonio Pizzi (Tenerife) 31 |
| 1994–1995 | Iván Zamorano (Real Madrid) 27 |
| 1993–1994 | Romário (Barcelona) 30 |
| 1992–1993 | Bebeto (Deportivo La Coruña) 29 |
| 1991–1992 | Manolo Sánchez (Atlético Madrid) 27 |
| 1990–1991 | Emilio Butragueño (Real Madrid) 19 |
| 1989–1990 | Hugo Sánchez (Real Madrid) 38 |
| 1988–1989 | Baltazar (Atlético Madrid) 35 |
| 1987–1988 | Hugo Sánchez (Real Madrid) 29 |
| 1986–1987 | Hugo Sánchez (Real Madrid) 34 |
| 1985–1986 | Hugo Sánchez (Atlético Madrid) 22 |
| 1984–1985 | Hugo Sánchez (Atlético Madrid) 19 |
| 1983–1984 | Jorge da Silva (Real Valladolid) 17 Juanito (Real Valladolid) 17 |
| 1982–1983 | Poli Rincón (Real Betis) 20 |
| 1981–1982 | Quini (Barcelona) 26 |
| 1980–1981 | Quini (Barcelona) 20 |
| 1979–1980 | Quini (Sporting Gijón) 24 |
| 1978–1979 | Hans Krankl (Barcelona) 29 |
| 1977–1978 | Mario Kempes (Valencia) 28 |
| 1976–1977 | Mario Kempes (Valencia) 24 |
| 1975–1976 | Quini (Sporting Gijón) 18 |
| 1974–1975 | Carlos (Athletic Bilbao) 19 |
| 1973–1974 | Quini (Sporting Gijón) 20 |
| 1972–1973 | Marianín (Real Oviedo) 19 |
| 1971–1972 | Enrique Porta (Granada) 20 |
| 1970–1971 | José Eulogio Gárate (Atlético Madrid) 17 Carles Rexach (Barcelona) 17 |
| 1969–1970 | Amancio (Real Madrid) 16 Luis Aragonés (Atlético Madrid) 16 José Eulogio Gárate (Atlético Madrid) 16 |
| 1968–1969 | Amancio (Real Madrid) 14 José Eulogio Gárate (Atlético Madrid) 14 |
| 1967–1968 | Fidel Uriarte (Athletic Bilbao) 22 |
| 1966–1967 | Waldo (Valencia) 24 |
| 1965–1966 | Vavá (Elche) 19 |
| 1964–1965 | Cayetano Ré (Barcelona) 25 |
| 1963–1964 | Ferenc Puskás (Real Madrid) 20 |
| 1962–1963 | Ferenc Puskás (Real Madrid) 26 |
| 1961–1962 | Juan Seminario (Real Zaragoza) 25 |
| 1960–1961 | Ferenc Puskás (Real Madrid) 27 |
| 1959–1960 | Ferenc Puskás (Real Madrid) 26 |
| 1958–1959 | Alfredo di Stéfano (Real Madrid) 23 |
| 1957–1958 | Manuel Badenes (Real Valladolid) 19 Alfredo di Stéfano (Real Madrid) 19 Ricardo (Valencia) 19 |
| 1956–1957 | Alfredo di Stéfano (Real Madrid) 31 |
| 1955–1956 | Alfredo di Stéfano (Real Madrid) 24 |
| 1954–1955 | Juan Arza (Sevilla) 28 |
| 1953–1954 | Alfredo di Stéfano (Real Madrid) 27 |
| 1952–1953 | Telmo Zarra (Athletic Bilbao) 24 |
| 1951–1952 | Pahiño (Real Madrid) 28 |
| 1950–1951 | Telmo Zarra (Athletic Bilbao) 38 |
| 1949–1950 | Telmo Zarra (Athletic Bilbao) 25 |
| 1948–1949 | César (Barcelona) 28 |
| 1947–1948 | Pahiño (Celta Vigo) 23 |
| 1946–1947 | Telmo Zarra (Athletic Bilbao) 34 |
| 1945–1946 | Telmo Zarra (Athletic Bilbao) 24 |
| 1944–1945 | Telmo Zarra (Athletic Bilbao) 19 |
| 1943–1944 | Mundo (Valencia) 27 |
| 1942–1943 | Mariano Martín (Barcelona) 32 |
| 1941–1942 | Mundo (Valencia) 27 |
| 1940–1941 | Pruden (Atlético Madrid) 30 |
| 1939–1940 | Victor Unamuno (Athletic Bilbao) 26 |
| 1936–1939 | Not played due to |

| | Spanish Civil War |
|---|---|
| 1935–1936 | Isidro Lángara (Real Oviedo) 27 |
| 1934–1935 | Isidro Lángara (Real Oviedo) 26 |
| 1933–1934 | Isidro Lángara (Real Oviedo) 27 |
| 1932–1933 | Manuel Olivares (Real Madrid) 16 |
| 1931–1932 | Guillermo Gorostiza (Athletic Bilbao) 12 |
| 1930–1931 | Bata (Athletic Bilbao) 27 |
| 1929–1930 | Guillermo Gorostiza (Athletic Bilbao) 19 |
| 1928–1929 | Paco Bienzobas (Real Sociedad) 14 |

## BRAZIL: CAMPEONATO BRASILEIRO CHAMPIONS

| | |
|---|---|
| 2006 | São Paulo |
| 2005 | Corinthians |
| 2004 | Santos |
| 2003 | Cruzeiro |
| 2002 | Santos |
| 2001 | Atlético Paranaense |
| 2000 | Not played |
| 1999 | Corinthians |
| 1998 | Corinthians |
| 1997 | Vasco da Gama |
| 1996 | Grêmio |
| 1995 | Botafogo |
| 1994 | Palmeiras |
| 1993 | Palmeiras |
| 1992 | Flamengo |
| 1991 | São Paulo |
| 1990 | Corinthians |
| 1989 | Vasco da Gama |
| 1988 | Bahia |
| 1987 | Sport Club Recife |
| 1986 | São Paulo |
| 1985 | Coritiba |
| 1984 | Fluminense |
| 1983 | Flamengo |
| 1982 | Flamengo |
| 1981 | Grêmio |
| 1980 | Flamengo |
| 1979 | Internacional |
| 1978 | Guarani |
| 1977 | São Paulo |
| 1976 | Internacional |
| 1975 | Internacional |
| 1974 | Vasco da Gama |
| 1973 | Palmeiras |
| 1972 | Palmeiras |
| 1971 | Atlético Mineiro |

## BRAZIL: COPA DO BRASIL (BRASILIAN CUP)*

| | |
|---|---|
| 2007 | Fluminense |
| 2006 | Flamengo |
| 2005 | Paulista |
| 2004 | Santo André |
| 2003 | Cruzeiro |
| 2002 | Corinthians |
| 2001 | Grêmio |
| 2000 | Cruzeiro |
| 1999 | Juventude |
| 1998 | Palmeiras |
| 1997 | Grêmio |
| 1996 | Cruzeiro |
| 1995 | Corinthians |

| | |
|---|---|
| 1994 | Grêmio |
| 1993 | Cruzeiro |
| 1992 | Internacional |
| 1991 | Criciúma |
| 1990 | Flamengo |
| 1989 | Grêmio |
| 1968 | Botafogo |
| 1967 | Palmeiras |
| 1966 | Cruzeiro |
| 1965 | Santos |
| 1964 | Santos |
| 1963 | Santos |
| 1962 | Santos |
| 1961 | Santos |
| 1960 | Palmeiras |
| 1959 | Bahia |

* Known as Taça Brasil 1959–1968.

## BRAZIL: LEAGUE TOP SCORERS

| | |
|---|---|
| 2006 | Souza (Goiás) 17 |
| 2005 | Romário (Vasco da Gama) 22 |
| 2004 | Washington (Atlético Paranaense) 34 |
| 2003 | Dimba (Goiás) 31 |
| 2002 | Luís Fabiano (São Paulo) 19 |
| | Rodrigo Fabri (Grêmio) 19 |
| 2001 | Romário (Vasco da Gama) 21 |
| 2000 | Dill (Goiás) 20 |
| | Magno Alves (Fluminense) 20 |
| | Romário (Vasco da Gama) 20 |
| 1999 | Guilherme (Atlético Mineiro) 28 |
| 1998 | Viola (Santos) 21 |
| 1997 | Edmundo (Vasco da Gama) 29 |
| 1996 | Paulo Nunes (Grêmio) 16 |
| | Renaldo (Atlético Mineiro) 16 |
| 1995 | Túlio (Botafogo) 23 |
| 1994 | Márcio Amoroso (Guarani) 19 |
| 1993 | Guga (Santos) 15 |
| 1992 | Bebeto (Vasco da Gama) 18 |
| 1991 | Paulinho McLaren (Santos) 15 |
| 1990 | Charles (Bahia) 11 |
| 1989 | Túlio (Goiás) 11 |
| 1988 | Nilson (Internacional) 15 |
| 1987 | Muller (São Paulo) 10 |
| 1986 | Careca (São Paulo) 25 |
| 1985 | Edmar (Guarani) 20 |
| 1984 | Roberto Dinamite (Vasco da Gama) 16 |
| 1983 | Serginho (Santos) 22 |
| 1982 | Zico (Flamengo) 20 |
| 1981 | Nunes (Flamengo) 16 |
| 1980 | Zico (Flamengo) 21 |
| 1979 | César (América) 13 |
| 1978 | Paulinho (Vasco da Gama) 19 |
| 1977 | Reinaldo (Atlético Mineiro) 28 |
| 1976 | Dario (Internacional) 16 |
| 1975 | Flávio (Internacional) 16 |
| 1974 | Roberto Dinamite (Vasco da Gama) 16 |
| 1973 | Ramón (Santa Cruz) 21 |
| | Túlio (Botafogo) 19 |
| 1972 | Dario (Atlético Mineiro) 17 |
| | Pedro Rocha (São Paulo) 17 |
| 1971 | Dario (Atlético Mineiro) 15 |

## ARGENTINA: PRIMERA DIVISION CHAMPIONS*

| | |
|---|---|
| 2007C | San Lorenzo |
| 2006A | Estudiantes |

| | |
|---|---|
| 2006C | Boca Juniors |
| 2005A | Boca Juniors |
| 2005C | Vélez Sársfield |
| 2004A | Newell's Old Boys |
| 2004C | River Plate |
| 2003A | Boca Juniors |
| 2003C | River Plate |
| 2002A | Independiente |
| 2002C | River Plate |
| 2001A | Racing Club |
| 2001C | San Lorenzo |
| 2000A | Boca Juniors |
| 2000C | River Plate |
| 1999A | River Plate |
| 1999C | Boca Juniors |
| 1998A | Boca Juniors |
| 1998C | Vélez Sársfield |
| 1997A | River Plate |
| 1997C | River Plate |
| 1996A | River Plate |
| 1996C | Vélez Sársfield |
| 1995A | Vélez Sársfield |
| 1995C | San Lorenzo |
| 1994A | River Plate |
| 1994C | Independiente |
| 1993A | River Plate |
| 1993C | Vélez Sarsfield |
| 1992A | Boca Juniors |
| 1992C | Newell's Old Boys |
| 1991A | River Plate |
| 1990–1991 | Newell's Old Boys |
| 1989–1990 | River Plate |
| 1988–1989 | Independiente |
| 1987–1988 | Newell's Old Boys |
| 1986–1987 | Rosario Central |
| 1985–1986 | River Plate |
| 1985N | Argentinos Juniors |
| 1984N | Ferro Carril Oeste |
| 1984M | Argentinos Juniors |
| 1983N | Estudiantes |
| 1983M | Independiente |
| 1982N | Ferro Carril Oeste |
| 1982M | Estudiantes |
| 1981M | Boca Juniors |
| 1981N | River Plate |
| 1980M | River Plate |
| 1980N | Rosario Central |
| 1979M | River Plate |
| 1979N | River Plate |
| 1978M | Quilmes |
| 1978N | Independiente |
| 1977M | River Plate |
| 1977N | Independiente |
| 1976M | Boca Juniors |
| 1976N | Boca Juniors |
| 1975M | River Plate |
| 1975N | River Plate |
| 1974M | Newell's Old Boys |
| 1974N | San Lorenzo |
| 1973M | Huracán |
| 1973N | Rosario Central |
| 1972M | San Lorenzo |
| 1972N | San Lorenzo |
| 1971M | Independiente |
| 1971N | Rosario Central |
| 1970M | Independiente |
| 1970N | Boca Juniors |
| 1969M | Chacarita Juniors |
| 1969N | Boca Juniors |
| 1968M | San Lorenzo |

| | |
|---|---|
| 1968N | Vélez Sársfield |
| 1967M | Estudiantes |
| 1967N | Independiente |
| 1966 | Racing Club |
| 1965 | Boca Juniors |
| 1964 | Boca Juniors |
| 1963 | Independiente |
| 1962 | Boca Juniors |
| 1961 | Racing Club |
| 1960 | Independiente |
| 1959 | San Lorenzo |
| 1958 | Racing Club |
| 1957 | River Plate |
| 1956 | River Plate |
| 1955 | River Plate |
| 1954 | Boca Juniors |
| 1953 | River Plate |
| 1952 | River Plate |
| 1951 | Racing Club |
| 1950 | Racing Club |
| 1949 | Racing Club |
| 1948 | Independiente |
| 1947 | River Plate |
| 1946 | San Lorenzo |
| 1945 | River Plate |
| 1944 | Boca Juniors |
| 1943 | Boca Juniors |
| 1942 | River Plate |
| 1941 | River Plate |
| 1940 | Boca Juniors |
| 1939 | Independiente |
| 1938 | Independiente |
| 1937 | River Plate |
| 1936 | River Plate |
| 1935 | Boca Juniors |
| 1934 | Boca Juniors |
| 1933 | San Lorenzo |
| 1932 | River Plate |
| 1931 | Boca Juniors |

* In 1999 the championship was split into two tournaments: Apertuna (August to December) and Clausura (February to June).

Championship was previously split into two tournaments in 1967–1986: Metropolitano (open only to teams affiliated to the national association) and Nacional (open to teams from the provinces).

## ARGENTINA: LEAGUE TOP SCORERS

| | |
|---|---|
| 2007C | Martín Palermo (Boca Juniors) 11 |
| 2006A | Mauro Zárate (Vélez Sársfield) 12 |
| | Rodrigo Palacio (Boca Juniors) 12 |
| 2006C | Gonzalo Vargas (Gimnasia) 12 |
| 2005A | Javier Cámpora (Tiro Federal) 13 |
| 2005C | Mariano Pavone (Estudiantes) 16 |
| 2004A | Lisandro López (Racing Club) 12 |
| 2004C | Rolando Zárate (Vélez Sársfield) 13 |
| 2003A | Ernesto Farías (Estudiantes) 12 |
| 2003C | Luciano Figueroa (Rosario Central) 17 |
| 2002A | Néstor Silvera |

|  |  |
|---|---|
| | (Independiente) 16 |
| 2002C | Fernando Cavenaghi (River Plate) 15 |
| 2001A | Martín Cardetti (River Plate 17) |
| 2001C | Bernardo Romeo (San Lorenzo) 15 |
| 2000A | Juan Pablo Ángel (River Plate) 13 |
| 2000C | Esteban Fuertes (Colón) 17 |
| 1999A | Javier Saviola (River Plate) 15 |
| 1999C | José Luis Calderon (Independiente) 17 |
| 1998A | Martín Palermo (Boca Juniors) 20 |
| 1998C | Roberto Sosa (Gimnasia) 17 |
| 1997A | Rubén Da Silva (Rosario Central) 15 |
| 1997C | Sergio Martínez (Boca Juniors) 15 |
| 1996A | Gustavo Reggi (Ferro Carril Oeste) 11 |
| 1996C | Ariel López (Lanús) 12 |
| 1995A | José Luis Calderon (Estudiantes) 13 |
| 1995C | José Oscar Flores (Vélez Sársfield) 14 |
| 1994A | Enzo Francescoli (River Plate) 12 |
| 1994C | Hernán Crespo (River Plate) 11 |
| | Marcelo Espina (Platense) 11 |
| 1993A | Sergio Martínez (Boca Juniors) 12 |
| 1993C | Rubén Da Silva (River Plate 13 |
| 1992A | Alberto Acosta (San Lorenzo) 12 |
| 1992C | Diego Latorre (Boca Juniors) 9 |
| 1991A | Ramón Angel Díaz (River Plate) 14 |
| 1990–1991 | Esteban González (Vélez Sársfield) 18 |
| 1989–1990 | Ariel Cozzoni (Newell's Old Boys) 23 |
| 1988–1989 | Oscar Dertycia (Argentinos Juniors) 20 |
| | Néstor Raúl Gorosito (San Lorenzo) 20 |
| 1987–1988 | José Luis Rodriguez (Deportivo Español) 18 |
| 1986–1987 | Omar Palma (Rosario Central) 20 |
| 1985–1986 | Enzo Francescoli (River Plate) 25 |
| 1985N | Jorge Comas (Vélez Sársfield) 12 |
| 1984N | Pedro Pablo Pasculli (Argentinos Juniors) 9 |
| 1984M | Enzo Francescoli (River Plate) 24 |
| 1983N | Armando Husillos (Loma Negra) 11 |
| 1983M | Víctor Ramos (Newell's Old Boys) 30 |
| 1982N | Miguel Juárez (Ferro Carril Oeste) 22 |
| 1982M | Carlos Manuel Morete (Independiente) 20 |
| 1981M | Raúl Chaparro (Instituto) 20 |
| 1981N | Carlos Bianchi (Vélez Sársfield) 15 |
| 1980M | Diego Maradona (Argentinos Juniors) 25 |
| 1980N | Diego Maradona (Argentinos Juniors) 17 |
| 1979M | Diego Maradona (Argentinos Juniors) 14 |
| | Sergio Fortunato (Estudiantes) 14 |
| 1979N | Diego Maradona (Argentinos Juniors) 12 |
| 1978M | Diego Maradona (Argentinos Juniors) 22 |
| | Luis Andreucci (Quilmes) 22 |
| 1978N | José Omar Reinaldi (Talleres) 18 |
| 1977M | Carlos Álvarez (Argentinos Juniors) 27 |
| 1977N | Alfredo Letanu (Estudiantes) 13 |
| 1976M | Mario Kempes (Rosario Central) 21 |
| 1976N | Norberto Eresuma (San Lorenzo de Mar del Plata) 12 |
| | Luis Ludueña (Talleres) 12 |
| | Víctor Marchetti (Atlético Unión) 12 |
| 1975M | Héctor Scotta (San Lorenzo) 32 |
| 1975N | Héctor Scotta (San Lorenzo) 28 |
| 1974M | Carlos Manuel Morete (River Plate) 18 |
| 1974N | Mario Kempes (Rosario Central) 25 |
| 1973M | Oscar Más (River Plate) 17 |
| | Hugo Curioni (Boca Juniors) 17 |
| | Ignacio Peña (Estudiantes) 17 |
| 1973N | Juan Gómez Voglino (Atlanta) 18 |
| 1972M | Miguel Ángel Brindisi (Huracán) 21 |
| 1972N | Carlos Manuel Morete (River Plate) 14 |
| 1971M | Carlos Bianchi (Vélez Sársfield) 36 |
| 1971N | Alfredo Obberti (Newell's Old Boys) 10 |
| | José Luñis (Juventud Antoniana) 10 |
| 1970M | Oscar Más (River Plate) 16 |
| 1970N | Carlos Bianchi (Vélez Sársfield) 18 |
| 1969M | Walter Machado (Racing Club) 14 |
| 1969N | Rodolfo Fischer (San Lorenzo) 14 |
| | Carlos Bulla (Platense) 14 |
| 1968M | Alfredo Obberti (Los Andes) 13 |
| 1968N | Omar Wehbe (Vélez Sársfield) 13 |
| 1967M | Bernardo Acosta (Lanús) 18 |
| 1967N | Luis Artime (Independiente) 11 |
| 1966 | Luis Artime (Independiente) 23 |
| 1965 | Juan Carlos Carone (Vélez Sársfield) 19 |
| 1964 | Héctor Rodolfo Viera (San Lorenzo) 17 |
| 1963 | Luis Artime (River Plate) 25 |
| 1962 | Luis Artime (River Plate) 25 |
| 1961 | José Sanfilippo (San Lorenzo) 26 |
| 1960 | José Sanfilippo (San Lorenzo) 34 |
| 1959 | José Sanfilippo (San Lorenzo) 31 |
| 1958 | José Sanfilippo (San Lorenzo) 28 |
| 1957 | Roberto Zarate (River Plate) 22 |
| 1956 | Juan Alberto Castro (Rosario Central) 17 |
| | Ernesto Grillo (Independiente) 17 |
| 1955 | Oscar Massei (Rosario Central) 21 |
| 1954 | Ángel Berni (San Lorenzo) 19 |
| | Norberto Conde (Vélez Sársfield) 19 |
| | José Borello (Boca Juniors) 19 |
| 1953 | Juan José Pizzuti (Racing Club) 22 |
| | Juan Benavidez (San Lorenzo) 22 |
| 1952 | Eduardo Ricagni (Huracán) 28 |
| 1951 | Santiago Vernazza (River Plate) 22 |
| 1950 | Mario Papa (San Lorenzo) 24 |
| 1949 | Llamil Simes (Racing Club) 26 |
| | Juan José Pizzuti (Banfield) 26 |
| 1948 | Benjamín Santos (Rosario Central) 21 |
| 1947 | Alfredo di Stéfano (River Plate) 27 |
| 1946 | Mario Boye (Boca Juniors) 24 |
| 1945 | Ángel Labruna (River Plate) 25 |
| 1944 | Atilio Mellone (Huracán) 26 |
| 1943 | Luis Arrieta (Lanús) 23 |
| | Ángel Labruna (River Plate) 23 |
| | Raúl Frutos (Platense) 23 |
| 1942 | Rinaldo Martino (San Lorenzo) 25 |
| 1941 | José Canteli (Newell's Old Boys) 30 |
| 1940 | Delfín Benitez (Racing Club) 33 |
| | Isidro Langara (San Lorenzo) 33 |
| 1939 | Arsenio Erico (Independiente) 40 |
| 1938 | Arsenio Erico (Independiente) 43 |
| 1937 | Arsenio Erico (Independiente) 47 |
| 1936 | Evaristo Barrera (Racing Club) 32 |
| 1935 | Agustín Cosso (Vélez Sársfield) 33 |
| 1934 | Evaristo Barrera (Racing Club) 34 |
| 1933 | Francisco Varallo (Boca Juniors) 34 |
| 1932 | Bernabé Ferreyra (River Plate) 43 |
| 1931 | Alberto Zozaya (Estudiantes) 33 |

## USA: NORTH AMERICAN SOCCER LEAGUE CHAMPIONS

|  |  |
|---|---|
| 1984 | Chicago Sting |
| 1983 | Tulsa Roughnecks |
| 1982 | New York Cosmos |
| 1981 | Chicago Sting |
| 1980 | New York Cosmos |
| 1979 | Vancouver Whitecaps |
| 1978 | New York Cosmos |
| 1977 | New York Cosmos |
| 1976 | Toronto Metros–Croatia |
| 1975 | Tampa Bay Rowdies |
| 1974 | Los Angeles Aztecs |
| 1973 | Philadelphia Atoms |
| 1972 | New York Cosmos |
| 1971 | Dallas Tornado |
| 1970 | Rochester Lancers |
| 1969 | Kansas City Spurs |
| 1968 | Atlanta Chiefs |

## NORTH AMERICAN SOCCER LEAGUE TOP SCORERS

|  |  |
|---|---|
| 1984 | Steve Zungul (Golden Bay Earthquakes) 20 |
| 1983 | Roberto Cabanas (New York Cosmos) 25 |
| 1982 | Ricardo Alonso (Jacksonville Tea Men) 21 |
| 1981 | Giorgio Chinaglia (New York Cosmos) 29 |
| 1980 | Giorgio Chinaglia (New York Cosmos) 32 |
| 1979 | Giorgio Chinaglia (New York Cosmos) 26 |
| 1978 | Giorgio Chinaglia (New York Cosmos) 34 |
| 1977 | Steve David (Los Angeles Aztecs) 26 |
| 1976 | Derek Smethurst (Tampa Bay Rowdies) 20 |
| 1975 | Steve David (Miami Toros) 23 |
| 1974 | Paul Child (San Jose Earthquakes) 15 |
| 1973 | Warren Archibald (Miami Toros) 12 |
| | Ilija Mitic (Dallas Tornado) 12 |
| 1972 | Randy Horton (New York Cosmos) 9 |
| 1971 | Carlos Metidieri (Rochester |

Lancers) 19

**1970** Kirk Apostolidis (Dallas Tornado) 16

**1969** Kaiser Motaung (Atlanta Apollos) 16

**1968** John Kowalik (Chicago Mustangs) 30

Cirilo Fernandez (San Diego Toros) 30

## USA: MAJOR LEAGUE SOCCER CHAMPIONS – MLS CUP

**2007** Houston Dynamo
**2006** Houston Dynamo
**2005** Los Angeles Galaxy
**2004** DC United
**2003** San Jose Earthquakes
**2002** Los Angeles Galaxy
**2001** San Jose Earthquakes
**2000** Kansas City Wizards
**1999** DC United
**1998** Chicago Fire
**1997** DC United
**1996** DC United

## MLS TOP SCORERS

**2007** Luciano Emilio (DC United) 20
**2006** Jeff Cunningham (Real Salt Lake) 16
**2005** Taylor Twellman (New England Revolution) 17
**2004** Brian Ching (San Jose Earthquakes) 12
**2003** Carlos Ruiz (Los Angeles Galaxy) 15
**2002** Carlos Ruiz (Los Angeles Galaxy) 24
**2001** Alex Pineda Chacón (Miami Fusion) 19
**2000** Mamadou Diallo (Tampa Bay Mutiny) 26
**1999** Jason Kreis (Dallas Burn) 18
**1998** Stern John (Columbus Crew) 26
**1997** Jaime Moreno (DC United) 16
**1996** Roy Lassiter (Tampa Bay Mutiny) 27

## JAPAN: J–LEAGUE CHAMPIONSHIP

**2006** Urawa Red Diamonds
**2005** Gamba Osaka
**2004** Yokohama F. Marinos
**2003** Yokohama F. Marinos
**2002** Júbilo Iwata
**2001** Kashima Antlers
**2000** Kashima Antlers
**1999** Júbilo Iwata
**1998** Kashima Antlers
**1997** Júbilo Iwata
**1996** Kashima Antlers
**1995** Yokohama Marinos
**1994** Verdy Kawasaki
**1993** Verdy Kawasaki

## JAPAN: ALL–JAPAN FOOTBALL CHAMPIONSHIP*

**1991–1992** Yomiuri
**1990–1991** Yomiuri
**1989–1990** Nissan
**1988–1989** Nissan
**1987–1988** Yamaha Motors

**1986–1987** Yomiuri
**1985–1986** East Furukawa
**1984** Yomiuri
**1983** Yomiuri
**1982** Mitsubishi Motors
**1981** Fujita
**1980** Yanmar Diesel
**1979** Fujita
**1978** Mitsubishi Motors
**1977** Fujita
**1976** East Furukawa
**1975** Yanmar Diesel
**1974** Yanmar Diesel
**1973** Mitsubishi Motors
**1972** Hitachi
**1971** Yanmar Diesel
**1970** Toyo Kogyo
**1969** Mitsubishi Motors
**1968** Toyo Kogyo
**1967** Toyo Kogyo
**1966** Toyo Kogyo
**1965** Toyo Kogyo

* Amateur tournament played until the formation of the J–League. Amateur league was highest level of the sport in Japan until 1992.

## JAPAN: EMPEROR'S CUP*

**2006** Urawa Reds
**2005** Urawa Reds
**2004** Tokyo Verdy 1969
**2003** Júbilo Iwata
**2002** Kyoto Purple Sanga
**2001** Shimizu S–Pulse
**2000** Kashima Antlers
**1999** Nagoya Grampus Eight
**1998** Yokohama Flügels
**1997** Kashima Antlers
**1996** Verdy Kawasaki
**1995** Nagoya Grampus Eight
**1994** Bellmare Hiratsuka
**1993** Yokohama Flügels
**1992** Yokohama Marinos
**1991** Nissan
**1990** Matsushita
**1989** Nissan
**1988** Nissan
**1987** Yomiuri
**1986** Yomiuri
**1985** Nissan
**1984** Yomiuri Club
**1983** Nissan
**1982** Yamaha
**1981** NKK
**1980** Mitsubishi Heavy Industries
**1979** Fujita Industries
**1978** Mitsubishi Heavy Industries
**1977** Fujita Industries
**1976** Furukawa Electric
**1975** Hitachi
**1974** Yanmar Diesel
**1973** Mitsubishi Heavy Industries
**1972** Hitachi
**1971** Mitsubishi Heavy Industries
**1970** Yanmar Diesel
**1969** Toyo Industries
**1968** Yanmar Diesel
**1967** Toyo Industries
**1966** Waseda University
**1965** Toyo Industries

**1964** Title shared between Yawata Steel and Furukawa Electric
**1963** Waseda University
**1962** Chuo University
**1961** Furukawa Electric
**1960** Furukawa Electric
**1959** Kwangaku
**1958** Kwangaku
**1957** Chuo University
**1956** Keio BRB
**1955** All Kwangaku
**1954** Keio BRB
**1953** Kwangaku
**1952** All Keio University
**1951** Keio BRB
**1950** All Kwangaku
**1949** Tokyo University LB
**1946** Tokyo University
**1940** Keio BRB
**1939** Keio BRB
**1938** Waseda University
**1937** Keio University
**1936** Keio BRB
**1935** Seoul Shukyu–dan
**1933** Tokyo Old Boys 4
**1932** Keio
**1931** Tokyo University
**1930** Kwangaku
**1929** Kwangaku
**1928** Waseda University WMW
**1927** Kobe–Ichi Junior High School
**1925** Rijo Shukyu–dan
**1924** Rijo
**1923** Astra
**1922** Nagoya Shukyu–dan
**1921** Tokyo Shukyu–dan

* Not played 1926 due to Emperor Taisho's death; not played 1934 due to East Asian Games; not played 1941–1945 due to the Second World War; not played 1947–1948 due to post Second World War disorder.

## JAPAN LEAGUE TOP SCORERS

**2007** Magno Alves (Gamba Osaka) 26
**2006** Washington (Urawa Reds) 26
**2005** Araújo (Gamba Osaka) 33
**2004** Emerson (Urawa Reds) 27
**2003** Ueslei (Nagoya Grampus Eight) 22
**2002** Naohiro Takahara (Júbilo Iwata) 26
**2001** Will (Consadole Sapporo) 24
**2000** Masashi Nakayama (Júbilo Iwata) 20
**1999** Hwang Sun–Hong (Cerezo Osaka) 24
**1998** Masashi Nakayama (Júbilo Iwata) 36
**1997** Patrick Mboma (Gamba Osaka) 25
**1996** Kazuyoshi Miura (Verdy Kawasaki) 23
**1995** Masahiro Fukuda (Urawa Reds) 32
**1994** Frank Ordenewitz (JEF United Ichihara) 30
**1993** Ramón Díaz (Yokohama Marinos) 28

## AUSTRALIA: A–LEAGUE*

**2006–2007** Melbourne Victory
**2005–2006** Sydney FC
**2004–2005** Not played
**2003–2004** Perth Glory

**2002–2003** Perth Glory
**2001–2002** Olympic Sharks
**2000–2001** Wollongong City Wolves
**1999–2000** Wollongong City Wolves
**1998–1999** South Melbourne
**1997–1998** South Melbourne
**1996–1997** Brisbane Strikers
**1995–1996** Melbourne Knights
**1994–1995** Melbourne Knights
**1993–1994** Adelaide City
**1992–1993** Marconi Fairfield
**1991–1992** Adelaide City
**1990–1991** South Melbourne Hellas
**1989–1990** Olympic UTS
**1989** Marconi Fairfield
**1988** Marconi Fairfield
**1987** Apia Leichhardt
**1986** Adelaide City
**1985** Brunswick Juventus
**1984** South Melbourne Hellas
**1983** Budapest St. George
**1982** Sydney City Hakoah
**1981** Sydney City Hakoah
**1980** Sydney City Hakoah
**1979** Marconi Fairfield
**1978** West Adelaide Hellas
**1977** Sydney City Hakoah

* Known as Australian National Soccer League and played under a different format until 2004.

## AUSTRALIA A–LEAGUE TOP SCORERS

**2006–2007** Daniel Allsopp (Melbourne Victory) 11
**2005–2006** Alex Brosque (Queensland Roar) 8
Bobby Despotovski (Perth Glory) 8
Archie Thompson (Melbourne Victory) 8
Stewart Petrie (Central Coast Mariners) 8

# GLOSSARY

**AGGREGATE**
When a fixture is played over two legs, the aggregate is the scores of both games added together.

**ASSISTANT REFEREES**
The flag-carrying officials positioned on each touchline who help the referee.

**AWAY GOALS**
In games played over two legs, goals scored in the away match count extra if the aggregate score is tied.

**BENCH**
A bench at the side of the field to seat players who are waiting their chance to play or who have been removed from play due to injury or other reasons. A substitute is often referred to as being "on the bench."

**CAP**
An appearance for an international team. The term originated in England, where players were once presented with a white silk cap every time they played for their country.

**CENTER SPOT**
The point in the center of the field where the game starts and restarts after a goal.

**CHIP**
A pass or shot in which the bottom of the ball is struck with a short stabbing motion with no follow-through.

**CORNER FLAG**
A flag marking the corner arc.

**CORNER KICK**
An attacking dead ball situation arising when the defending team puts the ball over its own goal line between the corner flag and the goalpost.

**CROSS**
To kick or pass the ball across the field, usually into the penalty area to create a goalscoring opportunity.

**CRUYFF TURN**
A deceptive turn named after the world-famous Dutch player of the 1970s, Johan Cruyff, who perfected it.

**DEAD BALL**
A break in play, often due to a free kick or throw in.

**DISTRIBUTION**
Passing the ball to teammates. Good distribution is making the right type of pass at the best moment.

**DIVE**
An attempt by a player to convince the referee (falsely) that a foul has been committed against him by diving to the ground. This is against the Laws of the Game.

**DRAG-BACK**
When a player drags the ball behind him and executes a quick turn and change of direction.

**DRIBBLE**
Moving the ball with lots of small, quick kicks, usually with both feet.

**DUMMY**
To pretend to pass or shoot in one direction to deceive an opponent and then to move the opposite way.

**EIGHTEEN-YARD BOX**
The larger marked area around the goal, in which a penalty may be given.

**EXTRA TIME**
Additional period of time played at the end of a game that has resulted in a draw to try to decide the winner. Extra time is usually only played in a knockout competition where a winner must be decided.

**FAR POST**
The goal post farthest away from the point of attack.

**FIELD OF PLAY**
The soccer field; the surface on which the game is played and its markings.

**FOURTH OFFICIAL**
A game official who assists the referee in a number of different tasks. The fourth official may also be called on to replace any other official who cannot continue in a game.

**FOUL**
An infringement of the laws of soccer, such as when a player trips, kicks, or pushes an opponent (accidentally or deliberately).

**FREE KICK**
When play is stopped by the referee and a kick awarded to the opposing side, usually due to a foul or infringement.

**FREE TRANSFER**
When a player transfers from one team to another after the contract has expired, so that no transfer fee is paid. It is also known as the Bosman ruling.

**FRIENDLY GAME**
A game where there is no trophy, prize, or ranking dependent on the result. This is sometimes called an exhibition game.

**GOAL**
1. The nets supported by two posts and a crossbar at each end of the field, where the goalkeepers stand.
2. When the ball crosses the line into the goal area and a team scores.

**GOAL KICK**
A kick awarded to the defending team when the ball has crossed the goal line last touched by an attacking player, but no goal has been scored.

**GOAL LINE**
The line linking the corner flags with the goal posts.

**GOLDEN BOOT**
Award given to the top scoring player in a particular soccer competition.

**GOLDEN GOAL**
A way of deciding the winner when a game in a knockout contest ends in a draw. The first goal scored in overtime, known as a "golden goal", wins the game instantly. If there is no golden goal in 30 minutes of overtime, a penalty shootout decides the game.

**HALFWAY LINE**
The marked-out line that separates one half of the field from the other.

**HANDBALL**
A type of foul. It is illegal for an outfield player to touch the ball with his or her hand in open play.

**HAT TRICK**
Three goals scored by the same player in one game. When a player scores two goals in one game it is sometimes referred to as a "brace".

**INFRINGEMENT**
To break one of the rules of the game.

**INTERCEPT**
To steal possession of or get in the way of an opponent's pass.

**INJURY TIME**
Time added at the end of a game to allow for time lost due to injuries, substitutions, or other stoppages. The fourth official notifies the teams how much time has been added.

**KICKOFF**
The way of starting each half of a soccer game. The kickoff is the first kick of the half that sets the ball in play. It is taken from the center spot. The kick that restarts play after a goal is scored is also known as a kickoff.

**GEAR**
The clothing worn by a player during a game, including shorts, shirt, socks, cleats, and shin pads.

## LEG
One game of a game between two teams that is played over two individual games. The winner is the team with the better aggregate score.

## LOCAL DERBY
A game between two local rival teams.

## MAN OF THE GAME
Award given to the player judged to be the most outstanding in a particular game.

## MARK
To position yourself close to an opponent so that it is difficult for him to receive or pass the ball.

## GAME
A competitive game, usually comprising two halves of 45 minutes.

## NEAR POST
The goal post nearest to the point of attack.

## NUTMEG
To kick the ball through an opponent's legs and then collect it on the other side. The word is thought to originate from the Victorian term "to nutmeg," meaning "to trick."

## OFFSIDE
When an attacker has moved beyond the second last defender as the ball is played forward.

## ONE-TWO
A quick back-and-forth pass between two players, also known as a wall pass.

## OWN GOAL
A goal scored accidentally by a player into his own net.

## PASS
When a player passes the ball to another member of his team during a game.

## PENALTY
A specific kind of free kick awarded when an attacker is fouled in the penalty area.

## PENALTY SHOOTOUT
A way of deciding the winner in a knockout competition where the game ends in a draw. The teams take turns shooting at the goal from the penalty spot. Usually the best of five wins, however, if the teams are level after five penalties they play until one team misses.

## PENALTY SPOT
The place from where the penalty is taken.

## FIELD
The field of play.

## PHYSIO
Short for a physiotherapist, a health worker who treats injuries during a game and helps players to recover from long-term injuries.

## PLAYMAKER
A player who creates attacking moves and opportunities for his team to score.

## POSSESSION
To have the ball.

## QUARTERFINALS
In a knockout competition, the four games that decide which four of the eight remaining teams will play in the semifinals.

## READING THE GAME
Playing the game intelligently, e.g., using tactical knowledge to improve positioning, passing, tackling, and intercepting.

## RED CARD
A player is shown this after an extremely serious foul or infringement, or after receiving two yellow cards in a game. They usually receive a suspension.

## REFEREE
The official in charge of the game, who checks that the laws of soccer are not broken.

## REPLAY
A game played between two teams for a second time at a later date, because the first game resulted in a draw.

## ROUND-ROBIN
A competition where all teams play each other in turn and the team with the highest points score is the winner. In some other competitions, the first round has the teams split into groups that then play round robins to decide which will go through to later rounds. The rest of the tournament is played as knockout rounds.

## RUNNER-UP
The team that finishes in second place in a competition.

## SCORE
To get a goal.

## SEMIFINALS
In a knockout competition, the two games that decide which two of the four remaining teams will play in the final.

## SENT OFF
When a player receives a red card and is sent from the field of play.

## SHIN PADS
Protective shields for the shins and ankles, usually worn underneath the socks.

## SHOOT
To aim a kick or pass at the goal.

## SILVER GOAL
A way of deciding the winner when a game in a knockout contest ends in a draw. The team leading after a fifteen-minute period of overtime wins the game, with the goal that gives it the lead known as a "silver goal". If the score is level, another fifteen-minute period is played. If the score is still level, the game is decided by a penalty shootout.

## SIX-YARD BOX
The small marked-out area around the goal.

## STOP TURN
A way of changing direction quickly by stopping the ball at high speed.

## SUBSTITUTE
A player who replaces another player during a game, either for tactical reasons or because the first player is injured or not playing well. Up to three substitutes are allowed in most games.

## SWERVE
To kick or strike across the back of the ball so that it bends in the opposite direction.

## TACKLE
To challenge a player fairly for the ball. A tackle can be block or sliding.

## THROW-IN
A throw from the touchline awarded by the referee when the opposition has kicked the ball out of play.

## TOUCHLINES
The two lines running down the length of the field

## TRANSFER
The movement of a player under contract from one team to another team.

## TRANSFER FEE
When a player transfers from one team to another, the team he is joining pays a sum of money, known as a transer fee, to the team he is leaving.

## VOLLEY
To kick the ball before it touches the ground, usually as a shot on goal.

## WALL
A line of two or more players defending their goal against a free kick.

## WARM DOWN
Period of gradual decrease in physical activity after a game or training session. Warming down allows the body to transition smoothly to a resting state.

## WARM UP
Preparation for a game or training session by gradual increase in physical activity. Warming up properly reduces the risk of injury and improves performance.

## YELLOW CARD
This is shown by the referee for a serious offence or persistant offending.

# INDEX

# ACKNOWLEDGMENTS

THE PUBLISHER WOULD LIKE TO THANK THE FOLLOWING FEDERATIONS AND CLUBS FOR THEIR KIND PERMISSION TO REPRODUCE THEIR LOGOS OR TEAM BADGES:

M.L.S. properties courtesy of Major League Soccer, L.L.C.

Accra Hearts of Oak Sporting Club, ADO Den Haag, All India Football Federation, Amsterdamsche Football Club Ajax, Arbil Football Club, Arsenal Football Club, ASEC Mimosas, AS Monaco Football Club, AS Nancy-Lorraine, Asociación Paraguaya de Fútbol, AZ Alkmaar, Bayer 04 Leverkusen, Blackpool Football Club, Bolton Football Club, Borussia Dortmund, Bulgarian Football Union, Canadian Soccer Association, Cantera Puma, Chelsea Football Club, Club Atlético Osasuna, Corporación Deportiva Once Caldas, Cotonsport Garoua, Croatian Football Federation, Dalian Shide, Danish Football Association, Federación Costarricense de Fútbol, Federación Mexicana de Fútbol Asociación, Fédération Camerounaise de Football, FC Basel 1893, FC Bayern Munich, FC Dallas, FC de Metz, FC Dynamo Kiev, FC Eintracht, FC Girondins de Bordeaux, FC Groningen, FC Lorient Bretagne Sud, FC Twente, Football Association of Wales, Football Federation Australia, Fulham Football Club, Galatasaray S.K., Go Ahead Eagles, Hamburger SV, Hanover 96, Hertha BSC Berlin, Invincible Eleven, Irish Football Association (www.irishfa.com), Israel Football Association, Japan Football Association, Jubilo Iwata Yamaha Football Club, Kazier Chiefs, Korea Football Association, Le Mans Union Club 72, Levante Unión Deportiva, Liberia Football Association, Middlesbrough Football Club, N.E.C., Newcastle United Football Club, New Zealand Football, Nottingham Forest Football Club, OGC Nice, Panathinaikos Football Club, Paris Saint-Germain Football Club, Portsmouth Football Club, Racing Club de Lens, Racing Club de Strasbourg, Real Madrid Club de Fútbol, Real Murcia, Real Racing Club de Santander, Real Valladolid Club de Fútbol, Real Zaragoza, Romanian Football Federation, Royal Netherlands Football Association, Royal Sporting Club Anderlecht, Royal Standard de Liège, Saudi Arabia Football Federation, Scottish Football Association, Singapore Armed Forces Football Club, SK Slavia Praha, SM Caen, Sparta Rotterdam, Sport Club Corinthians Paulista, Stade Rennais Football Club, Suwon Samsung Bluewings Football Club, Toulouse Football Club, UEFA, U.S. Soccer Federation, Vitesse, VVV-Venlo, Werder Bremen, Willem II Tilburg, Wolverhampton Wanderers Football Club.

THE PUBLISHER WOULD LIKE TO THANK THE FOLLOWING FOR THEIR KIND PERMISSION TO REPRODUCE THEIR PHOTOGRAPHS:

(Key: a-above; b-below/bottom; c-center; f-far; l-left; r-right; t-top)

Action Images: 11cl, 11fbl, 15tc, 12bc, 30br, 38bl, 38crb, 40-41c, 42br, 47tl, 57ca, 57ftl (friedel), 88cr, 125cl, 126fbr, 126tr, 127tl, 129bl; Reuters / Thomas Bohlen 124br; Andrew Budd 126br; Reuters/Claro Cortes IV WC 127cr; Jean Marie Hervio / Flash Press 102cb; Reuters / Enrique Marcarian 126ftl, 127ftr; Alex Morton 67c, 124ftr; John Sibley 127ftl; Sporting Picture 37br; Sporting Pictures 40cr, 124ftl, 125cr, 127tr; Boogertman + Partners Architects (Pty) Ltd: 63fcrb; Corbis: Toni Albir/epa 1; Jose L. Argueta/isiphotos.com 14bc; Yannis Behrakis / Reuters 2-3; Sandor Bojar/epa 45cb; Joao Luiz Bulcao 6-7; P. Caron/Corbis Sygma 148bl; Daniel Dal Zennaro/epa 36-37; Michael Dalder/Reuters 19tr, 126c; Tim De Waele 50c; Marcos Delgado/epa 90b; Duomo 122-123; Carlo Ferraro/epa 105crb; Andrew Fox 80-81; Marc Francotte/TempSport 39c; Maurizio Gambarini/epa 82-83; Mast Irham/epa 89b; Michael Janosz/isiphotos.com 11br; Youri Kochetkov/epa 46cb; Andres Kudacki 4-5, 59ca; C. Liewig/Corbis Sygma 35br; Christian Liewig 18-19, 96bl; Christian Liewig / Tempsport 69bl; Christian Liewig/TempSport 45bl, 110clb, 110-111 (b/g); Neil Marchand/Liewig Media Sports 60bl; Stefan Matzke/NewSport 37bc; Tannen Maury/epa 56crb, 91br; Thierry Orban 45cl; Gerry Penny 94-95; Jerome Prevost / TempSport 103cr; Jerome Prevost/TempSport 86bl; Ben Radford 22br; Stephane Reix/For Picture 39l, 46bl; Reuters 54bl, 71br; Reuters/Juan Carlos Ulate 90cl; Reuters/Kim Kyung-Hoon 18tr; Reuters/Marcelo Del Pozo 97cl; Jean-Yves Ruszniewski/TempSport 28bl, 52-53; Ruben Sprich/Reuters 44cb; Darren Staples/Reuters 11tr, 16tl; John Todd/ISI 19br; Underwood & Underwood 10bl; Horacio Villalobos 51tc; Jens Wolf/epa 35c; Wu Xiaoling/Xinhua Press 26clb; Getty Images: 37tl, 104cl, 104-105 (b/g), 106r, 106-107 (background), 107clb, 107tr, 109crb, 116c, 116r, 117cb, 123clb, 125fcl, 126cl, 126fbl, 126tl, 127fbl, 127fbr; AFP 34bl, 53br, 68cra, 83tl, 86tl, 114cb, 114crb, 115cr, 115tc, 120c, 121clb, 126ftr; AFP Photo / Timothy A. Clary 57ftl (keller); AFP Photo/Alfredo Estrella 99bl; Arif Ali / AFP 121tc; Allsport UK 91ca; Allsport UK/Allsport 11c; Vanderlei Almeida/AFP 98br; Odd Andersen / AFP 66br; Torsten Blackwood / AFP 77b; Bagu Blanco 111tc; Bongarts 122l, 124bl, 124cl; Lutz Bongarts 72clb; Shaun Botterill 35tl, 74br, 118tr; Shaun Botterill/Allsport 90cr; Shaun Botterill/Allsport Uk 87tl; Simon Bruty 97; Gerard Burkhart/AFP 99cl; David Cannon/Allsport 32cb, 34cl, 38br, 101tr; Central Press/Hulton Archive 42cl; Denis Charlet / AFP 103cl; Phil Cole 27clb; Jonathan Daniel 56-57; Stephane De Sakutin / AFP 102cl, 102-103; Adrian Dennis 79br; Adrian Dennis/AFP 27cr; Khaled Desouki / AFP 118br, 119r; Denis Doyle 43fcrb; Stephen Dunn 57br; Stephen Dunn/Allsport 91bl; Evening Standard/Hulton Archive 61bl, 75br; Evening Standard/Stringer/Hulton Archive 10cb; Franck Fife/AFP 16fcrb; Stu Forster 41tc, 59bc; Stu Forster/Allsport 62cr; Fox Photos 100cb; Fox Photos/Hulton Archive 12cl; Gallo Images 118clb; Bru Garcia/AFP 111crb; John Gurzinski/AFP 99cb; Martyn Harrison/AFP 93cl; Alexander Hassenstein/Bongarts 63bc; Patrick Hertzog/AFP 34cr; Mike Hewitt 96cb; Tobias Heyer/Bongarts 46br; Hulton Archive 58cl, 98cb; isifa/Filip Singer 113crb; Karim Jaafar / AFP 121cr; Jose Jordan/AFP 111cra; Keystone/Hulton Archive 34clb, 42c; Saeed Khan / AFP 78cr; Toshifumi Kitamura / AFP 79bl; Pornchai Kittiwongsakul / AFP 78tl; James Knowler 93tr; Natalia Kolesnikova/AFP 112c; Dima Korotayev/Epsilon 112; David Leah/Allsport 35bl; Alex Livesey 87bl; Pierre-Philippe Marcou/AFP 13bl; Marty Melville 120cl; Rabih Moghrabi / AFP 66cl; Dean Mouhtaropoulos 112cr; Peter Muhly/AFP 43bl; Guang Niu 76bc; Mark Nolan 120r; Ralph Orlowski 49tr; Ryan Pierse 100cl; Steve Powell/Allsport 36cl; Gary M. Prior 26br; Gary M. Prior/Allsport 65bc; Ben Radford 67clb, 72cr; Mark Ralston /AFP 121cra; Cesar Rangel/AFP 110r; Andreas Rentz / Bongarts 76cr; Holm Roehner/Bongarts 13tl; Martin Rose/Bongarts 39c; Evaristo Sa/AFP 13br; Issouf Sanogo/Afp 11bl; Roberto Schmidt/AFP 42bl; Antonio Scorza/AFP 90c, 98bl; Michael Steele 43cl; Chung Sung-Jun 24c; Henri Szwarc / Stringer / Bongarts 66bl; Mark Thompson/Allsport 62cl; Mirek Towski/Time Life Pictures 51br; Pius Utomi Ekpei / AFP 119c, 119cla; Friedemann Vogel/Bongarts 113cl; WireImage 117tl, 117tr; Toru Yamanaka 121cla; Mary Evans Picture Library: 9bl, 9r, 9t, 10tl, 10cl, 10cr; Central Press/Stringer/Hulton Archive 10br; The National Soccer Hall of Fame, Oneonta, NY: 10fcr, 56bl; PA Photos: 50bl, 79tl, 83cr; Abaca Abaca Press 125br; Africa Visuals 62bl, 63tc; AP Photo/ Claudio Cruz 99br; AP Photo/Anja Niedringhaus 92l; AP Photo/ Ariel Schalit 88br, 88c; AP Photo/Ben Curtis 88bl; AP Photo/Carlo Fumagalli 52bl; AP Photo/Eugene Hoshiko 92cr; AP Photo/Fernando Llano 51l; AP Photo/Hans Punz 59br; AP Photo/Jae C. Hong 93br; AP Photo/Jon Super 101c; AP Photo/Massimo Pinca 105tc; AP Photo/Nasser Nasser 64br, 64c; AP Photo/Roberto Candia 58r; AP Photo/Vincent Thian 89ca; Bernat Armangue/AP25clb; Matthew Ashton / EMPICS Sport 66cr, 73cla; Matthew Ashton/Empics Sport 13ca, 32br, 75cl, 75cr, 82tl, 89cl, 91cl, 127br; Mark Baker / AP 77clb; Barratts 78bl, 82cra, 125ftr, 127fcl; Gregorio Borgia/AP 27cr; Bruno Press 109tr; Jon Buckle/Empics Sport 54tr; Jon Buckle/Empics Sport/ 12bl; Buzzi 36cra, 105tl; Liewig Christian/Abaca 53c; Barry Coombs/EMPICS Sport 125tr; Cordon Press 111cla; Bas Czerwinski/AP 108cr; David Davies/PA Archive 83tr; Adam Davy / Empics Sport 72tr; Adam Davy/Empics Sport 12r, 46fcla, 62br, 63l; Adam Davy/Empics Sport/ 21tl; Sean Dempsey/PA Archive 108cb; DPA 36bl, 38cl, 39br, 127cl, 150-151; DPA Deutsche Press-Agentur 44c, 124tl; Mike Egerton / EMPICS Sport 77; Mike Egerton/EMPICS Sport 21br, 24cr, 28clb, 14r, 33bl, 47c, 51bc, 59cb, 75bl, 126cr; Mike Egerton/Empics Sport/ 24bl; Empics Sport 20fbr, 23cl, 54c, 64cr, 65bl, 74c, 77cl; Christophe Ena/AP 20cr; Nigel French/EMPICS Sport 108-109; Nigel French/Empics Sport/ 65crb; Simon Galloway/Empics Sport 44fcra; Petros Giannakouris/AP 86cl; Gouhier-Hahn-Orban/Cameleon/abacapress.com 24tl; Laurence Griffiths/EMPICS Sport 125tl; Janerik Henriksson/Scanpix 123br; Torbjorn Jakobsson/Scanpix 13tr; Petr David Josek / AP 41br; Jasper Juinen/AP 18bl; Keystone/Hulton Archive 83fcr; Ross Kinnaird/EMPICS Sport 125fcr; Christian Liewig 68cla, 68clb; David Mariuz/AP 29cl; Tony Marshall / EMPICS Sport 41bc, 67crb, 72bc, 76cl; Tony Marshall/Empics Entertainment 45cr; Tony Marshall/EMPICS Sport 21c, 21tc, 21tr, 30bl, 52tl, 53bc, 55br, 55tr, 65cl, 104cr, 106clb, 126fcl; Tony Marshall/Empics Sport/ 74bl; Clive Mason 25c; Ricardo Mazalan 41c; Taamallah Mehdi / ABACA 102-103; Peter Morrison/AP 47bc; Steve Morton/Empics Sport 55tc; Daniel Motz 83tr; Rebecca Naden/PA Wire 100cr; PA Archive 32cr, 40bl, 125bl, 125ftl; PA Wire 33br; PA/PA Archive 32bl; Photocome 89cr; Nick Potts/Empics Sport 96br; Presse Sports 50fbr, 86cr; Michael Probst/AP 27tl; Rangers FC 96ca; Brian Rasmussen/Scanpix 46tc; Michael Regan/Empics Sport 45tr; Martin Rickett/PA Archive 32-33; Martin Rickett/PA Wire 97br; Peter Robinson / Empics Sport 40br, 67br; Peter Robinson/Empics Sport 36br, 38cr, 45tl, 47tc, 52c, 52clb, 74cr, 87cr, 124cr, 124fbl, 125fbl, 126fcr; Peter Robinson/Empics Sport/ 83c; S&G 126bl; Jorge Saenz/AP 75clb; Marcio Jose Sanchez / AP 76tr; Neal Simpson / EMPICS Sport 103tl; Neal Simpson/EMPICS Sport 37ca, 57clb, 97bc, 125fbr; SMG 55bl, 96cr, 98cra; Howard Smith/International Sports Images 123tr; Michael Sohn/AP 16l, 19r, 46c; Jon Super/AP 18tr; Topham Picturepoint 50crb, 124fbr; Marcel Van Hoorn/AP 108cl, 108-109 (background); Geert Vanden Wijngaert/AP 22c; John Walton/Empics Sport 16cb; Aubrey Washington/EMPICS Sport 124tr; Haydn West 44br; Panapress: MAXPPP 69ca, 93bc; Reuters: 33c, 57ftl (howard), 99c, 107tl, 113tr, 114ca, 116clb, 131br; Sporting Pictures (UK) Ltd: 92br, 103cb; Wikipedia, The Free Encyclopedia: 8cla

Front Endpapers: Varley Picture Agency; Back Endpapers: Varley Picture Agency

Jacket images: Front: Corbis: Matt A. Brown/isiphotos.com fbl; Tannen Maury/epa bc. Getty Images: fbr; Shaun Botterill br. PA Photos: bl. Back: Corbis: Andy Rain/epa. Front Flaps: Corbis: Toni Albir/epa t. Back Flaps: PA Photos: AP Photo/Carlo Fumagalli t.

All other images © Dorling Kindersley
For further information see: www.dkimages.com